The Culture Puzzle

Cross-Cultural Communication
For English As A Second Language

Deena R. Levine
Jim Baxter
Piper McNulty

 Prentice Hall Regents, Englewood Cliffs, NJ 07632

Library of Congress Cataloging-in-Publication Data

Levine, Deena R.
  The culture puzzle.

  1. English language—Text-books for foreign
speakers. 2. Intercultural communication.
I. Baxter, Jim. II. McNulty, Piper. III. Title.
PE1128.L463 1987   428.3′4   87-1742
ISBN 0-13-195520-9

Editorial/production supervision
and interior design: Evalyn Schoppet
Cover design: H.B. Levine
Cover mechanicals: Lundgren Graphics, Ltd.
Manufacturing buyer: Margaret Rizzi

Printed in the United States of America

10   9   8   7   6

ISBN 0-13-195520-9 01

Prentice-Hall International (UK) Limited, *London*
Prentice-Hall of Australia Pty. Limited, *Sydney*
Prentice-Hall of Canada, Inc., *Toronto*
Prentice-Hall of Hispanoamericana, S. A., *Mexico*
Prentice-Hall of India Private Limited, *New Delhi*
Prentice-Hall of Japan, Inc., *Tokyo*
Prentice-Hall of Southeast Asia Pte. Ltd., *Singapore*
Editora Prentice-Hall do Brasil, Ltda., *Rio de Janeiro*

To our children

   Ilana, Kara

   Kenzo, Utana

   Sara Mei Wah, Claudia Lai Wah

For encouraging us to value the process as much as the goal.

Contents

Preface

The Culture Puzzle: Cross-Cultural Communication for English as a Second Language is unique in that it encompasses language learning and culture learning. Designed for the intermediate-level student, the text integrates the teaching and learning of language and culture in a systematic manner. *The Culture Puzzle* gives students opportunities to recognize common sources of cross-cultural miscommunication and conflict through examples of realistic interactions. As students master the skills and information presented in the text, they gain awareness of cultural differences and develop confidence in interacting with native speakers of English. Each chapter gives examples and presents skills that help students understand differences in communication styles across cultures. By the time students finish the text, they will have a basic understanding of commonly held American expectations for interaction in English.

The Culture Puzzle presents key concepts from the field of cross-cultural communication with immediate application for the ESL student. In nonacademic and nontheoretical language, the text lays out skills and information that students need for effective communication. Throughout the text, there are realistic examples of cross-cultural interactions between native and non-native speakers of English. Cross-cultural notes and U.S. culture notes describe patterns of communication and culture that help students understand their own and others' culturally influenced styles of communication.

The Culture Puzzle was written because cultural differences often create predictable communication difficulties for ESL students. To a large extent, the particular background of an individual student will determine the degree of difficulty that he or she may have with a specific cultural pattern of communication. For example, a student who comes from a culture where asking questions of teachers is acceptable usually does not have difficulty interacting in a similar manner with an American teacher or other authority figure. Conversely, someone from a culture in which students normally do not initiate discussion with teachers or ask questions of them will often find such typical interactions difficult. However, regardless of the degree of cultural similarity, most intermediate-level students benefit from explicit explanations of the cultural use of English among native speakers. In addition, intermediate-level speakers of English, whether they are immigrants, refugees, business people or foreign students, need intensive skill practice in cross-cultural communication.

As educators in the fields of English language and cross-cultural communication training, we are aware that the acquisition of skills for culturally different patterns of interaction can require personal change and can initially create discomfort. For instance, people who have learned in their native cultures never to volunteer information or give opinions in classes or at meetings may be uncomfortable interacting in this way with Americans. *The Culture Puzzle* provides explanations of American cultural expectations, but students are not asked to copy American behavior. We believe that once students have a clear understanding of effective communication in English, they can ultimately make their own decisions about how they may adapt their communication styles in cross-cultural situations. In this text, we hope to convince students and teachers that communication, language and culture cannot be separated. We hope that students, while developing their competence in conversation, reading, and vocabulary, will also realize that effective communication depends on both language fluency and cultural fluency.

Acknowledgments

We owe our thanks to many people who have directly and indirectly contributed to *The Culture Puzzle: Cross-Cultural Communication for English as a Second Language.* First, a special acknowledgment is given to IRI International in Redwood City, California, where we met and worked as a team. In particular, we owe much to Clifford Clarke, Sheila Ramsey, and King Ming Young, who contributed a great deal to our professional growth. We also acknowledge the opportunities we had with IRI International to develop materials that later became the basis for portions of the text. In particular, we would like to mention the "Take One/Take Two" methodology, which led to the videotape production entitled "Take Two: English for Intercultural Communication," directed by Jim Baxter. We have adapted this methodology for the cross-cultural interactions that appear throughout *The Culture Puzzle.*

There are many other individuals and organizations we would like to thank for their interest, assistance, and ideas: Dr. Mara Adelman (Northwestern University), coauthor of *Beyond Language;* Linda Barker (formerly with the Bronx Community College); Professor A. Hirata (University of Toyama); Dr. Ann Johns (San Diego State University); Professor T. Okuhara (University of Toyama); Professor Randolph Quirk (University of London); Larry Smith (East-West Center, Honolulu); Claire Stanley (The Experiment in International Living, Vermont); and Dianne Walker (formerly with the Center for Applied Linguistics, Bangkok, Thailand). In addition to these individuals, we wish to thank the staff, students, and volunteers in the following organizations and institutions: De Anza College, Cupertino, California; IRI International; the Lao Family Community Programs of San Francisco, California; University of California, Berkeley Extension; the United Nations High Commissioner on Refugees Cultural Orientation Program, Hong Kong; and Youth for Understanding International Exchange.

We would also like to thank the people who helped turn the manuscript into the textbook: Hillel Levine, for his many hours of designing graphics for the book and the cover; Susan Levine, for suggesting the cover design; Claudine Baxter, for her ability to create graphics depicting the communication problems of nonnative speakers of English; Mel Lipsett, for suggesting the title; Frederick McNulty, for checking overall clarity of the text; Jau Ping, Liang, for further editing the manuscript for limited English speakers; Evalyn Schoppet, for her careful copy editing; and Brenda White, for coordinating the production of the book in a most patient manner.

Finally, we would like to thank our spouses, Michael Lipsett, Claudine Baxter, and Ed Leung, for their support and encouragement.

To the Teacher:
Guide to Using the Text

The Culture Puzzle: Cross-Cultural Communication for English as a Second Language is a textbook which integrates language learning and culture learning. It emphasizes cross-cultural knowledge and skills for English as a second language, while developing students' fluency in oral communication and reading. The themes and content of the text provide an awareness of cross-cultural communication. The skill practice sections serve as a foundation for effective communication. Each unit includes information on aspects of U.S. culture that directly influence the communication style and expectations of American speakers of English. The book is written primarily in informal English, although the unit readings are written in a slightly more formal style. The cross-cultural interactions and notes are drawn from the experiences of immigrants, refugees, foreign students and foreign business people in the U.S. The text is designed for use in English language classes both in the U.S. and abroad, and provides material for a variety of English language programs, including conversation, oral skills, reading, vocabulary, culture and cross-cultural communication. The structure and language in *The Culture Puzzle* are geared toward intermediate-level students. However, advanced students can also gain important cultural information from the text.

For an overview of the book and as a way to prepare to teach from *The Culture Puzzle,* teachers should read the four major readings in the final chapter of each unit.

METHODOLOGY

A basic assumption of the text is that through studying examples of cross-cultural differences in communication, students will become more aware of how easy it is to misinterpret the words or behavior of someone from a different culture. The text helps students identify ways to avoid misinterpretations in their own interactions with Americans and with people from other cultures. By illustrating ineffective and effective *cross-cultural* interactions, rather than interaction among native speakers of English, students become aware of the knowledge and skills that are needed for successful communication. Students learn from examples and analyses of examples, as well as by direct explanation.

The communicative approach of the book spans both language and cultural fluency. Different levels of cultural fluency among students may require that the presentation of the material be adapted in the same way that English in textbooks is adapted to students' levels of language fluency. The "Unit Foundations" at the beginning of each unit give an overview of concepts and broad principles underlying the cultural information presented. Asking students to discuss these foundations and to provide examples illustrating the foundations can give the teacher an idea of the depth of students' overall cultural knowledge.

FORMAT AND EXPLANATION OF CHAPTER PARTS

The units are divided into chapters. Except for the final reading chapter in each unit, the chapters contain the following components:

- Chapter Introduction
- Cross-Cultural Interactions
- Questions and Discussion
- Interaction Summaries/Analyses

- Focus on U.S. Culture
  - Exercises and Skill Practice
  - Phrases and Expressions
  - U.S. and Cross-Cultural Notes

The first four components stress broad *cross-cultural* learning; the remaining component focuses on aspects of U.S. culture.

Chapter Introduction   This includes a brief introductory paragraph about the chapter, followed by "Culture Learning Questions" which ask about the students' own cultural backgrounds and their experiences with people from different cultures.

Cross-Cultural Interactions   There are two cross-cultural interactions contained in the section following the chapter introduction. These are conversations in which one speaker is an American native speaker of English and the other is not. The first conversation exemplifies cultural differences or ineffective communication and is *not* a model for students to copy. It is labeled "Original" with a note indicating that there is a revised interaction. The second cross-cultural interaction, labeled "Revised," includes examples of the skills that students will learn later in the chapter and thus serves as a model for learning. Through the juxtaposition of these two interactions, students are given clear examples of effective communication in a cross-cultural context. The culture of the non-native speaker in these dialogues is not specified in order to avoid creating feelings of self-consciousness among students.

Questions and Discussion   This section includes: (1) comprehension questions that check the students' understanding of the first cross-cultural interaction; (2)

analysis questions that ask the students to try to explain the cultural behavior in the interaction; and (3) cross-cultural discussion questions intended to stimulate interest in the students' cultural backgrounds. The last set of questions is designed to heighten cultural awareness so that as students become more cognizant of their own cultural backgrounds, they will be able to better understand the cultural behavior of others.

Interaction Summaries/Analyses   The second cross-cultural interaction is either followed by a summary or by an analysis entitled, "What Is Happening." The analysis, appearing alongside the revised interaction, explains what the speakers are doing differently and what skills they are using.

Focus on U.S. Culture   This section begins with a set of questions entitled, "How much do you already know about U.S. culture?" These questions can function as a brief pretest and a partial preview to the rest of the "Focus on U.S. Culture" section.

Exercises and Skill Practice   In the text, the term "exercises" refers to activities that ask students to analyze and discuss the cultural information presented. "Skill practice" refers to activities in which students practice language and communication skills.

Phrases and Expressions   These are lists of culturally appropriate ways of using English in given contexts. Before students practice using the phrases and expressions, they should repeat them after the teacher, who models appropriate intonation for each.

U.S. Culture Notes   These brief explanations give information on U.S. cultural attitudes, behavior, communication styles and expectations of American English speakers. Many of the notes introduce the skills and exercises that follow them. These notes are primarily discussion starters and secondarily reading passages. If the reading level is too high for some students, teachers may wish to paraphrase the notes aloud.

Cross-Cultural Notes   These short paragraphs present cultural contrasts and anecdotes from immigrants, refugees, business people, and foreign students who have had experience interacting with Americans, either in the U.S. or in other countries. The information in the cross-cultural notes has been verified through discussions with people from the culture or cultures mentioned. Nevertheless, students may disagree with the information presented if they have not had similar experiences or if they have made different observations. Such disagreements should be welcome, as these can stimulate discussion on differing perceptions of cultural behavior. An attempt has been made to balance the cultures represented in the cross-cultural notes. It should be noted, however, that it is often easier to recognize contrasts between Eastern and Western cultures. Therefore, notes about European or Latin American cultures, for example, are less frequent than examples from Middle Eastern and Asian cultures.

Glossed Vocabulary   The words that are glossed (i.e., defined at the bottom of the page) throughout the chapters help the intermediate-level student quickly understand the interactions and information presented. These glossed words, unlike the glossed words in the final reading chapter of each unit, are not accompanied by vocabulary exercises. There is some repetition of important glossed words throughout the text to accommodate teachers who may not present chapters sequentially.

The final chapter in each unit contains the following:

Reading Preview Activities   The reading preview activities consist of an outline of the reading, with questions that preview the reading. There are additional suggestions for previewing the reading, as well as a pronunciation guide for the new vocabulary in the text. If students complete all of these activities before starting the reading, they will have a clear idea of the subjects to be covered in the reading text. Lower-level intermediate students may also benefit from completing the vocabulary exercises in the post-reading activities before they begin the reading.

Reading Text   The final chapter in each of the four units contains a reading which may be taught over several class sessions. To assist the intermediate-level student, readings are divided into parts, each with subheadings. The division of the reading into parts enables students to complete the readings in small segments. The readings can be assigned as homework or can be introduced and covered in class. Key concepts are written in the margin and are summarized at the end of each part so that students can understand and review the material easily. The language in the reading text is not simplified, so as to retain a natural, idiomatic style. Intermediate-level students, however, will be able to understand the readings because of the many glossed words, key concepts, and subheadings of the text. The content of the readings is appropriate for students in advanced-level courses or in courses such as cross-cultural communication and American culture.

Glossed Vocabulary in the Readings   The glossed vocabulary at the bottom of each page consists of those words which will be least familiar to intermediate-level students. The glossed words appear in the reading preview section with pronunciation guides and reappear in the exercises in the post-reading section. The reading text contains some glossed words introduced in previous chapters. It is expected that some teachers will want to present the reading text first, and for this reason, important words are glossed even if they have already been glossed in preceding chapters.

Post-Reading Activities   These consist of questions that check students' comprehension of the material as well as questions about cross-cultural similarities and differences. Many of the questions in the post-reading activities may be used as a basis for writing assignments.

Vocabulary Exercises   These include matching, word forms, fill-in-the-blanks, choose-the-best-explanation, and synonym/antonym exercises. The words in these exercises appear with pronunciation guides in the reading preview activities and are glossed in the reading.

IMPORTANT NOTE: The teacher may want to vary the order of presentation of the chapters. For example, the final reading chapter in each unit may be introduced first. The readings reinforce information from earlier chapters in the unit by expanding concepts and giving additional examples. Presented first, the reading texts serve as a foundation for the rest of the chapters in that unit. Presented last, they serve as a summary of many of the skill practices in the preceding chapters.

Answer Key   There is a separate booklet containing the answers to questions in the text. Some answers are included at the end of the chapters when they contain cultural information that will clearly benefit the students.

COMMUNICATING ACROSS CULTURES

UNIT I FOUNDATIONS

- Language fluency is not always enough for good communication. It is also necessary to understand people's cultures.
- Much of culture is hidden. This hidden part influences communication and behavior.
- What is right or "normal" in one culture may be wrong or not "normal" in another culture.

UNIT I CONTENTS

Chapter 1. "Addressing People" will introduce you to:

- using forms of address
- greetings and farewells
- making introductions

Chapter 2. "Complimenting and Showing Appreciation" covers:

- choosing words for complimenting
- starting conversations with compliments
- giving and receiving gifts

Chapter 3. "Expressing Emotions" looks at:

- cross-cultural differences
- using nonverbal and verbal communication

Chapter 4. "Reading Text and Activities" contains:

- Reading Text: Communicating Across Cultures
- Comprehension, vocabulary, and discussion questions

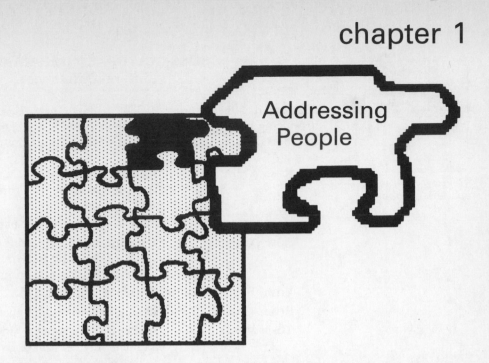

chapter 1

Addressing People

Introduction   There are many things that we do in our own culture that we never ask questions about. We do things without thinking about them because we have always done them in the same way. When we are in another culture or with people from a different culture, we see that people do things in many different ways. One of the first differences we notice is the *forms of address* that are used in the culture. The language that people use to address each other tells us many things about a culture. For example, the language of addressing people gives cultural information about *customs, relationships,* and *communication style,* both *verbal* and *nonverbal.* In this chapter, you will learn mainly about addressing people in American English, but you also will learn about addressing people in other cultures. The *focus* of this chapter is on addressing people, and in addition, there is information on introductions, *greetings,* and *farewells.*

CULTURE LEARNING QUESTIONS

1. Do Americans address you in the same way that people from your own culture address you? If so, is this way comfortable for you? Explain your answer.
2. Think of the way people address each other in your language and culture. What can people learn about your language and culture by the way people address each other (for example, age, respect, position in society)?

forms of address—use of titles or special words that go along with people's names (example: Mr. or Mrs.)
customs—usual ways of behaving, cultural habits
relationships—people's connections to each other
communication style—the way people communicate and talk to each other
verbal—with words
nonverbal—without words
focus—major part
greetings and *farewells*—"Hello's" and "Goodbye's"

CROSS-CULTURAL INTERACTION 1A:
Cultural Differences

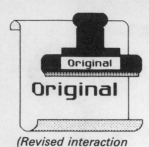

(Revised interaction appears on page 5.)

Situation: It is the first day of English class. Rose Arno, an American teacher, is introducing herself to the class. The students in the class, all from countries other than the U.S., are introducing themselves to their new teacher.

Rose Arno:	"I would like to introduce myself. My name is Rose Arno. If you want, you can use Mrs. or Ms. with my name."
Naima Moud:	"How do you spell your name, Mrs. Rose?"
Rose Arno:	"It's Mrs. Arno." (writing on the board) "R-O-S-E A-R-N-O. Now I'd like you to give your names. Let's start with the first person in the front row."
Yoshi Imada:	"My name is Imada."
Rose Arno:	"Imada, could you also give us your last name?"
Yoshi Imada:	"Imada is my last name. In my country, most people call me by my last name. Even my friends at work use my last name."
Rose Arno:	"Would you like us to use your first name or last name in class?"
Yoshi Imada:	(thinking) "I don't know yet. I will tell you."
Rose Arno:	"O.K. That's fine. Let's continue with the second student. What is your name?"
Magdalena Chavez:	"My name is Magdalena Chavez, but people call me Lena, Teacher. That's my *nickname*."
Rose Arno:	"O.K. We'll call you Lena, and please call me Rose or Mrs. Arno." (The teacher continues to ask the students to introduce themselves.)

QUESTIONS AND DISCUSSION

Comprehension

Write T (true) or F (false) in the space provided.

1. _____ The teacher said that the students could call her "Mrs. Arno" or "Miss Arno."

2. _____ Naima Moud called the teacher "Mrs. Rose" instead of "Mrs. Arno."

3. _____ The first student who introduced himself gave his first name only.

4. _____ Yoshi Imada's friends at work (in his own country) use his last name and not his first.

5. _____ Rose Arno did not want to use Magdalena's nickname to address her.

(Note: The answers to this exercise can be found in the separate Answer Key.)

nickname—a shortened or special name a person uses

Analysis: Can You Explain?

1. Why does the teacher say that the students can use "Mrs." or "Ms." to address her?
2. Do you think that it might be difficult for some of the students to call the teacher by her first name?
3. Why do you think Yoshi Imada doesn't answer the teacher's question right away? (He says, "I don't know yet. I will tell you.")
4. The teacher says to Magdalena Chavez, ". . . please call me Rose or Mrs. Arno." Why does she say that?

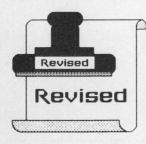

TALK ABOUT YOUR OWN LANGUAGE AND CULTURE

1. How do students address teachers in your culture?
2. How do teachers address students?
3. How do you introduce yourself in your language and culture? Which name or names do you give?
4. Are there special words that are used for men and women in your own language? Are different words used for married men and women (such as Mrs.)?
5. Do you address people younger than you differently than people older than you?

Summary of Cross-Cultural Interaction 1A: Cultural Differences

There are many ways of addressing teachers and students and introducing oneself in other cultures. In many parts of the world, students must show politeness and respect to teachers; one way of doing this is not to use the teacher's first name. Some teachers in the U.S. don't think it is rude if their students call them by their first names. This may be their way of having a close *informal* relationship with students. In the U.S., one way to show closeness and friendliness is to use a person's first name. This is why Rose Arno prefers to use the students' first names. In the U.S., it is not *appropriate* for adults to call their teachers "Teacher" as Magdalena did. Only young children call their teacher "Teacher."

CROSS-CULTURAL INTERACTION 1B

In the original cross-cultural interaction (1A), the students address the teacher and introduce themselves as they would in their own countries. The following interaction shows the students addressing the teacher and introducing themselves as American students would. The first interaction does not show wrong ways of communicating; it shows culturally different ways.

Rose Arno: "I would like to introduce myself. My name is Rose Arno. If you want, you can use Mrs. or Ms. with my name."

---

informal—not formal, not according to fixed customs or rules
appropriate—correct, acceptable

Naima Moud: "Mrs. Arno, how do you spell your name?"
Rose Arno: "A-R-N-O. Now I'd like you to give your names. Let's start with the first person in the front row."
Yoshi Imada: "My name is Yoshi Imada."
Rose Arno: "Thank you. Let's continue with the second student. What is your name?"
Magdalena Chavez: "Magdalena Chavez, but people call me Lena, Mrs. Arno. That's my nickname."
Rose Arno: "O.K. Lena." (The teacher continues to ask the students to introduce themselves.)

Summary of Cross-Cultural Interaction 1B

In the revised interaction, the students use Mrs. and the teacher's last name to address her. They may not have felt comfortable using her first name, so they chose to address her in a way that was more usual for them. The students introduce themselves by giving their first names and then their last names. Finally, Magdalena Chavez does not call the teacher, "Teacher."

It isn't always easy to change one's way of addressing people. For some people, it can take years. In the U.S., one of the most difficult things for many newcomers to do is to use people's first names.

FOCUS ON U.S. CULTURE
Cultural Notes, Exercises, and Skill Practice

HOW MUCH DO YOU ALREADY KNOW ABOUT U.S. CULTURE?

Write T (true) or F (false) in the space provided.

1. _____ When you want to address a teacher in class (for example in an adult school or college), you can say, "Teacher" without saying his or her name.
2. _____ If you are not sure if a woman is married, you can use "Ms." and her last name.
3. _____ "Mr." is used for married men only.
4. _____ When you are introducing yourself to an employer or teacher, you never give your last name.
5. _____ Teachers usually call students by their last names.
6. _____ If someone introduces himself to you and gives his first name, you can call him by his first name.

Note: The answers to this exercise can be found throughout the chapter and in the separate Answer Key.

NOTE TO STUDENTS

Remember that the information presented in this book about culture and communication in the U.S. is general. There are many kinds of Americans, and many ways of doing things. The information that follows is usually true for many Americans, but not for all Americans.

SECTION 1. USING FORMS OF ADDRESS

In general, Americans don't use special forms of address (or titles) as often as people in other countries. However, there are times when special forms of address are used. The following special forms of address are used before a person's last name.

Dr. (Doctor):   medical doctors (those with an M.D. degree), professors, scientists and researchers (those who have a Ph.D)

Mrs. (pronounced "Missus"):   married women only (some married women prefer Ms.)

Miss: unmarried women only (some unmarried women prefer "Ms.")

Ms. (pronounced "Miz"):   married or unmarried women (some married women prefer Mrs.)

Mr. (pronounced "Mister"):   married or unmarried men

Professor: college or university teachers (used with or without the last name)

Note: "Teacher" as a form of address is only used by children.

CROSS-CULTURAL NOTE

In Vietnam, people often use special forms of address. A person calls his older brother or sister "older brother" or "older sister" without using a name.

CULTURE PUZZLE #1

Read the situation and choose the appropriate answer or answers. There may be more than one possible answer for each culture puzzle.

What would you do if you met a woman and you didn't know if she should be called "Mrs.," "Miss" or "Ms.?"

    a) You could use "Ms."
    b) You could try not to use her name.
    c) You could check the woman's left hand to see if she's married.

Can you think of anything else you could do?

(Answers are given at the end of the chapter.)

CULTURE PUZZLE #2

What would you do if someone told you to use his or her first name, but you felt uncomfortable doing this?

    a) You could continue to use the person's last name without explaining why you are doing this.
    b) You could try to use the person's first name even though you are uncomfortable doing this.
    c) You could ask the person. "Is it O.K. if I use your last name?" Then you could explain that you are not used to using people's first names.

(Answers are given at the end of the chapter.)

CROSS-CULTURAL NOTE

In Japan, co-workers or classmates do not usually call each other by their first names. They use the last name followed by a title ("San").

CROSS-CULTURAL NOTE

In North Africa, men often call each other "Mister" ("As-sa-id") with the first name. Sometimes when Americans are in North Africa, they are addressed in this way, for example, "Mister Michael."

U.S. CULTURE NOTE

Often people call each other by their first names where in other countries people use last names. For example, many employees call their bosses (supervisors or managers) by their first names. This is not considered *rude.* Many bosses prefer this. Even though they are in a higher position than the employees, bosses sometimes want to be treated as *equals.*

rude—not polite, impolite
equals—people of the same status or rank; one person is not higher than the other

Contact Assignment

Ask two or three Americans how they address the following people. That is, ask them what words or names they use when they speak to the following people:

- parents
- boss or supervisor
- an older man or woman
- a grandparent
- mother-in-law or father-in-law
- a clerk in a store
- a student in a class

Report to the class and compare answers with those of the other students. Discuss cross-cultural differences.

SECTION 2. GREETINGS AND FAREWELLS

U.S. CULTURE NOTE

It is sometimes difficult to know when to shake hands with Americans. In business situations, men always shake hands when they first meet each other. Recently, especially in the business world, women have begun shaking hands, too. In social situations when two people meet, they often shake hands. You may find that younger women shake hands more often than older women do.

CULTURE PUZZLE #3

What would you do if someone introduced you to another person and you didn't know if you should shake hands?

a) You could keep your hands in your pockets in order to avoid shaking hands.

b) You could wait and see what the other person does and then you could do the same (shake or don't shake hands).

c) You could be the first person to give your hand.

(Answers are given at the end of the chapter.)

U.S. CULTURE NOTE

When Americans shake hands, they usually only shake hands for a few seconds. When they shake, they shake hands firmly, not loosely. "He shakes hands like a dead fish" refers to someone whose handshake is not firm enough. In the American culture, a weak handshake is a sign of a *weak character*. In other countries people shake hands differently. They may take the other person's hand loosely and may shake it for more than a few seconds.

weak character—a weak person; usually refers to someone's personality

Cross-Cultural Exercise: Greetings and Farewells

Demonstrate with a student from your culture greetings and farewells in your own language. Do exactly what you would do in your own culture, using the same words and nonverbal communication as you would use. (You can translate for the students after your demonstration.) If there are no students from your culture in the class, tell the class (and show) what you would say and do.

As you watch other students, look for the following cultural differences:

- *Amount of touching.* Is there any touching?
- *Kind of eye contact.* Do they look each other in the eye the whole time?
- *Distance between people.* How far apart from each other do they stand?
- *Type of facial expressions.* Is there a lot of smiling? What kind of expressions do they have on their faces?
- *Amount of gesturing.* Do they use their hands while speaking?

Suggestions for Demonstrations

Choose one or more of the following:

1. A boss and employee greet each other after not seeing each other for a couple of weeks. They have a short conversation and then say goodbye.
2. A teacher and student greet each other after a summer away from school. They have a short conversation and then say goodbye.
3. A husband and wife greet each other after not seeing each other for one day. (Is there a difference if the greeting is in the home or in public, such as in a restaurant or on a street?) Demonstrate also a husband and wife saying goodbye to each other for the day.

4. Two good friends greet each other after not seeing each other for a long time. They have a conversation and then say goodbye.

5. Two people who don't know each other very well greet each other in a store. They have a brief conversation and then say goodbye.

U.S. CULTURE NOTE

When Americans greet each other, introduce each other, and have conversations, they usually stand about an arm's distance (about eighteen inches) to two feet (twenty-four inches) apart. This is not always a comfortable distance for people in other cultures, who may prefer less or more distance.

CROSS-CULTURAL NOTE

Latin Americans, North Africans, and Middle Easterners are examples of cultural groups that *tend* to stand closer together when talking than Americans do. People from some Asian cultures tend to stand farther apart when talking than Americans do. In Japan, a person usually stands farther from a boss or a teacher than from a friend.

tend to—usually do (*Note:* When we say people in one culture *tend* to do something, it means that many people do it. There are always people in a culture who do not do what others do.)

Cross-Cultural Exercise: Distance Between People

Demonstrate with a person from your culture a comfortable conversational distance (a good distance to stand for talking). Then, with a student from another culture (whose comfortable distance is different), have a conversation. What happens? How do you feel? What does the other person do?

SECTION 3. MAKING INTRODUCTIONS

CULTURE PUZZLE #4

Read the situation and choose the appropriate answer or answers. There may be more than one possible answer.

What would you do if you were talking to a friend and then a third person (who you didn't know) came along and began talking to your friend?

    a) You could introduce yourself by saying something like: "I don't think we've met. I'm . . . (give your name)."

    b) You could ask your friend to introduce you. You could say something like, "I don't think I've met your friend."

    c) You could not say anything and wait for your friend to introduce you.

(Answers are given at the end of the chapter.)

Phrases To Introduce Yourself —————————————————————————

Repeat the following phrases and sentences after your teacher says them.

Informal	*Informal or Formal*	*Formal*
"Hi, I'm Lani."	"Hello. My name is Michael."	"Let me introduce myself. My name is George. . . ."
"Nice to meet you." (after someone has told you his name.) "I'm Belle."	"It's nice to meet you. My name is Joe."	"I don't believe we've met. I'm Mel Maurice."

Phrases To Introduce Others —————————————————————————

Repeat these phrases and sentences after your teacher says them.

Informal	*Informal or Formal*	*Formal*
"Meet my friend, Rachel." "Rachel, meet Josh."	"I'd like you to meet my friend, Rachel Levine."	"I'd like to introduce you to Rachel Levine, a friend of mine."
"Let me introduce you two. Josh . . ." (*gesturing with your hand toward Josh.*) ". . . Rachel." (*gesturing toward Rachel.*)	"Let me introduce you to Rachel. Josh, this is Rachel. Rachel, this is Josh."	"I don't believe you two have met. Josh, this is Rachel Levine. Rachel, this is Josh Brown."
"This is Rachel. This is Josh."	"Have you met Rachel? Josh this is Rachel Levine."	"Mr. Waxman, have you met Ms. Lipsett?"

Skill Practice: Introducing Other People

Using the phrases to introduce others, practice making introductions in the following situations. Use appropriate forms of address and first names or last names where needed.

Situations

1. Two students and a teacher are entering a classroom. One student knows the teacher, but the other does not.
2. Three parents are waiting outside the school to pick up their children. One parent knows the other two parents, but they don't know each other.
3. Someone in a company is introducing a new employee to the vice-president of the company.
4. A relative comes to visit you while a friend of yours is at your house.

Skill Practice: Introducing Yourself

Using the phrases to introduce yourself, practice making introductions in the following situations. After you introduce yourself, add a sentence or two and have a short conversation:

For example: (in a bank)

"Hi, I'm Phil Moser, a customer of this bank.
I'd like to open another bank account."

1. You meet a neighbor in a store. You have seen and greeted each other, but you don't know each other's names.
2. You are at a party and only know the host and hostess. They are both busy and haven't introduced you to anybody. (This is a common situation.) Introduce yourself to someone at the party and begin a conversation.
3. You are in the foreign student office in a college. You have come there with a problem.
4. You see a job announcement in the newspaper and are interested in finding out about it.
5. You are calling a doctor's office to set up an appointment.

CHAPTER SUMMARY

In this chapter you looked at cultural differences in the areas of:

*   addressing people
*   use of first and last names

- greetings and farewells
- nonverbal communication: distance between people and handshaking

You practiced and used English in the following areas:

- forms of address
- introductions of yourself and others

ANSWERS TO CULTURE PUZZLES IN CHAPTER 1

Culture Puzzle #1

a) Yes. Since Ms. is used with either married or unmarried women, it can be used safely with both. You can ask the woman what she prefers to be called.

b) Yes. By avoiding using the person's name, you can also avoid using a special form of address (such as Ms., Mrs., or Miss). It is not always necessary to use a person's name when speaking to that person.

c) No. This is not always an accurate way of finding out whether a woman is married. She may wear a ring on her left hand and *not be* married or she may not wear a ring and *be* married. Even if the women is married, she may prefer to be called Ms.

Culture Puzzle #2

a) No. If you do this, some people might not understand why you continue to call them by their last name when they told you to use a first name. They might want to know your reasons.

b) Yes. When you try something new, it may be difficult at first. After awhile you may find that it is not so difficult to do.

c) Yes. People are interested in learning about others' customs. Many people can accept cultural explanations and appreciate hearing them. You could explain, for example, to a teacher: "Would you mind if I used your last name? In my country, it is polite for students to use their teachers' last names."

Culture Puzzle #3

a) No. If the person wants to shake hands with you, this would be rude.

b) Yes. If the other person extends his or her hand, then shake it immediately. If he or she does not, then there is no need to shake hands.

c) Yes. It is not considered wrong to shake hands in introductions. Some women, particularly older ones, may not be used to shaking hands in an introduction. Most, however, will shake hands if you extend your hand first.

Culture Puzzle #4

a) Yes. This is common. Your friend should remember to introduce you, but if he or she doesn't, it is not rude to introduce yourself. This may make you and the third person feel more comfortable.

b) Yes. This is also common. This is a way of reminding your friend to introduce you.

c) No. This is not the best idea. If you are not introduced, then you may not feel comfortable talking to the third person (and vice versa). The other person may be shy about introducing himself or herself and would probably appreciate your introduction.

Note: Answers to other exercises can be found in the separate Answer Key.

chapter 2

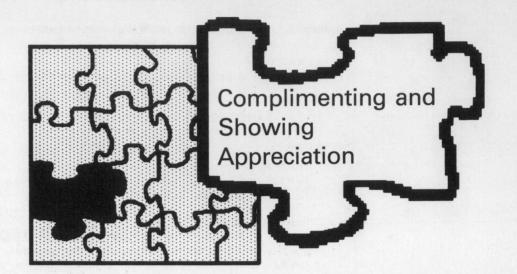

Complimenting and Showing Appreciation

Introduction Every language has certain *rules of speaking* and every culture has rules about how people should interact with each other. These rules are not usually written down, but are learned by people living together in one culture. In your own culture, you don't need to think very much about how to interact with other people because the rules are a part of you. When you learn about other cultural ways of doing things, you start to think about what you've been doing in your own language and culture. *Complimenting* and *showing appreciation* are examples of two areas where ways of interacting can differ across cultures. People compliment and show appreciation in many ways. This chapter will explain cultural differences and will provide you with language and information about complimenting and showing appreciation in American English.

CULTURE LEARNING QUESTIONS

1. In your own language and culture, when do people give compliments? How frequently are compliments given?
2. Have you noticed any cultural differences between the way people compliment in your culture and in U.S. culture? Explain your answer.
3. Have you had any experiences with people from another culture which show differences in customs relating to showing appreciation (example: gift-giving and receiving)?

rules of speaking—rules about the way people use their language; these rules are usually not written down, but are understood by native speakers of a language

complimenting—saying something to show another person that you like or approve of something; praising

showing appreciation—showing people that you like them or like something they did for you (in this chapter, showing appreciation focuses mainly on giving and receiving gifts)

16

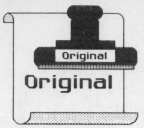

Original

(Revised interaction appears on page 18.)

CROSS-CULTURAL INTERACTION 2A:
Cultural Differences

Situation: Jonathan is a teacher in an adult school class in the United States. After class, he is speaking to Anh, one of his students.

Jonathan: "Anh, your English is improving. I am pleased with your work."

Anh: (looking down) "Oh, no. My English is not very good."

Jonathan: "Why do you say that, Anh? You're doing very well in class."

Anh: "No, I am not a good student."

Jonathan: "Anh, you're *making progress* in this class. You should be proud of your English."

Anh: "No, it's not true. You are a good teacher, but I am not a good student."

Jonathan: (He is surprised by her response and wonders why she thinks her English is so bad. He doesn't know what to say and wonders if he should stop giving her compliments.)

QUESTIONS AND DISCUSSION

Comprehension

Write T (true) or F (false) in the space provided.

1. _____ Anh is not a good student.
2. _____ Anh thinks that Jonathan is not a very good teacher.
3. _____ Jonathan thinks that Anh should be proud of her English.
4. _____ Jonathan does not understand why Anh thinks she is not a good student.
5. _____ Anh complimented Jonathan.

Analysis: Can You Explain?

1. Why do you think Anh says her English is not good?
2. Why do you think that Anh looks down when she says, "Oh, no, my English is not very good."
3. Why is Jonathan surprised when Anh says, "No, it's not true. I am not a good student."?
4. Jonathan doesn't know what to say when Anh disagrees with him. He wonders if he should stop giving her compliments. What do you think?

TALK ABOUT YOUR OWN LANGUAGE AND CULTURE

1. How does Anh's way of responding to compliments compare with the way people respond in your language and culture?
2. Does a teacher praise students often when they do well? Or does a teacher not say anything when students do good work?

making progress—improving; getting better

3. When Jonathan compliments Anh, she does not *make eye contact* with him. Can you think of times when people in your own culture do not make eye contact with teachers or other people who are of a *higher status?*

Summary of Cross-Cultural Interaction 2A: Cultural Differences

Jonathan is surprised when Anh says that her English is not good. He *expects her to say* "Thank you" (showing that she accepts the compliment). Instead she disagrees with (or denies) the compliment. This is her way of responding to compliments in her own culture. In Jonathan's culture (in the U.S.), most people say "Thank you" in response to a compliment. With her teacher, Anh behaves in a way that is natural and *proper* in her own culture. She is *modest and humble*. She does not look at her teacher at all times because that, too, is another way to show modesty. Jonathan should not stop giving compliments to Anh. Most people enjoy receiving compliments. He should understand that there are culturally different ways of responding to compliments. At the same time, it would be helpful for Anh to understand that many Americans are *not used to* people denying or disagreeing with compliments.

CROSS-CULTURAL INTERACTION 2B

The following interaction shows Anh responding in a way that is culturally familiar to Jonathan.

Jonathan: "Anh, your English is improving. I am pleased with your work."

Anh: (making eye contact) "Thank you. I have learned a lot in this course."

Jonathan: "You're doing well and I can really see progress."

Anh: "I enjoy studying English. I do homework every night."

Jonathan: "I can see that. *Keep up the good work.*"

Anh: "I'll try. You are a good teacher. You have helped me a lot."

Summary of Cross-Cultural Interaction 2B

In this interaction, Anh accepts her teacher's compliment with a direct "Thank you." This makes Jonathan feel comfortable because this is what he expects to hear. Anh also gives some extra information which adds to the conversation ("I have learned a lot in this course."). In giving the extra information she is helping to keep the conversation going. This is something that Americans often do. That

---

make eye contact–look at someone in the eyes
higher status—higher position; not at the same level
expects her to say—thinks she will say
proper—correct, acceptable
modest and humble—shy with and respectful of people of a higher status; does not wish to appear proud.
not used to—not accustomed to; not familiar with
Keep up the good work—keep doing good work; continue your good work

is, they turn compliments into conversations. Anh thanks Jonathan for his teaching. This seems natural to Jonathan, since Anh accepted his first compliment with a "Thank you."

FOCUS ON U.S. CULTURE
Cultural Notes, Exercises, and Skill Practice

HOW MUCH DO YOU ALREADY KNOW ABOUT U.S. CULTURE?

Write T (true) or F (false) in the space provided.

1. _____ When someone gives a compliment, the receiver immediately denies it (for example, "No, it's not true.").

2. _____ If a guest compliments something in another person's home, the host or hostess gives that thing to the guest.

3. _____ Americans (particularly American women) begin many conversations with compliments. They might say, for example, "You look nice today. Is that a new dress?"

4. _____ If an American compliments a woman's dress, for example, he or she usually asks how much it cost.

5. _____ It is *disrespectful* <u>not</u> to give a teacher a gift at the end of a course.

6. _____ Money is commonly given as a gift (for example, students give money to their teachers or employees to their supervisors).

7. _____ It is more polite to open a gift after the giver has gone away than to open it in front of him or her.

Note: The answers to the above can be found throughout the chapter and in the separate Answer Key.

SECTION 1. CHOOSING WORDS FOR COMPLIMENTING

The kinds of things people compliment and the words they use to compliment differ from culture to culture. The following lists what Americans commonly compliment.* Read the list and in the blank write "Yes" if this is a common compliment in your language and culture, or write "No" if it is not.

What Americans Compliment	*Common in Your Language/Culture*
1. Physical Appearance Example: "You have a beautiful smile." "Your hair looks nice."	_____

---

disrespectful—not respectful; not polite; rude

*The authors wish to thank Nessa Wolfson for her article entitled: "Compliments in Cross-Cultural Perspective" (*TESOL Quarterly*, Vol. 15, No. 2, June 1981, pp. 117–124) which provided the basis for parts of section 1 and 2.

2. Personality
   Example: "You have a good sense of humor."
   "He's got a great personality."

_____

3. Family Member
   Example: "Your wife is beautiful."
   "Your children are cute."

_____

4. Abilities
   Example: "You gave an excellent speech."
   "You teach very well."

_____

5. People's Things (possessions)
   Example: "Your car is nice."
   "You have a beautiful home."

_____

6. Meals, Food
   Example: "The dinner is great."
   "I love this dish."

_____

In American English, a limited number of words, mostly adjectives, are often used when people give compliments. The following adjectives can be used to describe things or people:

nice	beautiful
good	great
pretty	interesting
wonderful	fantastic

"Great," "wonderful," and "fantastic" all sound like strong compliments, but many Americans use them to describe everyday objects and events. For example, someone might say, "That's a great car," instead of "That's a nice car." This a common way of complimenting, but to some people from different countries these compliments seem *exaggerated* and *insincere*.

There are other adjectives that are more specific than the ones in the list above.

attractive: pretty, good-looking, handsome

tasty, delicious: very good food

gorgeous: very pretty or attractive; used for people, clothes, and other objects

Skill Practice: Choosing Words for Complimenting

Choose an appropriate word or words from the adjectives listed above and fill in the blanks. Use the correct part of speech.

exaggerated—expressed too strongly, overstated
insincere—not sincere, not honest

Examples

"That hat looks *good* on you."
"The dinner was *delicious*."

1. (two co-workers) "The speech you gave yesterday at work was _____."

2. (two friends) "That's a _____ dress. Is it new?"

3. (teacher/parent) "Your child's work is _____. You should be proud of her."

4. (two neighbors) "What a _____ car!"

5. (boss/employee) "You did an _____ job. I really appreciate it."

6. (two friends) "The picnic today was _____. Let's do it again soon."

7. (mother/daughter) "You look _____ today. The dress _____ you."

8. (teacher/student) "I _____ your composition very much. There were very few mistakes."

9. (guest/host) "The meal is _____. I really _____ the noodle salad."

10. (husband/wife) "The meal turned out _____. Everyone _____ it."

Cross-Cultural Exercise: Varieties of Compliments

Listed below are compliments that are typical of different languages and cultures.* Read them and write "English" in the blank if the compliment sounds like one that you might hear Americans give. Do any of the other compliments sound like ones you might hear in your language?

Example

"Your child is very intelligent." *English*

(Note: This compliment can be heard in many languages, including English, but it is not a compliment that is common in all languages.)

1. "She is like the moon and has beautiful eyes." _____

2. "I like your jacket. It suits you." _____

3. "You're such a good cook." _____

4. "Your earrings are pure gold, aren't they?" _____

5. "Wow! What did you do to your hair? Not bad!" _____

6. Son: "It was delicious, Mother. I hope your hands never have pain." _____

7. Husband to wife: "You must be tired after doing all the shopping." _____

*The authors wish to thank Nessa Wolfson for the examples of compliments across cultures. (*Ibid.*)

8. "Your shoes are nice." Response: "It is your
    eyes which can see them that are nice."   _____

9. "Your party was great. We loved it!"   _____

10. "Not a bad-looking dress you're wearing."   _____

(Answers are given at the end of the chapter.)

> **U.S. CULTURE NOTE**
>
> People from different cultures sometimes don't understand why Americans
> give so many compliments. In many cultures, too many compliments would
> seem insincere. For example, many Japanese people think that Americans
> give too many compliments. A Japanese woman said that she might give a
> compliment once a week. An American women said that she gives at least one
> compliment a day!

SECTION 2. STARTING CONVERSATIONS WITH COMPLIMENTS

Americans often say "Thank you" after they receive compliments and add a
sentence or two which can lead into a conversation. For example:

First Friend: "I like your earrings."
Second Friend: "Thanks, I got them in Mexico last year."

or

Boss: "The report you wrote is great. It has all the information I
            need."
Employee: "Thank you. I hope you have everything you need to start the
            project."

Even when some Americans disagree with a compliment, they will often say,
"Thanks" and add a sentence or two. For example:

Guest: "The cake is delicious."
Host: "Thanks, but it didn't turn out exactly right,"

> **CROSS-CULTURAL NOTE**
>
> A Chinese woman from Hong Kong, after fourteen years in the U.S., said, "It is
> still difficult for me to say, 'Thank you' when someone gives me a compliment.
> I still want to say, 'No, no, it's not true." I like when people compliment me,
> but I don't feel modest or humble if I accept a compliment with a "Thank you."

One of the reasons Americans seem to compliment frequently is to start a
conversation. The following is an example of a compliment that quickly turns into
a conversation.

> Sara: "I like your table."
> Mark: "Thanks. I made it myself."
> Sara: "Really? I didn't know that you work with wood."
> Mark: "I've been doing this for the past year."
> Sara: "Did you take a class in woodworking?"
> Mark: "No, I taught myself from books."
> Sara: "That's great!"

The second compliment at the end ("That's great!") means "That's a nice thing to do."

Skill Practice: Turning Compliments into Conversations

In pairs, begin a conversation with a compliment.

Example

> Maria: "You did a nice job on the project the boss asked you to do."
> Kara: "Thanks. It took about two weeks to do it."
> Maria: "That's not bad. It takes some people four weeks to do that job."
> Kara: "Really? I didn't think it was that hard."
> (The conversation continues.)

The following are suggestions for compliments (or think of your own).

1. (two neighbors)   one compliments the other's garden
2. (guest/host)   the guest compliments the meal
3. (student/teacher)   the student compliments the teacher's style of teaching
4. (two friends)   one compliments the other's clothes
5. (two students)   one compliments the other's English
6. your choice

CULTURE PUZZLE #1

Read the situation and choose the appropriate explanation or explanations. There may be more than one possible answer.

Situation: An American woman received a letter from a Japanese friend who had just gotten married. The Japanese woman wrote in her letter, "My husband is not very handsome. Your husband is much more handsome than mine." The American woman was very surprised by what her friend wrote.

Why do you think the American was surprised?

a) The American saw a picture of her friend's husband and thought that he was very handsome.
b) The American didn't think her own husband was handsome.
c) In the U.S., it is disrespectful to say that your husband is not handsome.

Why do you think the Japanese woman wrote, "My husband is not very handsome"?

a) The Japanese woman was trying to tell her American friend that she did not like her husband very much.

b) It is more common in Japan to *not* compliment one's husband than to compliment him. From a Japanese point of view, the woman was not being rude.

c) The Japanese woman didn't think her husband was handsome, but she liked his personality.

(Answers are given at the end of the chapter.)

U.S. CULTURE NOTE

In many cultures when people have a close relationship (for example, two close friends or a husband and a wife), they may not feel that it is necessary to give compliments to the other person. That is, they may not *verbalize* their thoughts. This is usually *not* true in the U.S. Even when people know each other well, they will verbalize their thoughts (for example, give compliments).

SECTION 3. GIVING AND RECEIVING GIFTS

In some countries, there are many rules about giving gifts. When do you give a gift? To whom do you give a gift? For what reasons do you give a gift? In the U.S., there are no exact rules about gift giving, but there are some general customs. The list below includes occasions when many people give gifts and includes the types of things people give. Remember that rules and customs around gift giving in the U.S. are general; it is *up to the individual* to decide when to give a gift and what to give.

Occasion	Typical Gifts
a meal at someone's home	a bottle of wine, flowers, candy
an overnight stay at someone's home	an object from your country (for example, a vase or dish), gifts for the children
friends' birthdays, particularly the "big" birthdays (21, 25, 30, 40. 50 . . . 75, 80, etc.)	books, records, clothing, decorations for the house, photo albums. (This depends on the person who is giving the gift.)
religious ceremonies such as Baptism (Christian), Confirmation (Christian), or Bar/Bat Mitzvah (Jewish)	books, religious objects. (For these occasions, it is a good idea to ask people for suggestions.)
weddings	items for the home such as dishes, pots, towels, blankets, photo albums
showers (baby showers, wedding showers)	baby showers: sheets, blankets, diaper bags, baby toys. wedding showers: usually small things for the kitchen
birth of a baby	clothes, toys, stuffed animals, things for the baby's room

verbalize—say with words
up to the individual—it is the choice of each person; it depends on the person

CROSS-CULTURAL NOTE

In some countries, giving money to a teacher or supervisor to show appreciation is usual. A group of Vietnamese students gave a money tree (a tree made out of paper with dollar bills attached) to an American teacher. She appreciated the gift, but was also surprised. She had never before received money from students as a gift. Her American students usually thanked her for her teaching at the end of a course, but they rarely gave her a gift and they never gave her money.

Cross-Cultural Exercise: When To Give Gifts

There are times when a gift is appropriate and times when it is not. In the following exercise, decide in which situations you would give a gift. Discuss what you would do in *your own culture* and *in the U.S.*

1. You have studied English with a tutor (private teacher) for about two months. Your tutor cannot continue because of a busy schedule. You will be meeting with your tutor for the last time.

   Would you give a gift? (yes/no)   my culture _____   U.S. _____

   If yes, what would you give? _____

2. Your supervisor at work just gave you your six-month performance review (evaluation). He gave you an excellent review and an increase in salary.

   Would you give a gift? (yes/no)   my culture: _____   U.S. _____

   If yes, what would you give? _____

3. A teacher has helped you after class when you had difficulty in a subject. She stayed more than an hour after class on three different days to help you. You appreciate her extra help.

   Would you give a gift? (yes/no)   my culture _____   U.S. _____

   If yes, what would you give? _____

4. It is one of your co-worker's birthdays. You don't know this person very well, but you like him and you know that other people will be getting presents for him.

   Would you give a gift? (yes/no)   my culture _____   U.S. _____

   If yes, what would you give? _____

5. You have a small problem with your car and your neighbor, a mechanic, looks at the car. He finds the problem in a couple of minutes and fixes it right away.

   Would you give a gift? (yes/no)   my culture _____   U.S. _____

   If yes, what would you give? _____

6. You have been sick for a few days. One of your neighbors has been bringing food for your family every day.

   Would you give a gift? (yes/no)   my culture _____   U.S. _____

   If yes, what would you give? _____

(Answers are given at the end of the chapter.)

Contact Assignment

Ask an American you know what he or she would do in the above six situations. If, in any of the situations, the American would not give a gift, ask what he or she would *say* to express appreciation. If you have the opportunity to ask more than one American, including both men and women, note the variety of responses. Write down what people tell you and share the responses with the class.

Phrases and Expressions for Showing Appreciation

Repeat these after your teacher says them:

"Thank you very much for doing what you did. You really helped me a lot."

"I really appreciate your help. It meant a lot to me."

"Thanks for all you've done. It was a great help."

"I couldn't have done it without you. Thank you very much."

"I hope I can help you someday the way you helped me."

U.S. CULTURE NOTE

A *non-U.S.-born* employee gave his American supervisor a gift of $200 (two hundred dollars). The employee told the supervisor, "I appreciate you and my job so much that I want you to have this." The American supervisor told his employee that he couldn't accept the gift. The employee said, "You must accept the gift or I will quit." The supervisor told him, "You have to understand that I cannot accept this gift." The supervisor was confused and felt very bad about it when he heard that his employee quit the job.

CULTURE PUZZLE #2

What would you do if you gave your boss or teacher an expensive gift and he or she said, "I'm sorry. I really can't accept this gift."

a) You could say, "If you don't accept this gift, I'll quit," or, "I won't take this class anymore."

b) You could try to find out the person's reasons for not accepting the gift.

c) You can insist many times on giving the gift until the person accepts it.

(Answers are given at the end of the chapter.)

Note: Read the following U.S. Culture Note for an explanation of Culture Puzzle #2.

non-U.S.-born—not born in the United States

> ### U.S. CULTURE NOTE
>
> Most of the time Americans do accept gifts that people give to them. However, in the workplace, supervisors or bosses sometimes feel uncomfortable accepting gifts and are not always allowed to do so. The following are some of the reasons:
>
> - They do not want to feel that they have to do something special or different for the employee who gave a gift.
> - They don't want their other employees to think that they have *favorites* among the employees.
> - They may find it difficult to criticize their employee's work if they've just received a gift from him or her.
> - Many companies have a *policy* that says that a supervisor is not allowed to accept gifts from employees.

CHAPTER SUMMARY

In this chapter, you looked at cultural differences in the areas of:

- when, why, and what people compliment
- gift giving and receiving

You practiced language and communication skills in the areas of:

- giving compliments
- starting conversations with compliments
- showing appreciation

ANSWERS TO CULTURE PUZZLES AND CROSS-CULTURAL EXERCISES IN CHAPTER 2

Cross-Cultural Exercise: Varieties of Compliments

1.	Arabic	6.	Farsi (Iranian)
2.	English	7.	Indonesian
3.	English	8.	Farsi
4.	Japanese	9.	English
5.	English	10.	English

Culture Puzzle #1

Why do you think the American was surprised?

a) No. Even if this were true, she wouldn't have expected a wife to say this about her husband. To the American, the Japanese woman insulted her husband.

b) No. Even if this were true, she wouldn't expect such a negative statement (i.e., from the American point of view) from the Japanese woman.

c) Yes. A statement like this about one's spouse (i.e., in the U.S.) would be considered very disrespectful. If an American woman said this about her husband, people might think that they didn't have a good relationship.

favorites—people who are favored; people who are liked more than others
policy—a rule; a formal instruction guiding behavior

Why do you think the Japanese woman wrote, "My husband is not very handsome."?

    a) No. This would not be a Japanese way of saying that she didn't like her husband.

    b) Yes. In Japan, a person would be considered boastful and not modest enough if she (or he) complimented family members in front of others. Instead, some Japanese (particularly those who are more traditional than others) might say something slightly negative just to show that they are being modest and not overly proud.

    c) No. See b).

Cross-Cultural Exercise: When To Give Gifts

(All of the following answers apply to U.S.)

1. In this situation, it would not be necessary to give a gift, particularly if you have been paying for the private classes with the tutor. If not, you might want to bring something to the last class, such as candy or some food from your country.

2. In this situation, it is definitely *not* an American practice to bring a gift to the supervisor. It is the supervisor's job to supervise you; you are the one who worked hard to earn the excellent review. In this situation, the supervisor might not understand why you are bringing a gift.

3. In this situation, a teacher would not expect a gift, but would expect you to thank him or her sincerely for the extra time spent. Most likely, the teacher's reward would come from your understanding the difficult subject.

4. In this situation, your co-worker does not expect a present from someone he or she doesn't know well and it might even make him uncomfortable to receive one. Rather than giving individual presents, it is more usual for co-workers to buy a gift collectively. That is, each person contributes some money and one person buys a gift with the money.

5. In this situation, your neighbor wouldn't expect a gift, but it would be nice to bring him something like a bottle of wine. Your neighbor saved you time and money and spent some of his free time working.

6. In this situation, it would be a nice gesture to give a gift to your neighbor or to invite your neighbor's family over for a meal.

Culture Puzzle #2

    a) No. You need to understand the reasons why your boss or teacher will not accept the gift. From an American point of view, the reasons are good ones. (See U.S. Culture Note following Culture Puzzle #2.)

    b) Yes. This would show that you respect the person who is not accepting the gift. It would also show that you are open-minded.

    c) No. You can try to encourage the other person to accept the gift by offering it 2 or 3 times at the most. Insisting many times might cause the person to become angry.

Note: Answers to other exercises can be found in the separate Answer Key.

chapter 3

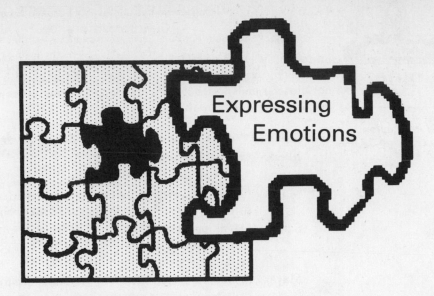

Introduction To understand other people, it is necessary to understand both their verbal and nonverbal communication. This is especially important when you want to understand the *emotions* that they are expressing. Although everyone experiences the same emotions, the way emotions are expressed can differ cross-culturally. There are also personal and cultural differences as to how much people want to talk about the way they feel.   Two emotions that are sometimes misunderstood and misread across cultures are sadness and anger. This chapter will explain cultural variations and give examples of some of the ways that Americans express sadness and anger.

CULTURE LEARNING QUESTIONS

1. If someone is upset or angry, do you think it is better for that person to talk about the way he or she feels? Is it better to keep feelings inside? Explain your answer.
2. If you see that someone is unhappy or upset, would you say anything about it? Would you ask the person why he or she was feeling that way?
3. Are there any expressions or idioms in your language that can help people understand cultural beliefs about expressing emotions? For example, in English the following are common.*

Get it off your chest.

Talk it out.

Get it out; don't hold it in.

---

emotions—feelings such as sadness, happiness, anger, etc.
*Note: All of these expressions refer to talking about feelings or problems; that is, not keeping silent about them.

Original

*(Revised interaction
appears on page 32.)*

CROSS-CULTURAL INTERACTION 3A:
Cultural Differences*

Situation: Maya, a non-U.S.-born employee, and her American co-worker, Sara, are leaving work to go home. The two are friendly with each other, but they are not close friends. Sara notices that Maya seems upset about something, so she decides to ask her about it.

Sara: "You seem upset about something. Is everything okay?"

Maya: "Everything's fine."

Sara: "Are you sure? You look upset."

Maya: (Thinking, "Why is she asking me how I feel? She shouldn't ask me so many questions.") "No, there's no problem." (She looks away.)

Sara: (Thinking to herself, "I'm just trying to help her and to show her that I'm interested in her.") "Well, I hope everything's okay. Remember, you can always talk to me."

Maya: (Thinking to herself, "Why should I talk to her?") "Okay."

Sara: (Thinking to herself, "I hope she talks to somebody. She'll feel better if she gets her feelings out.") "See you tomorrow."

QUESTIONS AND DISCUSSION

Comprehension

Write T (true) or F (false) in the space provided.

1. _____ Maya wanted to talk to Sara about the way she was feeling.
2. _____ Maya told Sara how she was feeling.
3. _____ Maya thought that it was okay that Sara was asking her questions.
4. _____ Maya was too busy to talk to Sara.
5. _____ Sara knew that she shouldn't ask Maya questions.

Analysis: Can You Explain?

1. Why do you think that Maya said, "No, there's no problem" when something was bothering her?
2. How do you think Sara felt when Maya didn't want to talk to her?
3. Do you think Sara should continue to ask Maya to talk about her problems? Why or why not?

*Note to the teacher: The differences in this interaction can also exist between people in one culture. It will help the student's understanding to know that two Americans can have an interaction similar to this one. However, there is a strong cultural dimension to the above interaction in that many Americans value "getting things out in the open" and "talking things out." It is helpful to remind students that cultural values exist even though not all people in a particular culture manifest those values.

TALK ABOUT YOUR OWN LANGUAGE AND CULTURE

1. If you were in the same situation as Sara (in Interaction 3A), would you try to get the other person to talk? How about with a close friend? Explain your answer.

2. How important do you think it is to "get things off your chest" (that is, to talk about problems)? Can you think of times when it is better not to talk about things?

Summary of Cross-Cultural Interaction 3A: Cultural Differences

Sara believes that it is *healthy* to let emotions out rather than to keep them in. She, like many Americans, thinks that people can feel better after they have talked about their feelings. Sara doesn't realize that her questions are making Maya uncomfortable. Maya probably thinks that it is strange for someone who is not a close friend to ask these kinds of questions. Maya may not even talk about her feelings with a close friend. Unfortunately, Sara does not understand these cultural differences and may feel that Maya is *rejecting* her efforts to make her feel better. In some cultures, people try to hide feelings of sadness or anger because they don't want to *burden* another person with their problems. In some cultures, *controlling one's emotions* is the sign of a strong person.

healthy—good; the right thing
rejecting—not accepting
burden—make problems for
controlling one's emotions—not letting such emotions as sadness or anger show; keeping emotions in

CROSS-CULTURAL INTERACTION 3B

In the following interaction, Maya still doesn't tell Sara how she is feeling, but she explains why she doesn't. As a result, both Sara and Maya are more comfortable this time.

Sara: "You seem upset about something. Is everything okay?"

Maya: "Everything's fine."

Sara: "Are you sure? You look upset."

Maya: "Well, something is bothering me, but I'm not used to talking about my feelings."

Sara: "You can always talk to me if you want. You might feel better if you do."

Maya: "Thanks, but in my culture we don't usually talk about our feelings with others.

Sara: "That's hard for me to understand, but I'm glad you explained it to me. I hope you feel better soon."

Maya: "Thanks. I'm sure I will."

Summary of Cross-Cultural Interaction 3B

Maya is able to prevent an uncomfortable interaction because she explains an important cultural difference between herself and Sara. Maya still doesn't answer Sara's questions, but this time Sara understands the reason. Even though it is difficult for Sara to understand the difference, she can accept it. In this interaction, she does not feel that Maya is rejecting her personally or her efforts to make Maya feel better.

FOCUS ON U.S. CULTURE
Cultural Notes, Exercises, and Skill Practice

HOW MUCH DO YOU ALREADY KNOW ABOUT U.S. CULTURE?

Write T (true) or F (false) in the space provided.

1. _____ When Americans are feeling sad or upset, most of the time they smile to hide their true feelings.

2. _____ Some American parents teach their sons and daughters different things about expressing emotion (for example, they sometimes tell their sons not to cry, but do not tell this to their daughters).

3. _____ It is unusual for Americans to express their anger directly to another person.

4. _____ If you seem upset about something, an American will never ask, "What's wrong?"

SECTION 1. CROSS-CULTURAL DIFFERENCES

People experience similar emotions all over the world, but sometimes express them differently. Children see their parents expressing such emotions as sadness and anger and, when they grow up, they express them in more or less the same way. In some parts of the world, people express these emotions very freely and you can *read their faces like a book.* In other parts of the world, it is not always as easy to know what another person is feeling. The culture puzzles and notes in this part of the chapter will illustrate some of these differences.

U.S. CULTURE NOTE

Boys and girls are sometimes taught different things about **expressing sadness.** Some American parents let their little girls cry, but feel uncomfortable when their sons cry. These parents may say, "Don't cry. Be a man!" This explains, in part, why men and women don't always express sadness in the same way. This is an example of how culture is learned, that is, **how children learn to express emotions from those around them.**

read their faces like a book—know what they're feeling just by looking at their faces

CULTURE PUZZLE #1

Read the situation and choose the appropriate explanation or explanations. There may be more than one possible answer.

Situation: Kim is an immigrant living in the United States. She is talking to Judy, an American neighbor. Judy asks Kim if she plans to go to the neighborhood picnic. Kim answers, "No, I won't be going." Smiling, Kim tells Judy, "Maybe you don't know this, but my husband *passed away* last month." Judy is surprised and saddened by the news and she expresses her *sympathy*. Later she thinks about her conversation with Kim. She felt that there was something strange about the conversation.

Judy felt that there was something strange about her conversation with Kim because:

a) An American woman whose husband had died recently would be wearing black clothing.
b) Most Americans would not smile when telling sad news.
c) An American would put a notice in the newspaper so that everyone would know about it.

(Answers are given at the end of the chapter.)

passed away—died
sympathy—feelings of sadness and caring

Cross-Cultural Exercise: Nonverbal Differences

Discuss the following questions and then do the observation activity that follows.

1. What do you think Kim's smile meant?
2. In the U.S., the usual meaning of the smile is happiness or friendliness. What else can a smile mean?

Observation Activity

1. Observe when and why people in your own culture smile, and then do the same for Americans and other cultural groups with which you are in contact. Write down your observations for both cultural groups.
2. Discuss cultural differences and possible misunderstandings that might occur because of these differences.

U.S. CULTURE NOTE

The "U.S." smile is famous. Many people from around the world refer to former U.S. president Jimmy Carter's smile. Americans are famous for saying "cheese" when they are being photographed. Americans notice right away when people don't smile in the same situations as those in which they smile. American businessmen think that Japanese businessmen look too serious in photos because they usually don't smile. Many Americans think that Russians don't smile enough or smile at the "wrong" time. Of course there is no "right" or "wrong" time to smile. People's cultural backgrounds often influence when and how often they smile.

CULTURE PUZZLE #2

Read the situation and choose the appropriate answer(s). There may be more than one possible answer.

Situation: Joe and Gary, both Americans, are friends. They have just *run into each other* at a store.

Joe: "Hey, Gary. How've you been?" (Joe is happy to see Gary. He slaps him on the back.)

Gary: "Oh, hi Joe. *How's it going?*" (Gary does not seem happy to see Joe.)

Joe: "Pretty good. *Everything okay* with you? It looks like something is bothering you."

Gary: "If you want to know the truth, I'm *pretty* angry at you."

Joe: "What did I do?"

Gary: "Well, I heard that you *went out with* Jennifer two nights ago. You know I've had my eye on her for a long time."

What do you think Joe's reaction will be?

---

run into each other—met by chance; see each other without having planned it
How's it going?—How is everything? How are you?
Everything okay?—Is everything okay?
pretty—very
went out with—went on a date with; took to (for example) a restaurant, the movies, etc.

a) Joe will *apologize* many times and will promise not to go out with Jennifer again.
b) Joe will say something like, "Wait a minute. You don't own her. You've never been out with her before."
c) Joe will get angry with Gary because Gary got angry with him.

(Answers are given at the end of the chapter.)

Cross-Cultural Exercise: Expressing Anger

Discuss the following questions and then do the role-play suggested in question 3:*

1. Could the situation with Gary and Joe occur in your country?
2. If so, what might Gary and Joe say to each other? Would Gary express his anger? Can you make a *cultural generalization* or does it depend on the person?
3. What would you say if you were either Gary or Joe? How would you express yourself? Discuss this answer and then role-play the situation.

U.S. CULTURE NOTE

Americans often ask each other, "What's wrong?" if they see by a person's expression that something is bothering him or her. Many people think that you should say what is wrong instead of just acting upset or angry. If a person acts upset, angry, or bothered, but doesn't say anything about it, some Americans think that person is being childish.

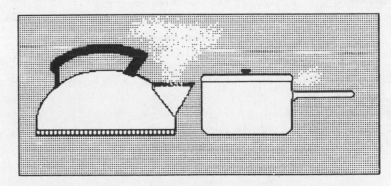

Some people "let off steam" easily; others keep most of it inside!

apologize—say "I'm sorry."
cultural generalization—a general statement about how many people act or behave in a particular culture; a statement about a cultural pattern
Note to the teacher: If your students are business people or older adults for whom this role-play may not be relevant, think of another situation in which one person is clearly angry at another. For example, ask what a supervisor, manager, or boss would do if one of his employees discussed a problem with the supervisor's superior rather than first bringing it up with the supervisor. Or, ask your students to think of times when they've been angry at another person. Compare cultural and individual responses.

CROSS-CULTURAL NOTE

In any one country, you will see people expressing anger in different ways, but there are generalizations that can be made. People from certain parts of the world are said to be "hot-blooded" or "hot-tempered." This means that they express their anger easily and quickly. In some parts of the world, people are taught that expressing anger is wrong and shows a lack of control. Imagine the kinds of things a married couple has to learn when the husband is from one side of the world and the wife is from another!

SECTION 2. USING NONVERBAL AND VERBAL COMMUNICATION

What can you say if you think that you are communicating nonverbally, but another person does not understand what you are trying to express? You might think that this person is rude or *insensitive*, but *this may not be the case*. If this happens, ask yourself the following questions:

1. Is my style of nonverbal communication familiar to this person?
2. Am I expecting this person to understand a way of communicating that he or she does not use with someone from the same culture?

U.S. CULTURE NOTE

American culture is a very verbal culture. Misunderstandings can occur when someone from a different culture tries to communicate nonverbally (without words), and the American doesn't notice or understand the nonverbal communication. This can also happen between two Americans.

CULTURE PUZZLE #3

Read the situation and choose the appropriate answer or answers. There may be more than one possible answer.

Situation: A Chinese man, a factory worker, is talking to a friend about his American boss. "My boss told me that he wanted me to work *overtime* this weekend. I really don't want to because my brother is arriving from Taiwan on Saturday, and I haven't seen him in five years. I told my boss about my brother last week. When he told me he needed me to work overtime, I said, 'Yes,' but I was not very happy. I'm sure he could see how I felt. He should have remembered that my brother was coming."

If the American boss had heard what his employee said, he would say something like:

a) "Oh, your brother's coming this weekend. I'm sorry that I forgot. Okay. I'm sure that I can find someone else to work overtime this weekend."

insensitive—not understanding of another person's feelings
this may not be the case—this may not be true
overtime—extra hours for which the employee gets paid more money

b) "Why didn't you tell me that you didn't want to work this weekend? You said 'Yes' when I asked you to work so I thought it was okay. I'm not a *mind reader*."

c) "I can't treat you differently from everyone else. If you work overtime, even when it is difficult for you, your *review* will be better."

(Answers are given at the end of the chapter.)

The situation above shows what can happen when one person thinks he is communicating clearly without words, but the other person does not understand the nonverbal communication. In this case, the Chinese man was upset and expected his boss to know that he was. This situation shows how important it is to verbalize (say in words) what you are thinking.

Phrases for Expressing Feelings

Repeat these after your teacher says them:

"Let me explain how I'm feeling."
"Let me explain how I feel."
"Let me tell you my reaction to that."
"It's not easy for me to say this, but I'm a bit upset about what happened."
'I will try to explain the way I'm feeling, but it's not easy to do."
"I am uncomfortable about what happened because. . . ."
"In my culture, we don't usually talk about this, but I'd like to let you know how I feel."

mind reader—someone who "reads" people's minds; someone who knows exactly what another person is thinking
review—performance review; evaluation of an employee's work (usually given every six months)

U.S. CULTURE NOTE

There are Americans who prefer not to express their emotions verbally or nonverbally. They may try to hide their emotions completely. In a culture made up of so many different types of people, it is not always easy or possible to describe how people react emotionally. In the area of expressing emotions, there can be differences between people of different generations, between men and women and among Americans of different cultural backgrounds. Yet, there is still a general belief that it is good to "talk things out" or "get things off your chest" when there is a problem.

CHAPTER SUMMARY

In this chapter, you looked at cultural differences in the areas of:

- expressing sadness and anger
- verbalizing feelings
- smiling and its meanings across cultures

ANSWERS TO CULTURE PUZZLES IN CHAPTER 3

Culture Puzzle #1

Judy felt that there was something strange about her conversation with Kim because:

  a) No. If a family member dies, most Americans would wear black only on the day of the funeral or memorial service, not for a full month after.
  b) Yes. Many Americans show sadness on their faces and do not smile to cover up sadness.
  c) No. Many Americans do put notices in the paper when a family member dies, but they wouldn't expect everybody (including neighbors) to read these notices.

Culture Puzzle #2

What do you think Joe's reaction will be?

  a) No. Joe would probably not apologize many times because, from his point of view, he may not feel that he has done anything wrong. Perhaps if Gary had asked Joe not to go out with Jennifer because he (Gary) was interested in her, then Joe might have apologized.
  b) Yes. This is very possible. Joe might also have said, "You should have asked me not to go out with her. We didn't agree on anything."
  c) Yes. This is also possible. Sometimes people react quickly and angrily when someone says so directly, "I'm angry at you."

Culture Puzzle #3

What do you think the American boss would say if he had heard what his employee said?

  a) No. The employee only mentioned that his brother was coming (before he was asked about overtime) and didn't say that he didn't want to work overtime. Even if the boss had remembered about the brother, he may have thought that this employee would still want the extra money by working overtime.
  b) Yes. This is very possible. The employee's nonverbal communication was not enough for him to know that the employee really didn't want to work. When most Americans hear the answer, "Yes," they think that "Yes" means "Yes."
  c) This is possible, although it depends on the personality of the boss. Some bosses can act this way; others do not.

Note: Answers to other exercises can be found in the separate Answer Key.

Reading Text and Activities

Contents:

Reading Preview Activities	**Post-Reading Activities**
Reading Outline	Reading Comprehension
Outline Questions	Vocabulary Exercises
Vocabulary	Going Beyond the Reading
Reading Preview Suggestions	
Reading Text	

READING TEXT: COMMUNICATING ACROSS CULTURES
Reading Preview Activities

Reading Outline   Read the outline of the text and discuss the questions following it.

Part I. Language Fluency and Communication

A. Two people from different cultures meet (examples are given in the reading).
B. Sometimes communication comes easily to them; other times it does not.
C. It is not enough to be fluent in the language spoken in another culture.
　　1. An example: An American in England.

Part II. Culture Learning

A. Understanding the new culture and learning to communicate comfortably in it are as important goals as learning the rules of the language.
B. Much of culture is hidden from sight; it cannot be seen.
　　1. Culture is like an iceberg.
　　2. Most of the iceberg is deep within the ocean just as much of culture is deep within people.

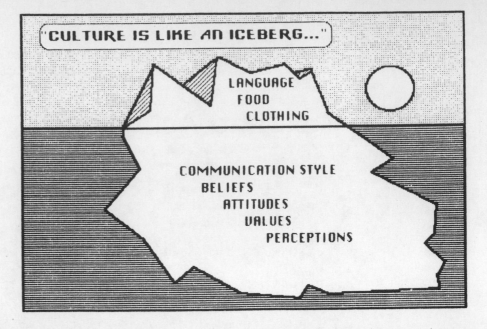

C. Some cultural differences can be seen right away; these are like the tip of the iceberg.

D. Learning to communicate well across cultures means becoming aware of the hidden parts of culture.

Part III. Cross-Cultural Understanding

A. In another language and culture, it can be especially difficult to explain one's ideas and feelings.

B. What is "right" in one culture may be "wrong" in another culture.

C. Understanding another cultural point of view means learning to see the submerged part of the iceberg and not forgetting that it is there.

OUTLINE QUESTIONS

Based on the outline and your own experiences, answer the following questions:

1. In the first part of the reading, the authors write, "Sometimes communication comes easily to two people from different cultures; other times it does not." What are some of the difficulties people have when they are not fluent in a language?

2. In the second part of the reading, the authors talk about the goals of a newcomer in another country. What were your goals when you first came to the U.S.? What did you need and want to learn right away?*

3. In the third part of the reading, the authors say that what is "right" in one culture may be "wrong" in another. From your own experience, can you think of any examples of this?

*Note to teachers outside of the U.S.: These questions need to be adapted for students who haven't traveled outside of their country. Ask them to discuss their thoughts as to what the immediate goals of a newcomer should be in a foreign country. Have them tell you what foreigners need to learn in their country.

VOCABULARY

Following is a list of vocabulary from the reading text in Unit I, *Communicating Across Cultures.* To help you with pronunciation, each word is divided into syllables. The stressed syllable is marked with an accent mark (´). The words are grouped by part of speech (nouns, verbs, etc.) in the order in which they appear in the reading. Practice saying these words after your teacher says them. Each word is glossed (defined) at the bottom of the page the first time it appears in the reading. The definition gives the meaning of the word as it is used in the reading. These words also appear in the post-reading activities.

PART I

Nouns
IMMIGRANT   im´-mi-grant
OVERSEAS   o-ver-seas´
ENGLISHMAN   Eng´-lish-man

Verbs
GUARANTEE   gua-ran-tee´
BOTHERING   both´-er-ing
COMPLIMENT   com´-pli-ment
SUPPOSE   sup-pose´
ASSUME   as-sume´

Adjectives
BRIEF   brief
FLUENT   flu´-ent

Adverbs
PERHAPS   per-haps´

Two-Word Verbs/Idioms
GET ALONG WITH   get a-long´ with
QUITE A BIT   quite´ a bit´

PART II

Nouns
GOALS   goals
STAGE   stage
CHALLENGE   chal´-lenge
ICEBERG   ice´-berg
ACCENT   ac´-cent
PHYSICAL FEATURES   phys´-i-cal fea´-tures
HABITS   ha´-bits
VALUES   val´-ues
BELIEFS   be-liefs´

Verbs
INVOLVES   in-volves´
OBSERVE   ob-serve´
CONSISTS OF   con-sists´ of
INFLUENCES   in´-flu-en-ces

Adjectives
HUGE   huge
HIDDEN   hid´-den
SUBMERGED   sub-merged´
DEEP WITHIN   deep´ with´-in
OBVIOUS   ob´-vi-ous
VERBAL   ver´-bal
NONVERBAL   non´-ver´-bal
AWARE   a-ware´

PART III

Nouns
BEHAVIOR   be-hav´-ior

Verbs
EXIST   ex-ist´
MISCOMMUNICATE   mis-com-m´u-ni-cate

Adjectives
SIMILAR   sim´-i-lar
NORMAL   nor´-mal

Two-Word Verb
FIGURE OUT   fig´-ure out´

Conjunctions
ALTHOUGH   al-though´

Reading Preview Suggestions

Before you begin to read the text, *Communicating Across Cultures,* do the following:

1. Read the titles of each part (parts I, II, and III).
2. Read the subheadings within each part of the reading.
3. Read the sentences in the margins.

4. Read the first sentence of each paragraph.
5. Read the key concepts at the end of each part.
6. Read the glosses (definitions) at the bottom of each page.

READING TEXT: COMMUNICATING ACROSS CULTURES

Part I. Language Fluency and Communication

1. Two people from different cultures meet. Let's say one is American, born in the U.S., and the other is from another country. *Perhaps* the person from the other country is an *immigrant* now living in the U.S., or maybe he is a foreign student staying in the U.S. for only a couple of years. He could be a businessman from *overseas* on a *brief* visit or he may be a tourist. Or, perhaps in a country outside of the U.S., it is an American who has met a citizen of that country.

2. Sometimes communication comes easily to them; other times it does not. If the non-U.S.-born person is *fluent* in English or if the American speaks the other's language, then conversation is not so difficult.

3. It is important to remember, however, that fluency in a language does not *guarantee* perfect communication all the time. Even two people who speak the same language can have difficulty.

4. **An Example: An American in England.** An American has traveled to England and is staying with a friend. During his stay, the American decides to talk to the *Englishman* about some things that are *bothering* him.

In another culture, a person may feel uncomfortable and not know why.

American:	"I feel uncomfortable with many of the people here, but I'm not sure why. I speak the same language, so there shouldn't be any problem. Back home, I usually *get along with* people. You know that I'm very friendly."
Englishman:	"Yes, that's true, but you're friendly in the way that Americans are friendly."
American:	"I'm not sure I understand what you mean."
Englishman:	"Well, for example, at the meeting we went to the other night, you immediately called people by their first names. We do that here, but not when we first meet someone."
American:	"That's how we make people feel comfortable. People feel friendlier toward each other when they use first names."
Englishman:	"It's different here. For example, when you met my boss at the meeting, you should have used his last name. There's something else that you do that English people don't often do."
American:	"What's that?"

perhaps—maybe
immigrant—a person who comes to a new country to live
overseas—countries beyond or across the seas
brief—short
fluent—can speak a language very well
guarantee—promise; mean something will happen for sure
Englishman—man from England
bothering—making someone feel worried or upset
get along with—have a good relationship with, be friendly with

Englishman: "You touch people on the shoulder *quite a bit,* especially when you *compliment* them."

American: "I guess I've never thought about that before. I *suppose* that is what I do at home."

Effective communication in another culture means knowing both the language and the culture.

5. This is an important lesson for the American. He speaks the same language as the English do, so he *assumes* that he won't have any problems. He doesn't stop to think that he may have to do things differently. Luckily for him, he has someone who can help him understand the people that he meets. He quickly learns that in England he needs to be able to do more than speak English.

Key Concepts in PART I _____

Communication across cultures: This phrase refers to communication between people from different cultures.

Ability to speak another language: Speaking another language fluently does not guarantee perfect communication.

_____

Part II. Culture Learning

Learning to communicate comfortably with people is as important as learning the rules of a language.

6. Fluency in another language is one of the most important *goals* of a newcomer to another country. In addition, understanding the culture and learning to communicate comfortably with the people of that culture are as important as learning the rules of the language. Language learning and culture learning go together and may take a long time.

7. Sometimes people feel that they know a culture after a few weeks or months. People do learn a lot when they first begin living in another culture, but this is only the first *stage* of learning. It usually *involves* things like learning everyday activities and some basic customs.

Much of culture is hard to see.

8. To really learn another culture, people have to go beyond the first stage. This is a *challenge* because it is often difficult to know what to learn. Much of what we call "culture" is hard to see.

Culture is deep within people.

9. **Culture is like an iceberg.**   Picture in your mind a *huge iceberg* in the ocean. The only part of the iceberg that you see is the tip. You don't see the rest of the iceberg because it is *hidden* from sight, *submerged* below the water. It's easy to forget that it is there. Most of the iceberg is deep within the ocean, just as much of culture is *deep within* people.

quite a bit—a lot; many times
compliment—to say something nice about someone
suppose—guess, think something is probably true
assumes—thinks something will probably be true
goals—major things you want to do
stage—step or level
involves (something)—includes (something)
challenge—something difficult, but also exciting or enjoyable
huge—very, very big
iceberg—a very large piece of ice floating in the ocean
hidden—cannot be seen; out of sight
submerged—under water
deep within—way inside

10. When you meet someone from another culture, certain cultural differences are *obvious*. You hear another language or you hear your own language spoken with an *accent*. You see different foods, clothes, and sometimes *physical features* of people. You *observe* new customs or *habits,* such as the use of chopstick or bowing or kissing on both cheeks when greeting. These differences are interesting and important, but they are usually not too difficult to understand. They are visible so they are seen easily and quickly.

The hidden part of culture influences a person's way of thinking and communicating.

11. The part of culture that is like the submerged part of the iceberg *consists of* assumptions, communication styles, *values,* and *beliefs* about what is right and wrong. The hidden part of culture *influences* much of a person's way of thinking and communicating. It is the meaning behind his or her *verbal* and *nonverbal* language. Learning to communicate well with people from other cultures involves becoming *aware* of the hidden part of culture.

Key Concepts in PART II

Culture learning: Culture learning takes time. A person cannot learn a culture in a few weeks or months.

Culture is hidden: Like an iceberg, much of culture is hidden from sight. You may not think much about the parts that you don't see.

The submerged part of culture: This part includes people's assumptions, styles of communication, values, and beliefs about what is right and wrong.

Part III. Cross-Cultural Understanding

In another language and culture, it can be especially difficult to explain one's ideas and feelings.

12. When deep cultural differences *exist,* a person may misunderstand someone from another culture. In another language and culture, it can be especially difficult to explain one's ideas and feelings. For these reasons, it takes more time to make sure that people have understood each other. We know that even in one's own culture, people often *miscommunicate*. There are many reasons for this. If people are tired or in a hurry or are uncomfortable with each other, they may not say what they really mean. One may say something with one meaning in mind and the other person may hear it completely differently. However, often (*although* not always) people from the same cultural background can *figure out* why there was a misunderstanding because they have *similar* ways of communicating and behaving.

obvious—very easy to see or understand
accent—the special pronunciation of a person who is speaking in a second language
physical features—shape or color of nose, mouth, eyes, skin
observe—notice, watch (noun: *observation*)
habits—usual and repeated behavior or customs
consists of—is made of; includes
values—beliefs and ideas that you consider important or desirable
influences—has an effect on
beliefs—things you believe; things you feel are true or right
verbal—with words or speaking
nonverbal—without words or speaking
aware—be aware of; have knowledge or understanding (noun: *awareness*)
exist—be; be real
miscommunicate—not communicate well, or not understand someone (noun: *miscommunication*)
although—but; however
figure out—think about until you understand
similar—almost the same (noun: *similarities*)

13. *Right in one culture; wrong in another culture.* When two people grow up in different parts of the world, they may have different ideas of what is usual, or "right" or "*normal.*" They may find that what is right in one culture is wrong in another. They may find out that their "normal" *behavior* is seen as strange.

Understanding another cultural point of view doesn't mean agreeing with it.

14. At first it may be difficult to understand another cultural way of thinking. Understanding it doesn't mean agreeing with it. It just means being able to say, "I understand what he did (or said) from his cultural point of view." Understanding another cultural point of view means learning to see the submerged part of the iceberg and not forgetting that it is there.

Key Concepts in PART III

Cross-cultural understanding: It takes more time in another culture to make sure that people have understood each other.

Right and wrong: When two people grow up in different parts of the world, they may have a different idea of what is usual, "right," or "normal."

POST-READING ACTIVITIES

READING COMPREHENSION EXERCISES

True/False

Read each statement. Then, according to the reading, decide whether the statement is true or false. Write T (true) or F (false) in the space provided.

1. _____ When two people speak the same language, there are no communication problems. (Part I)
2. _____ The example in Part I shows what happens when someone goes to another country and does not speak the language of that country.
3. _____ Cross-cultural communication takes place between people from two different cultures. (Part I)
4. _____ The American and English cultures are exactly the same. (Part I)
5. _____ A person can't really know or learn a culture in a few months. (Part II)
6. _____ When people from different cultures communicate with each other, they are usually aware of the hidden parts of culture. (Part II)
7. _____ People from the same culture always understand why they have communication problems. (Part III)
8. _____ In another language and culture, it is more difficult to explain one's ideas and feelings than in one's own culture. (Part III)

normal—usual; not strange
behavior—the way people act

9. _____ If something is wrong in one culture, then it is wrong in every culture. (Part III)

10. _____ When you live in another country, it is always necessary to agree with the way people do things. (Part III)

Multiple Choice

Circle the letter next to the one best answer. Try to answer each question without looking at the reading. Then, if you cannot answer the question, reread the paragraph indicated.

1. Fluency in another language doesn't mean that: (Paragraph 3)
   a) communication will be perfect all the time.
   b) two speakers will have difficulty understanding each other.
   c) two speakers are from the same culture.

2. The American in England had some problems because: (Paragraphs 4 and 5)
   a) he was an unfriendly person.
   b) he had language problems.
   c) he wasn't familiar with British culture.

3. Culture learning takes a long time because: (Paragraph 8)
   a) much of culture is hard to see.
   b) icebergs are not visible.
   c) there are so many basic customs.

4. The tip of the iceberg is like: (Paragraphs 9 and 10)
   a) the hidden parts of culture.
   b) the obvious and visible parts of culture.
   c) beliefs about right and wrong.

5. The submerged part of the iceberg is like: (Paragraph 11)
   a) the parts of culture that are easily seen.
   b) the hidden parts of culture that are not easily seen.
   c) different kinds of food.

6. People from the same culture may miscommunicate because: (Paragraph 12)
   a) they don't understand each other's language.
   b) they can never explain their ideas and feelings.
   c) they may be tired or in a hurry or uncomfortable with each other.

7. When two people grow up in different parts of the world: (Paragraph 13)
   a) they always have different ideas about what is right and wrong.
   b) they may have different ideas about what is right and wrong.
   c) they will always behave differently.

8. Understanding another cultural point of view involves: (Paragraph 14)
   a) agreeing with everything that is different in the new culture.
   b) changing one's own behavior completely.
   c) learning to see the hidden parts of culture.

VOCABULARY EXERCISES

Matching

Draw a line from each verb in the left column to the matching definition in the right column. The first one is done for you.

1. bother
2. assume
3. involve
4. influence
5. miscommunicate
6. exist

   a. be, be real
   b. say something nice about someone
   c. think something will probably be true
   d. not communicate well or not understand
   e. worry; upset
   f. promise; say that something will happen for sure

7. observe
8. compliment
9. guarantee

   g. include something
   h. have an effect; shape or change
   i. notice; watch

Word Forms

Choose the correct word in the parentheses ( ) and fill in the blanks in the following sentences. The first one is done for you.

1. (hide/hidden)
   In some cultures, people sometimes *hide* their true feelings because they don't want to make others feel uncomfortable.

2. (assume/assumptions)
   When you are talking to a person from another culture, you may make _____ about their actions.

3. (immigrants/immigrate)
   Many Americans are _____; they've come to the U.S. from other countries.

4. (challenge/challenging)
   Learning to live and work in a new culture can be very _____.

5. (miscommunication/miscommunicate)
   I helped a friend of mine with something. He never said, "thank you" to me. I thought he didn't appreciate what I did for him. This was an example of a misunderstanding or _____. Later I learned that close friends in his country don't feel they need to say "thank you" to each other.

6. (similar/similarities)
   Some aspects of European culture are _____ to aspects of American culture, but some things are very different.

7. (belief/believe)
   Some people _____ that it is good to be open and honest about feelings and opinions.

8. (behavior/behave)
   Parents teach their children how to _____ according to personal and cultural beliefs.

Fill In the Blanks

From the list of adjectives below, choose the correct word and fill in the blanks in the sentences following the list. Use each word only once.

brief   observe   nonverbal
fluent   normal   aware
obvious

1. Even if you go to a foreign country for a _____ visit, it is still important to understand the way the people live.

2. When the American touched the English people on their shoulders, he was not _____ that his actions made them uncomfortable.

3. In some cultures, it is considered _____ to kiss a friend on the cheek when you meet him or her. In other cultures, this is not acceptable (right or correct) behavior.

4. Smiling, shaking hands and making eye-contact are all examples of _____ communication.

5. You will learn much about U.S. culture if you _____ the behavior of the Americans you know.

6. Some differences between cultures are _____, but many other differences are not so easy to see.

7. Even if a person is _____ in a foreign language, he or she may still have communication problems.

Choose the Best Explanation

Each sentence below contains an italicized word or phrase from the reading. Read each sentence and the three possible explanations. Choose the one explanation that best matches the meaning of the sentence. Circle the letter next to that explanation. The first one is done for you.

1. He is easy to *get along with*.
   a) He's easy to be friendly with.
   b) He does not need many friends.
   c) He enjoys traveling to foreign countries.

2. He gave me *quite a bit* of help.
   a) He gave me a lot of help.
   b) He helped me because he was quiet.
   c) He gave me very little help.

3. It's difficult to *figure out* what to do.
   a) It's difficult to do this math problem.
   b) It's difficult to choose the best action.
   c) It's difficult to draw the picture.

4. *Although* he has lived here for only a few years, he is very comfortable in this culture.
   a) He has lived here for many years, so he knows a lot about the culture.
   b) He has lived here a short time and does not understand this culture.
   c) He has not lived here for a long time, but he is comfortable.

5. The American teachers laugh and joke with their students. *Perhaps* this is normal behavior for them.
   a) Of course this is normal behavior.
   b) You can be sure that this is not normal behavior.
   c) Maybe this is normal behavior.
6. If you meet an older American woman who does not offer to shake hands, I *suppose* it is better for you not to offer to shake her hand.
   a) I am sure it is better. . . .
   b) I guess maybe it is better. . . .
   c) I agree with you that it is better. . . .

GOING BEYOND THE READING

Each group of questions is based on a quote from the reading text. Read the questions and then discuss them in small groups or with the entire class. After the questions have been discussed, choose a topic related to one of the questions and write a composition.*

1. *"Language learning and culture learning go together and may take a long time."* (Paragraph 6)
   a) Do you think an American would have a difficult time learning your culture and language?
   b) How long do you think it would take him or her to accomplish this?
   c) What things do you think would be easiest to learn about your language and culture?
   d) What things do you think would be especially difficult?
2. *"Sometimes people feel that they know a culture after a few weeks or months."* (Paragraph 7)
   a) How long do you think it takes to fully understand another culture?
   b) How can people best understand and learn a new culture?
   c) How long do you think it takes to speak a language well?
   d) What is the best way to learn another language? Discuss your experiences.
3. *"The hidden part of culture influences much of a person's way of thinking and communicating."* (Paragraph 11)
   a) What else, besides people's cultures, influences their way of thinking and communicating?
   b) What were the most important influences on your way of thinking and communicating when you were growing up?
4. *"We know that even in one's own culture, people often miscommunicate."* (paragraph 12)
   a) Think about why people miscommunicate in your language and culture. What are some of the reasons?
   b) What do people do in your culture when there is miscommunication, such as a misunderstanding or misinterpretation?
   c) Would you do the same things if you had problems of miscommunication with people from different cultures?

*Note to the teacher: Some students may prefer to write out answers to questions that they feel are personal ones. In this case, you may want to use this exercise as a writing exercise.

5. *"At first it may be difficult to understand another cultural way of think-ing. Understanding it doesn't mean agreeing with it."* (paragraph 14)

   a) Do you agree with this statement? Explain your answer.

   b) Do you think that people have to change when they live in another culture? Do you agree that "When in Rome, do as the Romans do"? (This expression means that it is necessary to do what the people of another culture do when you are in their country.)

   c) Can you think of any situations where a person should not change? Or a situation where a person might not be *able* to change? Explain your answer.

Interacting in English

UNIT II FOUNDATIONS

- Learning another language also means learning another way of interacting and communicating.
- When two people interact, each one influences what the other person says or does.
- Successful communication in English requires that people tell each other when they understand and when they don't understand.

UNIT II CONTENTS

Chapter 5. "Showing That You Understand" gives you the opportunity to read about and practice five skills for effective communication with Americans:

- giving feedback
- interrupting
- asking for focused repetition
- asking for meaning
- checking bits of information

Chapter 6. "Guiding the Conversation" presents four different skills that you can use to help guide conversations:

- asking for focused explanation
- holding your turn
- correcting misunderstandings
- summarizing

Chapter 7. "Interacting in a Group" discusses ways of:

- getting into the conversation
- participating in group discussions and meetings

Chapter 8. "Reading Text and Activities" contains:

- Reading text: *Interacting in English*
- comprehension, vocabulary, and discussion questions

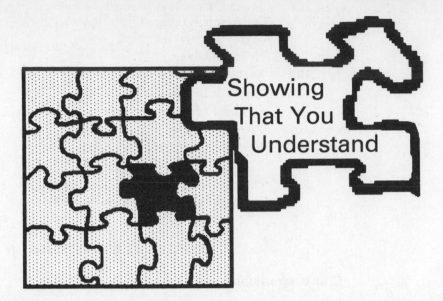

chapter 5

Showing
That You
Understand

Introduction   When you talk to people, how do you show that you are listening? How do you show that you understand or don't understand? There are many personal as well as cultural differences in this area of communication. As people learn another language, it is obvious that they need to learn grammar and pronunciation rules. Less obvious is the need to learn how people *interact* as they speak and listen in the new language. Chapter 5 presents information and skills that will help you interact *effectively* in English. Specifically, this chapter discusses listening and showing understanding in English.

CULTURE LEARNING QUESTIONS

1. Compare the way Americans interact in English with the way people interact in your native language. What similarities and differences have you observed?
2. Sometimes when people use another language, they say that they don't always feel like themselves. Do you feel this way when you interact in English? If so, what do you think makes you feel this way?

CROSS-CULTURAL INTERACTION 5A:
Ineffective Communication

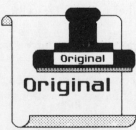

Original

Original

(Revised interaction appears on page 57.)

Situation: Tak works in the United States for Western Business Machines Company, which makes machines such as typewriters and adding machines. Tak works in the Sales Department. His supervisor, Bill, is an American. At this moment, Tak is working at his desk. Bill walks up to him.

Bill: "Hey, Tak, can you do something for me?"
Tak: (He turns and looks at Bill, but says nothing.)

interact—communicate back and forth; respond and speak to another person, both verbally and nonverbally
effectively—well; successfully

Bill: "Maria Garcia from Alameda Hospital just called. There's a problem. The hospital ordered two new typewriters last month, but they haven't received them yet."

Tak: (He says nothing.)

Bill: "So, anyway, can you find out what the problem is *A.S.A.P.?*"

Tak: (Tak nods his head). "Yes."

Bill: "Get hold of Pierre in Shipping and ask him about it, okay?"

Tak: (Tak says nothing.)

Bill: "You got that, Tak?"

Tak: "Yes."

Bill: "Okay, thanks." (Bill turns and walks away. He thinks to himself, "I wonder if Tak really understood me?")

QUESTIONS AND DISCUSSION

Comprehension

Write T (true) or F (false) in the space provided.

1. _____ Maria Garcia called Bill today to order two typewriters for Alameda Hospital.
2. _____ Bill wants Tak to find out why Alameda Hospital did not receive the two typewriters.
3. _____ Pierre works for Alameda hospital.
4. _____ When Bill says, "You got that, Tak?" he means, "Do you understand?" and "Do you know what to do?"

Analysis: Can You Explain?

1. At the end of the interaction, why does Bill ask, "You got that, Tak?"?
2. As he walks away, Bill says to himself, "I wonder if Tak really understood me?" Why doesn't Bill feel sure that Tak understood him?
3. Tak only says, "Yes" when Bill asks questions. Why doesn't Tak say anything else?

TALK ABOUT YOUR OWN LANGUAGE AND CULTURE

1. How do people show that they are listening to another person? Describe what a person does (nonverbally) and says.
2. What do people say or do to let another person know that they haven't understood something?
3. If you have the opportunity, tape record a short conversation between two people in your native language. Answer the following questions:
   - How do the speaker and listener interact?
   - Are there any interruptions?
   - Is there silence?
   - Are there sounds that the listener makes to show that he or she is listening and understanding?

A.S.A.P.—as soon as possible.

Play the tape for your classmates or have a conversation with someone from your culture in front of them. What are their observations and comments?

Summary of Cross-Cultural Interaction 5A: Ineffective Communication

In some cultures, including American culture, people usually say something to the speaker to show that they are listening and that they understand. This is a kind of *feedback*. Americans also sometimes interrupt the speaker to ask questions so that they can be sure that they understand. In Interaction 5A Bill expects Tak to show, with words, that he is listening, and to ask questions to make sure that he understands. When Tak doesn't do these things, Bill wonders, "Does he understand me?" Bill begins to *lose confidence in Tak*. Bill needs to be sure that Tak understood him and knows what to do. Bill would like Tak to interact in a way that Bill expects or is used to.

CROSS-CULTURAL INTERACTION 5B

The following dialogue is a more successful version of Cross-Cultural Interaction 5A. Read the dialogue, and then the explanation in the "What is Happening" column.

	Dialogue	*What is Happening*
Bill:	"Hey, Tak, can you do something for me?"	
Tak:	(He turns and looks at Bill). "Oh, Hi, Bill. Can I do what? What was your question?"	Tak did not hear Bill approach his desk. He is not sure what Bill said. He asks Bill to **repeat** his question.
Bill:	"Uh, can you do something for me?"	
Tak:	"Oh. Sure."	Tak gives Bill **feedback** that means "I understand, I will do it."
Bill:	"Maria Garcia from Alameda Hospital just called, and they've got a problem. They . . ."	
Tak:	"I'm sorry, what hospital?"	Tak **interrupts** to ask Bill to repeat the name of the hospital.
Bill:	"Uh, Alameda Hospital. Anyway, the hospital ordered two typewriters last month . . ."	
Tak:	(He nods his head). "Uh huh."	Tak gives Bill **feedback** that means "I'm listening."
Bill:	". . . but they haven't received them yet."	

feedback—answer; response; ways to show "I'm listening," "I understand," or "I don't understand."
lose confidence in Tak—think that Tak cannot do the job; think that he is not capable

Dialogue		*What is Happening*
Tak:	"So you mean we sent the typewriters but the hospital never received them?"	Tak **checks** what Bill said.
Bill:	"Well, that's what we don't know. Maybe we didn't send them."	
Tak:	"Oh, I see."	Tak gives **feedback** that means "I understand."
Bill:	"So, can you get hold of Pierre over in Shipping and find out?"	
Tak:	"Uh, . . . hold up?"	Tak **asks for the meaning** of "get hold of" by trying to repeat what he heard. He says "hold *up*" instead of "hold *of*" because he didn't hear Bill clearly.
Bill:	"Huh? Oh, *get hold of* Pierre . . . uh . . . call him, or go see him."	
Tak:	"Oh, I see. So . . .I'll call Pierre right away and ask him if he sent the typewriters."	Tak gives Bill **feedback** that means "I understand." Finally, Tak **summarizes** Bill's request.
Bill:	"Great. Thanks for doing this, Tak."	
Tak:	"Sure. No problem."	

FOCUS ON U.S. CULTURE
Cultural Notes, Exercises, and Skill Practice

HOW MUCH DO YOU ALREADY KNOW ABOUT U.S. CULTURE?

Write T (true) or F (false) in the space provided.

1. _____ If you do not understand what someone says, it is often all right to interrupt and ask for an explanation.

2. _____ Most Americans can speak at least one language besides English. Therefore, they understand how difficult it can be to speak English as a second language.

3. _____ It is usually all right to repeat, briefly, what another person says so that you can be sure that you understood them.

4. _____ Americans generally depend on verbal rather than nonverbal language to express themselves.

SECTION 1. GIVING FEEDBACK

Bill: "The hospital ordered two typewriters last month."
Tak: "Uh huh." (He nods his head.)
Bill: Get hold of Pierre . . . uh . . . call him, or go see him."
Tak: "Oh, I see."

In Cross-Cultural Interaction 5B, Tak gives Bill feedback. Tak uses sounds and words to show Bill, "I'm listening," "I understand," and "I don't understand."

U.S. CULTURE NOTE

Americans use verbal feedback often. The U.S. is considered a "verbal" culture. If Americans do not receive a lot of verbal feedback, they may feel that the other person is not listening, is bored or angry, or that he or she disagrees. Americans ask for feedback when they say things like:

"You got that?"   "Do you understand?"
"Am I making myself clear?"   "Okay. Any questions?"
"You know?"   "Okay?"
"Do you know what I mean?"

Phrases and Sounds Used to Give Feedback ——————————————

"Oh. Sure"   "Yeah . . ."   "Well . . ."
"Uh huh."   "Uhm hmm . . ."   "Uh . . ."
"Oh. I see."   "Hmm?"   "All right."
"Okay."   "I understand."   "I don't understand."

Here are some *non*verbal ways to give feedback:

Make eye contact with the speaker.
Smile.
Nod your head.
Look confused when you don't understand.
Look surprised when something surprises you.

CROSS-CULTURAL NOTE

People show that they are listening in different ways. Japanese speakers use a listening sound that sounds something like "mm mm" to show that they are paying attention to the speaker. They make this sound very often when listening. When a Japanese uses this listening sound in a conversation in English with an American, the American may think the Japanese listener is saying, "Okay! Okay! I understand! Hurry up and finish talking!" Of course, this is not what the person means.

Skill Practice: Giving Feedback

The following dialogue takes place between a supervisor and an employee in a hotel kitchen. The supervisor is explaining to the employee how to use the dishwasher. Read the dialogue with a partner. One student reads the part of the employee; the other reads the supervisor's part. Every time the employee sees a blank line (_____), he or she will give feedback that means, "I'm listening and I understand." The employee will use the following phrases:

Uh huh.   Oh, I see.   Okay.   Uhm hmm.   All right.

After you read the dialogue, answer the questions following it.

Supervisor: "Okay, for this job you need to wear gloves."
Employee   _____ (Employee finds a pair of gloves and puts them on.)
Supervisor: "All right. Now, first you make sure that this light is off." (The supervisor points to the light.)
Employee: _____
Supervisor: "And then you move this part . . ."
Employee: _____
Supervisor: ". . . like this and open the door carefully and watch out for the steam."
Employee: _____
Supervisor: "Wait a few seconds for the dishes to cool down . . ."
Employee: _____
Supervisor: ". . . and then you can unload everything."
Employee: _____

Questions:

1. Look at the interaction above, and answer the following questions.
    • Did the listener give feedback after every sentence?
    • Did the listener ever give feedback in the middle of the speaker's sentence?

2. Now think about your own language and culture and answer the following questions.
   - How often do you give feedback when you are listening? In the middle of the sentence? Only at the end of the sentence? After two or three sentences?
   - Are you completely quiet when you listen?
   - Do you give nonverbal feedback?

If you're not sure of the answers to these questions, try reading the dialogue in your language with someone from your culture. Compare how you do it in your own language with the way the employee does it in English.

U.S. CULTURE NOTE

If an American is not getting feedback that shows, "I understand" or "I don't understand," the American often begins to feel very uncomfortable. He or she might begin to talk more quickly and with fewer pauses. This is done because people often feel uncomfortable with silence and will try to "fill the silence" with words. When this happens, the American is usually hoping that the other person will "break in" to give a response or ask a question. The American may not be comfortable stopping or slowing down and waiting for the other person to interact.

SECTION 2. INTERRUPTING

Bill: "Maria Garcia from Alameda Hospital just called, and they've got a problem. They . . ."

Tak: "I'm sorry, what hospital?"

U.S. CULTURE NOTE

The word "interrupt" usually has a negative meaning in English. A person who interrupts does not let the other speaker finish speaking. Americans often become impatient or angry with someone who interrupts too often. However, in an interaction with someone from another culture, it is sometimes necessary to interrupt politely to ask a question. Most Americans will expect you to ask right away if you don't understand something they have said.

Cross-Cultural Exercise: Interrupting

In this exercise, you will compare patterns of interaction (the way people communicate) in your own language and culture with those among Americans in the U.S. Specifically, you will look at interruptions.

Read each of the following sentences and decide if the interaction described would be common among people from your culture. Then indicate whether you think the interaction would be common among Americans. Put a check (√) in the appropriate columns.

Situation: Imagine that you are at a small business meeting or in a small class with about ten people. You don't understand what the speaker (either the leader of the meeting or the teacher) is saying. Would you interrupt the speaker? How would you do it? When would you do it?

	Common in my language and culture	*Common among Americans*
1. Interrupt right away, in the middle of the person's sentence, to ask a question.	_____	_____
2. Interrupt at the end of the sentence.		
3. Interrupt nonverbally only (for example, look confused). Do not speak.	_____	_____
4. Do not interrupt the speaker. Wait to talk to the speaker another day,	_____	_____
5. Interrupt if necessary, but apologize several times.	_____	_____
6. Do not interrupt the speaker. Ask another person questions later.	_____	_____
7. Do not interrupt the speaker. Ask another person questions while the speaker is talking.	_____	_____
8. Never interrupt the speaker because the interruption means that he or she didn't explain clearly. This would insult the speaker.	_____	_____

(Answers are given at the end of the chapter.)

CROSS-CULTURAL NOTE

Attitudes toward interrupting and asking questions are different across cultures. Although many American parents may not like constant interruptions, they generally encourage their children to ask questions. In some cultures, questions from children are not appreciated. One Hispanic woman said that she and her friends get upset with their children if they ask too many questions. Some Chinese parents of American-born children apologize if their children talk too much and ask too many questions.

Phrases for Interrupting Politely

"Excuse me, but I didn't quite understand."
"I'm sorry, but I have a question."
"Could I ask a question?"
"Sorry to interrupt, but I didn't understand."
"Could I interrupt for a quick second?"
"Just a quick interruption, if it's okay."

Skill Practice: Interrupting

For this skill practice, close your books and listen to the teacher. The teacher will read a paragraph. Every time you hear a word or phrase that you don't understand, say, "Excuse me, but what does _____ (new word or phrase) mean?" Try to repeat the word that you don't understand. After you do the skill practice, answer the questions following it.

Example:

Teacher: "I am going to talk about American attitudes toward quitting a job."

Student: "Uh, excuse me, but what does 'quitting' mean?"

To the teacher: The students should close their books while you read the following paragraph. Use the glosses below to explain words that students ask about.

I am going to talk about American attitudes toward *quitting a job.* Sometimes people decide that they do not want to continue working at their *present job* and they decide to quit. It is important that they understand the *terms of the contract* when they quit. Usually it is necessary to *give at least two weeks' notice* before quitting. If you belong to a *union,* you can talk to the *shop steward* about any *grievances* you may have. Sometimes the union can help you get better *wages* or *working conditions.* If your company has an *Employee Relations Department,* you can talk to someone there about your problems.

quitting a job—leaving a job.
present job—job you have now
terms of the contract—what your contract (work agreement) says
give at least two weeks' notice—tell the employer that you plan to quit two weeks before you will quit.
union—organization of workers
shop steward—the union representative who works at your company
grievances—complaints.
wages—pay, salary
working conditions—work hours, safety on the job, etc.
Employee Relations Department—section of the organization or company that takes care of employees' problems at work

Questions:

- Did you give your teacher nonverbal signals that you wanted to interrupt?
- Did the teacher notice your signals?
- Did you have to speak to get the teacher to stop and let you ask a question?
- Did you have any difficulty interrupting the teacher?

CROSS-CULTURAL NOTE

A Chinese student in an English as a Second Language class in the U.S. said the following: "My English teacher tells me I should interrupt and ask questions when I don't understand, but for me, it is very rude to interrupt someone. I *would rather* ask a friend later if I don't understand something.

U.S. CULTURE NOTE

Many Americans feel that verbal communication is more important than non-verbal communication, particularly between people like supervisors and employees and teachers and students. They sometimes feel that spoken communication is clearer than nonverbal communication. They don't want to have to guess what a person is thinking or feeling. Many people believe that it is a person's responsibility to say *what is on his mind.*

would rather—prefer; feel that it is better
what is on his mind—what he is thinking about

SECTION 3. ASKING FOR FOCUSED REPETITION

> Bill: "Hey, Tak, can you do something for me?"
> Tak: "Oh, hi, Bill. Can I do what?"

In this example from Cross-Cultural Interaction 5B, Tak didn't hear Bill clearly. He asks Bill to repeat a specific part of the sentence. When you ask someone to repeat something, it helps to tell them exactly what word or phrase you need to hear again. This skill is called focused repetition. Focused repetition is like focusing a camera. You choose exactly what you want to take a picture of, then you focus the camera so that the part you need is clear. With focused repetition, you tell the speaker exactly what you want to hear.

CROSS-CULTURAL NOTE

An immigrant in the U.S. said, "When I say to my American boss, 'Please repeat,' he often repeats everything he said before, only louder, and faster. Why doesn't he speak more slowly when he repeats? Why does he repeat so many sentences? Usually, after he repeats, I *still* don't understand."

U.S. CULTURE NOTE

Many Americans have never had to learn a second language, either for business or for daily life. As a result, they may not be skilled in communicating with people who speak English as a second language. If someone says, "I don't understand," the American may not know what part of the sentence was confusing. The American probably wants to ask, "What don't you understand; everything I just said, or just part of what I said?"

Skill Practice: Asking for Focused Repetition

Read the following two excerpts from conversations between a head waiter and a new *bus boy* in a restaurant.

A   Head Waiter: "That table needs another butter knife."
    Bus Boy: "Another . . .?"

In this example, the bus boy repeats the word "another" so that the head waiter will repeat the *next* word, "butter knife." Note that the word "another" is stretched and said with a "question voice" (rising intonation).

The following is another way of asking for focused repetition:

B   Head Waiter: "Take another butter knife to that table."
    Bus Boy: "Another what?"
    Head Waiter: "Another butter knife."

bus boy—person who clears and sets tables in a restaurant.

In this example, the bus boy uses the question word, "what?" to ask a focused question. Question words are:

Who   What   Where   When   Why   How

Practice repeating the examples above after your teacher says them. Think of other examples using classroom objects. For example:

A: "The eraser is on the desk."
B: "On the . . .?   or   "The eraser is where?"

Ways To Ask for Focused Repetition

1. Use question words.
    For example: "*Where* do you want me to put it?"
2. Repeat the word(s) that came just before the word you want repeated. Make your voice rise as it would with a question. For example:
    A: "Put the eraser next to the ashtray."
    B: "Put it next to the . . .?" (The speaker will then say, "ashtray.")
3. If you cannot repeat the words the other person has said, ask the speaker directly. For example:
    "Could you say that last part again?"
    "Could you repeat what you said after _____?" (Say the part of the sentence that you can say.)

*Skill Practice: Asking for Focused Repetition**

Do this skill practice with a partner. One partner, B, will close the book. The other partner, A, will read each sentence below aloud.

*   If you are person A, when you see three X's (XXX) in the sentence, cover your mouth and say the word(s) in parentheses. Person B should not hear this word (or words) clearly.
*   If you are person B, do one of the following two things to make the speaker repeat the unclear word(s).
    1. Repeat the word or words before the unclear one(s) and use a question voice.
    2. Use a question word in place of the unclear word(s).
*   If you are person A, repeat the word or words, but clearly this time.

Example #1
A: "Give me the XXX (chalk)."
B: "Give you the. . . .?"
A: "Chalk."
B: "Oh, okay."

Note to the teacher: In this skill practice, the students must decide which question word to use. If this is difficult for your students, preview the exercise as follows: Write "what, who, when, where, how" on the board and read aloud each sentence from the exercise (do not read the "missing" word). Then ask students to say the corresponding question word, without asking the whole focused repetition question. After students have correctly identified all the question words, do the exercise with the students. Have them repeat the exercise in pairs.

Example #2

A: "My brother is feeling XXX (ill)."
B: *"Feeling how?"*
A: "Ill."
B: "Oh. That's too bad."

Student A will read the following sentences. Student B will ask focused repetition questions using the two patterns shown in the examples above. Students should take turns being A and B.

If you are student B, close your book.

1. A: "I think my child has the XXX (measles)."
2. A: "We have to come to work tomorrow at XXX (6:30)."
3. A: "There's a lot of traffic XXX (on Highway 20)."
4. A: "Give these to Mr. XXX (Baxter)."
5. A: "That box goes XXX (under) the table."
6. A: "These have to be lined up XXX (straight)."
7. A: "Don't forget to XXX (fill out) your time card."
8. A: "I'll see you XXX (the day after tomorrow)."

U.S. CULTURE NOTE

It is not usually considered polite to ask a one-word question such as "What?" or "Who?"

SECTION 4. ASKING FOR MEANING

Bill: "Can you get hold of Pierre over in Shipping and find out?"
Tak: "Uh, . . . hold up?"
Bill: "Huh? Oh, get hold of Pierre . . . uh . . . call him, or go see him."

Tak asks for the meaning of the phrase "get hold of" by trying to repeat what he heard Bill say. He does not repeat correctly, because he does not know the idiom "get hold of." Bill understands what Tak wants to ask, repeats the idiom ("get hold of"), and explains the meaning.

Look at the following interaction between the head waiter and the bus boy:

Head Waiter: "When you put out the salad, put the *cole slaw* on the left."
Bus boy: "The cold salad?"
Head Waiter: "No, the cole slaw . . . that salad there . . . the one with cabbage."

The bus boy asks about the word "cole slaw." Because he doesn't know this word, he cannot pronounce it correctly. He tries to pronounce what he *thinks* he heard, and the head waiter understands what to explain.

cole slaw—a salad made from chopped cabbage, mayonnaise, vinegar, and other ingredients.

Ways To Ask for Meaning _____

1. Try to repeat the word or phrase that you didn't understand. Use a question voice: "Cold salad?"
2. Ask for spelling: "Cole slaw? How do you spell that?"
3. Say: "Cole slaw? What does that mean?"
   "Uh . . . I don't understand. Cole slaw?"
   "Excuse me, what does 'cole slaw' mean?"

_____

Skill Practice: Asking for Meaning

Work with a partner or have the teacher follow student A's direction. Student A will choose one of the following topics and tell student B about it. Student B will interrupt whenever he or she needs to ask about the meaning of a word or phrase. Student B should use the phrase: "Excuse me, what does _____ mean?"

Topics:

1. How to cook a dish from your country.
2. How to use a machine that the other person doesn't know how to use.
3. How weddings are celebrated in your country.
4. How to set your watch if it has stopped running.
5. About an important date in the history of your country.
6. How to fix something that's broken.
7. A topic of your own choice.

*"Where's your son tonight?"

SECTION 5. CHECKING BITS OF INFORMATION

Bill: "Anyway, the hospital ordered two typewriters last month, but they haven't received them yet."

Tak: "So you mean we sent the typewriters but the hospital never received them?"

Bill: "Well, that's what we don't know. Maybe we didn't send them."

In Cross-Cultural Interaction 5B, Tak interrupts to check what Bill said because he's not sure that he understood Bill's idea. When he checks, he repeats what Bill said, but in his own words. You can check the meaning of ideas, or the meaning of specific words and phrases.

U.S. CULTURE NOTE

In American culture it is usually okay to interrupt the other speaker so that you can make sure you understood what the speaker said.

Phrases and Expressions for Checking ————————————————

Checking Ideas:

"So you mean . . . *they never received the typewriter?*"

"So *the hospital is still waiting for the typewriters?*"

"Do you mean *that they haven't received them yet?*"

"In other words *they still haven't received them?*"

"So you want me to *call Pierre?*"

Checking Words:

"You call this *cole slaw?*"

"It's called *cole slaw?*"

"I'm sorry, did you say *cole slaw?*"

Skill Practice: Checking Bits of Information

In the following dialogue, Ramesh is a factory worker and Sara is his American neighbor. Ramesh is talking to Sara about quitting his job. Sara is giving Ramesh some information, and he is checking to make sure he understands what Sara is saying. Read this dialogue with a partner. The checking phrases and techniques are in italics.

Ramesh: "I'm thinking about quitting my job."

Sara: "You are? Do you know about giving notice if you want to quit a job?"

Ramesh: "*Giving notice? Do you mean* I have to give my boss a letter telling him that I want to quit?"

Sara: "Not always. I think it's usually okay if you just talk to your boss and tell him you are going to leave . . ."

Ramesh: "I see."

Sara: ". . . but usually you need to give at least two weeks' notice."

Ramesh: "*So* I have to tell the boss two weeks before I plan to leave?"

Sara: "That's right. You know, maybe you should talk to the shop steward."

Ramesh: "Uh . . ." (he looks confused)

Sara: "You know, the union representative."

Ramesh: *"You call* the union representative the 'shop steward.'?"

Sara: "Yeah, that's right. If there's a problem, maybe the shop steward can help you get it fixed. Then you won't need to quit."
            "Also, you know, you should tell your job developer if you are planning to quit."

Ramesh: "Job developer? *You mean* the person from the training center, the one who got me the job?"

Sara: "That's right. Maybe your job developer can help you to get better working conditions."

Ramesh: "The job developer can help me even after I start working?"

Sara: "Yes, that's part of his job."

U.S. CULTURE NOTE

People in some cultures would say that Ramesh is doing too much "checking," and that he is talking when he should be listening. They might also say that Ramesh does not seem intelligent because he's asking too many questions. However, many Americans want to be reassured that non-native English speakers understand what they have said. Checking can give this reassurance.

Skill Practice: Checking Bits of Information

With a partner or the teacher, take turns explaining something to each other (for example, how something works, a grammatical construction in your language, etc.). Use checking phrases. Every time your teacher assigns you homework and gives you explanations, use checking phrases.

CHAPTER SUMMARY

In this chapter, you read about and practiced five skills for effective communication with Americans:

- giving feedback
- interrupting
- asking for focused repetition
- asking for meaning
- checking bits of information

The following are definitions, examples and phrases for each skill:

1. *Giving feedback:* Show the speaker that you are listening, that you understand, or that you don't understand.

Say:	*Do:*
"Oh. Sure."	Make eye contact with the speaker.
"Uh huh."	Smile.
"Oh. I see."	Nod your head.
"Okay."	Look confused when you don't understand.
"Yeah . . ."	Look surprised when something surprises
"Uhm hmm . . ."	you.
"Hmm?"	
"Well . . ."	
"Uh . . ."	
"All right."	
"I understand."	
"I don't understand."	

2. *Interrupting:* Say something while, or right after, a person speaks in order to understand what a speaker is saying.

   "Excuse me, but I didn't quite understand."

   "I'm sorry, but I have a question."

   "Could I ask a question?"

   "Sorry to interrupt, but I didn't understand."

   "Could I interrupt for a quick second?"

   "Just a quick interruption, if that's okay."

3. *Asking for focused repetition:* Get the speaker to repeat words or phrases that you didn't hear clearly.

   Use question words.

   Repeat the word(s) that came just before the word you want repeated.

   Make your voice rise as it would with a question.

   Ask the speaker directly: Could you say that last part again? or Can you repeat what you said after _____?

4. *Asking for meaning:* Get the meaning (or spelling) of a specific word or phrase.

Say:	*Do:*
"Uh . .I don't understand."	Try to repeat the word or phrase you
"Excuse me, what does	didn't understand. Use a question
_____ mean?"	voice.
"How do you spell that?"	

5. *Checking bits of information:* Check that you heard words, phrases or simple ideas correctly.

   "So you mean . . ."

   "So . . ."

   "Do you mean . . .?"

   "In other words . . ."

   "So you want me to . . ."

   "You call this . . .?"

   "It's called . . .?"

Answers to Cross-Cultural Exercise: Interruptions

1. For Americans, this would be considered rude.

2. Americans often do this.

3. This is done, but sometimes Americans will not notice unless you *say* something.

4. For Americans, it is best to ask questions at the time of the meeting or class. If you don't, the meeting leader or teacher may say, "Why didn't you ask me *then*?" (meaning at the time of the meeting or class).

5. When Americans are talking with each other, they may apologize, but not more than once (for example, "Sorry for interrupting, but I have a quick question.").

6. In most situations, except in formal meetings, Americans prefer to interrupt the speaker and ask questions directly.

7. Only in a large group. In a small group, asking another person a question while the speaker is talking would be considered rude.

8. Most Americans will not feel insulted if you ask a question because you didn't understand something. They will appreciate your interest.

Note: Answers to other exercises can be found in the separate Answer Key.

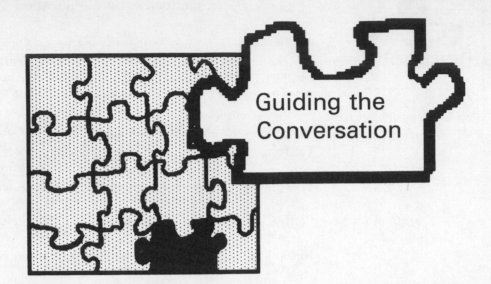

chapter 6

Guiding the
Conversation

Introduction   When a person is not a native speaker of a language, it is easy to *lose control of a conversation*. Native speakers may not give all the information you need to understand something, or they may interrupt you before you are finished speaking. They may misunderstand something you say, or you may misunderstand them. *Staying in control of the conversation* and *guiding* it are possible even if you are not a fluent speaker of the language. Chapter 6 will present information and skills that will help you to guide the conversation so that you are *confident* that you have communicated clearly. The context of the examples in this chapter is telephone conversations, but the skills apply to face-to-face interaction as well.

CULTURE LEARNING QUESTIONS

1. When you are speaking your own language with someone who is not a native speaker of the language, do you change the way you speak? For example, do you:
    *   talk more slowly?
    *   talk more loudly?
    *   use simpler words?
    *   repeat and explain?
    *   avoid long conversations?
    When people speak to you in English, do they do any of the above? How do you feel if and when they do these things?

2. Talk about your experiences speaking English on the telephone. What particular difficulties do you have? What, if anything, do you do to make telephone conversations easier?

lose control of a conversation—not be in control of a conversation; not understand; not be able to say anything
staying in control of the conversation—being able to participate in a conversation; being able to clarify what you don't understand; being able to finish saying what you want to say
guiding (the conversation)—directing; having some control over
confident—sure

Original

(Revised interaction appears on page 76.)

CROSS-CULTURAL INTERACTION 6A:
Ineffective Communication

Situation: Pierre is from France. Like Tak in Chapter 5, Pierre works for Western Business Machines Company. He works in the Shipping Department. At the moment, he is calling Maria Garcia at Alameda Hospital about the late typewriter delivery. The *receptionist* at the hospital answers the phone.

Receptionist: "Alameda Hospital."

Pierre: "Hello, is uh . . . " (He looks for a piece of paper on his desk.) " . . . is uh . . . *is Mr. somebody Garcia there?*"

Receptionist: "Um . . . we have several Garcias here. *Do you have a first name?*"

Pierre: "Uh . . . oh! Here it is!" (He finds the piece of paper.) "Maria Garcia."

Receptionist: "Maria Garcia's not in right now. She'll have to call you back."

Pierre: "What?"

Receptionist: "She's out. She'll have to call you back later." (The receptionist begins to sound irritated.)

Pierre: (He is confused. He doesn't say anything.)

Receptionist: "Do you want to leave a message?"

Pierre: "Uh . . . You see, uh . . . she ordered some uh, typewriters, but I don't think that we . . . we delivered them, and . . ."

Receptionist: "Why don't you just tell me your name and number and she will call you back?"

Pierre: "What? Oh, my name is Pierre Dupont. My company is Western Business Machines."

Receptionist: "Pierre Dupont, Western Machines . . . okay . . . give me your number." (The receptionist is speaking quickly.)

Pierre: (He thinks to himself, "No, it's Western *Business* Machines." He doesn't say anything.)

Receptionist: "Does she have your number?" (The receptionist sounds impatient.)

Pierre: "Oh, yes. Ah . . . my number is 733-2084."

Receptionist: "Okay. I'll give Ms. Garcia your message. Good-bye."

Pierre: "Ah . . . thank you. Good-bye." (Pierre hangs up the phone. He thinks to himself, "Sometimes I hate making phone calls.")

QUESTIONS AND DISCUSSION

Comprehension

Write T (true) or F (false) in the space provided.

receptionist—The person who answers the phone in an office
do you have a first name?—do you know the first name?

1. _____ In the conversation above, Pierre talks to Maria Garcia about the typewriters.
2. _____ At first, Pierre cannot remember Maria Garcia's first name because he does not have the piece of paper with her name on it in front of him.
3. _____ The receptionist says the name of Pierre's company correctly.
4. _____ Pierre cannot remember his own telephone number.

Analysis: Can You Explain?

1. The receptionist does not say the name of Pierre's company correctly. Why do you think Pierre doesn't give her the correct name?
2. Why do you think that the receptionist's voice began to sound irritated during the conversation?
3. How could Pierre have improved the conversation?

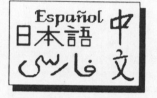

TALK ABOUT YOUR OWN LANGUAGE AND CULTURE

1. How frequently is the telephone used for business purposes? How about for *social* purposes?
2. How does a receptionist or secretary react when a caller is difficult to communicate with? Who, if anyone, is supposed to be polite?
3. Are business calls usually rushed? Do you need to give and receive information quickly? How about social calls? Explain your answer.

social—not related to business; involving friends

Summary of Cross-Cultural Interaction 6A: Ineffective Communication

In Cross-Cultural Interaction 6A, Pierre is not comfortable or confident. The receptionist becomes impatient when Pierre does not understand her and does not respond quickly and clearly. Pierre does not use common telephone dialogue phrases that would help the interaction. Furthermore, Pierre and the receptionist are not face to face, and this makes communication more difficult.

CROSS-CULTURAL INTERACTION 6B

The following interaction shows Pierre interacting more effectively with the receptionist. In this interaction, Pierre uses some of the skills discussed in Chapter 5. Read the dialogue and then the explanations in the "What is Happening?" column.

Dialogue	What Is Happening
Receptionist: (She answers the telephone.) "Alameda Hospital."	
Pierre: "Hello, this is Pierre Dupont from Western Business Machines." (He looks at a note on his desk.) "Could I speak to Maria Garcia?"	Pierre introduces himself and his company at the beginning of the conversation. Pierre knows Maria Garcia's full name before he telephones.
Receptionist: "Maria Garcia? I'm afraid she's not in right now. Can I . . ."	

Dialogue	*What Is Happening*
Pierre: "I'm sorry, she's not . . . ?"	Pierre **interrupts** to **ask for focused repetition** when he doesn't understand the phrase, "She's not in right now."
Receptionist: "She's not in . . ." (She waits for Pierre to respond.) "She's out. She'll have to call you back."	The receptionist repeats what she said before because Pierre guided her with a focused repetition question. Then she says the same thing in a different way.
Pierre: "She's out? . . . Oh, I see. Uh . . . will she be back today?"	Pierre *holds his turn* while he decides what he wants to ask.
Receptionist: "Yes. She'll be in the office later this afternoon."	
Pierre: "I see . . . uh . . . could I leave a message?"	Pierre **holds his turn** while he thinks of the correct phrase, "Could I leave a message?."
Receptionist: "Sure." (She waits for Pierre to speak.)	
Pierre: "Please tell her I called about the typewriter delivery."	Pierre knows the correct phrase to use to leave a message. He doesn't try to give a long message to the receptionist.
Receptionist: ". . . the typewriter delivery . . ."	The receptionist repeats Pierre's information as feedback that she understands him.
Pierre: "Uhm hmm . . ."	Pierre **gives feedback** that means, "that's correct."
Receptionist: "Okay . . . and what's your number?"	
Pierre: "My number is 733-2084."	
Receptionist: "733-2084. All right. And what's the spelling of your last name?"	
Pierre: "I'm sorry, could you speak a little more slowly?"	Pierre **controls the receptionist's speech** by asking her to slow down.
Receptionist: "Certainly. How do you spell your last name?" (She speaks more slowly.)	
Pierre: "D-U-, P-O-N-T."	
Receptionist: "All right, Mr. Dupont, and that was Western Machines Company . . . I'll give Ms. Garcia the message."	

holds his turn—to "hold your turn" means to save or keep your place in line, in a game or in a conversation. It means not letting someone interrupt you when you are speaking.

	Dialogue	*What Is Happening*
Pierre:	"Uh . . . it's Western *Business* Machines."	Pierre politely **corrects the receptionist's error.**
Receptionist:	"Oh, I'm sorry. Western Business Machines."	
Pierre:	"Yes, that's right."	Pierre **gives feedback.**
Receptionist:	"Okay, Mr. Dupont, I'll give her the message. Thank you for calling."	
Pierre:	"Excuse me . . . so . . . she'll call me back this afternoon?"	Pierre **summarizes** what he understood.
Receptionist:	"Yes, she should call you back before 5:00."	
Pierre:	"Okay. Thank you. Goodbye."	
Receptionist:	"Goodbye."	

Phrases and Expressions Used on the Telephone

The following phrases are commonly used for business conversations over the telephone. (These are lists of phrases, not dialogues.)

1. Phrases used by the person who is making the call.
   a) Hello, this is Pierre Dupont. May I speak to Maria Garcia?
   b) I'd like to make an appointment to see Dr. Meyers.
   c) Could I leave a message?
   d) Could you ask him to call me back?
   e) I'll try to call back after three.
   f) I'm returning Mr. Johnson's call.
   g) Do you know what time I can reach him?

2. Phrases used by the person receiving (answering) the call.
   a) Hello, Western Business Machines Company.
   b) Can I tell her who's calling?
   c) Would you like to leave a message?
   d) How do you spell that?
   e) She's not in right now.
   f) Could she call you back?
   g) Does she have your number?
   h) May I tell her what this is about?
   i) I'll give her your message.
   j) Just a moment, I'll connect you.
   k) One moment please.
   l) Please hold the line.
   m) Can you hold? (Would you like to wait?)
   n) Would you like to call back later?
   o) Can I call you back later?/Can you call me back later?
   p) I'm afraid you have the wrong number.

FOCUS ON U.S. CULTURE
Cultural Notes, Exercises, and Skill Practice

HOW MUCH DO YOU ALREADY KNOW ABOUT U.S. CULTURE?

Write T (true) or F (false) in the space provided.

1. _____ If someone (for example, a teacher or supervisor) has given you an explanation that you don't understand, it is not rude to ask questions about the explanation.

2. _____ If you are talking to someone and you can't think of what to say (for example, you've forgotten a word), it is better to be silent than to try and say something.

3. _____ If you do not answer a question quickly, most Americans will understand that you need time to think and time to translate from your language to English. They will wait patiently for you to speak.

4. _____ It is usually rude to correct misunderstandings. It is better to not say anything about them.

5. _____ It is helpful to summarize what a person has said because both you and he will know that you've understood.

SECTION 1. ASKING FOR FOCUSED EXPLANATION

Focused explanation is like focused repetition (Chapter 5), except that you are asking someone to give you more information or another explanation. It is not rude to do this in English and generally shows another person that you are interested in what he or she is saying. It also shows that you are trying to understand. Teachers, supervisors and co-workers will appreciate knowing that you are making an effort to understand what they are saying.

In the following conversation, David is teaching Sajia how to use a new computer terminal. Read the short conversation out loud.

David: "To operate the terminal, you need to plug in this cord, check to see if this light is on, and then wait for it to warm up."

Sajia: "I understand about the cord and the light, but can you explain the next thing you said?"

David: "Uh . . . you need to wait about 20 seconds before you can use it . . . before the words show on the screen."

Sajia: "Oh, I see."

David: "Then you press the 'enter' button and after that wait ten seconds for the red light to go off. Then you enter your program name, the date, and the new data that needs to be entered."

Sajia: "Press the 'enter' button, wait for the red light to go off, enter the program name and . . . what do I do next?"

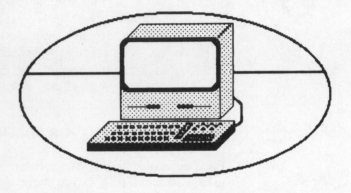

Ways To Ask for Focused Repetition

Repeat the following sentences after your teacher says them:

"I understand this, but could you explain the [other/next/first/last] thing you said?"

"I got what you said about the first part, but I didn't get the next part."

"Do you mean that I need to enter more than one piece of information in the computer? (Also: Did you mean . . . ?)"

"Can you give me an example of this?"

"I'm not sure [how/when/where] to enter the data."

Skill Practice: Asking for Focused Explanation

Do this skill practice in pairs. Student A will explain or describe something using the list of topics below. Student B will ask for focused explanations using the sentences listed above. For example:

COOKING RICE

A: "Put a little oil in a pot and sauté one cup of rice until the grains turn white. Then add two cups of water and let it simmer until all the water is gone."

B: "I understand about the water but can you explain the *first* thing you said? About the oil . . . ?"

A: "Oh. Okay. You put a little oil in a pot and heat it up, and then you add one cup of rice and stir it until every piece of rice becomes white."

B: "Okay. I see."

Topics:

1.   How to cook a dish from your country
2.   How to use a machine or piece of equipment
3.   How a certain holiday is celebrated in your country
4.   How to address people in your culture
5.   How to fix something that's broken
6.   A topic of your own choice

Skill Practice: Asking for More Information

Practice with the same topics you used above, but this time use the expression: "I'm not sure how (when/where/what) to. . . ."

Example: Cooking Rice

"I'm not sure how to make the rice turn white."

SECTION 2. HOLDING YOUR TURN

Receptionist: "She's not in . . . she's out. She'll have to call you back."

Pierre: "She's out? Oh, I see . . . uhm . . . could I leave a message?"

Here Pierre holds his turn by saying, "Oh, I see . . . uhm . . ." while he decides what to say next. Sometimes when you are talking with another person, you need time to think before you speak or before you answer a question. When you hold your turn, you are telling the other person that you have not finished speaking and that you will say something in a few seconds.

CROSS-CULTURAL NOTE

A Japanese man once told a friend, "Americans sometimes interrupt and seem impatient when I speak. Sometimes they don't give me time to decide what to say. I need time to think about what to say in English. I also need to think about how to say it to the person I'm talking with.

Dialogue:

Read the following conversation between Dan, an American man, and his Chinese co-worker, Moy. Then answer the questions following the dialogue.

Situation: Dan and Moy are working together on a new product design. Dan calls Moy at his home to talk about the design.

Dan: "Hello, Moy? This is Dan."

Moy: "Oh, hi, Dan. How are you?"

Dan: "Fine. Uh . . . have you had a chance to look over the designs I left on your desk?"

(There are 2 or 3 seconds of silence.)

Dan: "Moy? *Are you there?*"

Moy: "Yes. I'm sorry, *I didn't get to them.*"

Dan: "Oh, that's okay. Will you have a chance to take a look at them this weekend?"

(There are 2 or 3 seconds of silence.)

Dan: "Uhm . . . but if you don't get to them until Monday that's fine. Is that okay?" (There are two or three seconds of silence.)

Moy: "I think I can look at them tomorrow afternoon. Can I call you tomorrow night?"

Dan: "Sure. Talk to you then."

Moy: (He is silent for a couple of seconds.) "Okay. Goodbye."

Dan: "Bye." (As Dan hangs up the phone, he thinks to himself, "I guess Moy is angry that I want him to work over the weekend.")

Questions:

1. What did Moy do that made Dan think he was angry?
2. Do you think Moy was angry?
3. Why do you think Dan talked so much?
4. Why do you think Moy did not reply quickly to Dan's questions?

Read the summary below after you have answered the questions.

Summary of Dialogue: Moy is a little embarrassed that he hasn't had time to look at Dan's designs. He also realizes that he won't have time to look at them before tomorrow afternoon. He is not sure how to express this information politely in English. He needs time to think before he replies to Dan's questions. Unfortunately, while Moy is thinking, Dan hears only long silences. Dan becomes very uncomfortable with this silence, and he thinks Moy must be annoyed or angry.

U.S. CULTURE NOTE

In U.S. culture, if someone is asked a question, a verbal response is expected right away. If someone doesn't answer quickly, it can mean that he or she is annoyed, angry, doesn't care, or has no answer.

Here is another way that Moy could have responded to Dan. He is holding his turn and not being silent this time.

Dan: "Hello, Moy? This is Dan."

Moy: "Oh, hi, Dan. How are you?"

Dan: "Fine. Uh . . . have you had a chance to look over the designs I left on your desk?"

Moy: "Uh . . . well . . . to tell the truth, I didn't get to them."

Dan: "Oh, that's okay. Will you have a chance to take a look at them this weekend?"

Are you there?—Are you still on the phone?
I didn't get to them—I haven't been able to look at them

Moy: "Uh . . . this weekend? I think . . . uh . . . I can look at them to-
          morrow afternoon. Can I call you tomorrow night?"
Dan: "Sure. Talk to you then."
Moy: "Okay. Goodbye."
Dan: "Bye."

In this second dialogue, Moy helps Dan to feel more comfortable. Moy knows
that Dan needs and expects verbal feedback. Moy uses expressions to hold his
turn while he tries to decide what to say. Because he uses these expressions, Dan
does not make Moy uncomfortable with too much talking.

Ways To Hold Your Turn

"*This weekend?*" (Repeat part of the other person's question, with a ques-
tion voice.)
"Uh . . ."
"Well . . ."
"I think . . ."
"I'm not sure . . ."
"Let me see . . ."
"Let me think . . ."
"Just a 'sec' " (Just a second)
"Um, how can I say this . . ."
"Let me try to say this correctly . . ."
"Well, let me think for a minute . . ."

Ways To Delay Your Answer

Sometimes you really don't want to answer a question when someone asks it. You
want to think about it first and talk about it later. You need to *delay* your answer.

"How soon can you start this?"
"Uhm . . . can I get back to you on that?"
"Could you give me some time to think about that?"
"Let me get back to you about that tomorrow/this afternoon/after the meet-
ing/on Wednesday, etc."
"Uh . . . we're working on that. I'll have to get back to you."

Skill Practice: Holding Your Turn

Do this skill practice with a partner. Use phrases and expressions to hold your
turn or delay an answer before you respond to the questions below.

1. Your friend: "Have you ever been really upset with an American?"
    You: _____
2. Your teacher: "In your culture, do people often interrupt each other?
    Can anyone interrupt anyone else—for example, can a younger person
    interrupt an older person?"
    You: _____

delay—wait for a short time before you do something

3. Your supervisor: "Is work in this country like work in your native country? What are some of the differences?"

    You: _____

4. Your classmate: "What's your opinion of the government in this country?"

    You: _____

5. Now discuss any other topic of interest with your partner. Ask each other, "What's your opinion?" "What do you think?" Use ways to hold your turn while you are thinking of your answer.

Other Ways To Guide the Conversation _____

Repeat these sentences after your teacher says them:

"Could you speak a little more slowly, please?"
"I'm sorry, but I can't hear you very well."
"Could you speak louder, please?" ("More loudly" is also used.)
"Sorry, I didn't hear that."
"I'm sorry, but could you use simpler words?"
"I'm not a native speaker of English. Would you mind using simpler words? Thanks."

SECTION 3. CORRECTING MISUNDERSTANDINGS

Receptionist: "All right, Mr. Dupont, and that was Western Machines Company . . . I'll give Ms. Garcia the message."

Pierre: "Uh . . . it's Western *Business* Machines."

When the receptionist says the name of Pierre's company incorrectly, Pierre corrects her.

CROSS-CULTURAL NOTE

In some cultures, it is very rude to tell someone that they are wrong or that they have made a mistake, especially in front of other people. The person can become embarrassed, and can *"lose face."* In these cultures, people sometimes use nonverbal signals to let someone know when they have said something wrong. Over the telephone or face-to-face the person may use silence to let the speaker know that he or she has said something wrong. Americans may not always understand what the silence means.

CULTURE PUZZLE

Read the situation and choose the appropriate answer or answers. There may be more than one possible answer.

lose face—be shamed in front of others; make a mistake that people know about

What would you do if a stranger pronounced your name incorrectly? First, think about what you would do in your own language and culture, and then what you would do if you were talking in English with an American.

    a)   You wouldn't say anything.

    b)   You would say, "Excuse me, but my name is _____.

    c)   You would not say, "Excuse me." You would just say, "It's _____."

(Answers are given at the end of the chapter.)

U.S. CULTURE NOTE

In some cultures it is usually acceptable to say, "No, that's not right" or "I think you are wrong" even when you do not know the person very well. When an American corrects someone, he or she often begins with a "softening" sound, such as 'uh' or 'uhm,' or a word or phrase such as 'Well,' 'I think,' or 'Actually' before disagreeing with someone. For example, "I think you *may* be wrong," with an emphasis on "may" and not on "you."

Ways To Correct Misunderstandings _____

The following sentences show polite ways of correcting another person. Repeat these sentences after your teacher. The correction phrases and words are italicized.

    "*Uh,* it's Western *Business* machines."

    "*Uhm* . . . that's P-*O*-N-T."

    "*Uhm, well* . . . *actually* my name is pronounced [pronounce your name]."

    "I think the homework is *actually* due *tomorrow, not* the day after tomorrow.

    "*Actually,* I understood the opposite."

    "*I think you may be mistaken.* I heard that we do get the day off on Monday."

Skill Practice: Correcting Misunderstandings

Your teacher or a partner will say some things to you that are incorrect. Use the phrases listed above to correct the misunderstandings. For example:

    Teacher: "The bank closes at 3:00 on Fridays."

    You: "Uh . . . I think it closes at 5:00."

    1.   Your name is _____, right?

    2.   You're from _____, aren't you?

    3.   Haven't you been here for three years?

    4.   You already knew English before you came here, didn't you?

    5.   Class begins at 9:30.

    6.   The work day is usually 5 hours long.

Now with the other students, make incorrect statements and have them correct you.

SECTION 4. SUMMARIZING

> Pierre: "Excuse me . . . so . . . she'll call me back this afternoon?"

or

> *"In other words,* I should hear from her this afternoon."

The last skill that we will look at in Chapter 6 is the skill of summarizing. When we summarize, we briefly repeat what the other person said in order to show that we understood what we heard.

<table>
<tr><td>

CROSS-CULTURAL NOTE

A group of Japanese people were talking about the American phrase, "in other words". One Japanese woman said, "If I repeat your idea in my own words, then I feel that I am saying to you, 'Your explanation is not good enough.' I don't want to embarrass you. Even if I don't understand everything you say, I will not check my understanding or summarize what you say. I don't want you to think that I am criticizing your explanation."

</td></tr>
</table>

There are two reasons why it is important to summarize when you are speaking in a second language.

1. You can make sure that you understood everything correctly.
2. You can help the other person feel confident that you understood them.

For most Americans, it is usually acceptable to summarize what another person just said, especially on the job or in a class. In fact, it can be helpful to other listeners.

Ways To Summarize

Repeat these sentences after your teacher says them:

> *"Let me see. You said* to put another butter knife on the table."
> *"Let me see if I understand."* (Repeat the information or explanation briefly.)
> *"Okay. So* I put the cole slaw here?"
> *"Okay. So you want me to* put the knives on this table?"
> *"So you're going to* remove the napkins now?"
> *"So he will* call the bus boy? *Is that right?"*
> *"In other words, I need to* bring new dishes now."

Skill Practice: Summarizing

Work with a partner. One person will read one paragraph and the other person will summarize the most important points.

in other words—let me repeat or summarize what you just said, but in my own words

We're having a *pot luck dinner* at our house this weekend and we hope you can come. Can you bring a salad? We'll be starting at about 4:00 pm. I think we're going to do a barbeque outside. There'll be about 20 people, including kids, but some other people are also bringing salad, so you only need to bring enough for about ten people. If it looks like it's going to rain, give me a call. If it rains, we'll just have to do it another time.

• •

Many people who come to the U.S. from other countries come to New York City first. Many of these people think of New York as a typical American city. They think that all American cities must be like New York, and that all Americans must be like New Yorkers. Actually, New York is a unique and special place. It is different from most other American cities. New Yorkers have their own culture which is different from the culture of other cities and places in the U.S. If foreign visitors want to have a good understanding of American cities and American culture, they should visit several different places in different parts of the U.S. They shouldn't just visit New York.

CHAPTER SUMMARY:

In this chapter you looked at four different skills that you can use to help you guide the conversation. They are:

- asking for focused explanation
- holding your turn
- correcting misunderstandings
- summarizing

The following are definitions and examples of each skill:

1. *Asking for focused explanation:* Ask the speaker to explain what he said. Guide the speaker to use different words, an example or more details.

   "I understand this, but could you explain the other/next/first/last thing you said?"

   "I got what you said about the first part, but I didn't get the next part."

   "Do you mean . . . ?" or "Did you mean . . . ?"

   "Can you give me an example of this?"

   "I'm not sure how/when/where to. . . ."

2. *Holding your turn:* Show that you want to speak, but that you need time to think first.

"Uh. . . ."	"Let me think. . . ."
"Well. . . ."	"Just a sec. . . ."
"I think. . . ."	"Um, how can I say this?"
"I'm not sure. . . ."	"Let me try to say this correctly. . . ."
"Let me see. . . ."	"Well, let me think for a minute. . . ."

---

pot luck dinner—a dinner to which the guests bring a dish so that there is a variety of food and so that one person doesn't have to do all the cooking. This type of dinner party is very common in the U.S.

3. *Correcting misunderstandings:* If you feel your partner did not understand you correctly, interrupt and explain what you meant.

"Uh . . ."

"Uhm. . . ."

"Uhm, well . . . actually. . . ."

"Actually. . . ."

"I think you may be mistaken."

4. *Summarizing:* Repeat information or explanations briefly to show the speaker what you've understood.

"Let me see. You said. . . ."

"Let me see if I understand. . . ."

"Okay. So. . . ."

"Okay. So you want me to. . . ."

"So you're going to. . . ."

"So he will. . . ."

"In other words, I need to. . . ."

ANSWERS TO CULTURE PUZZLE IN CHAPTER 6

a) No. Sometimes it is best not to correct the person right away, especially if he or she is very busy. Also, if other people are present, the person may be embarrassed to find out they pronounced your name incorrectly. However, if the person pronounces your name incorrectly more than once, you should tell him or her. People come to the United States from all over the world, and have many different kinds of names. Most Americans are used to asking and telling people how to pronounce names.

b) Yes. If you want to be polite and formal, it is best to apologize first, and then say your name correctly.

c) Yes. If the situation is informal you can just say your name correctly without apologizing. Sometimes saying 'Excuse me' is *too* formal.

Note: Answers to other exercises can be found in the separate Answer Key.

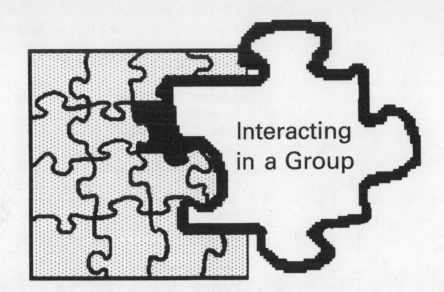

chapter 7

Interacting in a Group

Introduction You probably find yourself in situations where there are conversations or discussions among three or more people. These include class discussions, meetings at work, and social conversations. It is often difficult for non-native speakers of English to participate in group discussions and conversations when the others are native speakers of English. This chapter will apply skills presented in Chapters 5 and 6 to interaction in group contexts.

CULTURE LEARNING QUESTIONS

1. Which do you feel is more difficult, communication between two people or communication in a group?
2. Which is more difficult when you are speaking your own language? Which is more difficult when you are speaking English? Give examples from your own experience.

CROSS-CULTURAL INTERACTION 7A:
Ineffective Communication

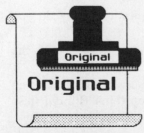

(Revised interaction appears on page 91.)

Situation: Bill is leading a staff meeting in a company in the U.S. There are eight people who are all American, except Anna, who is from Hungary. She is a supervisor in the manufacturing department. Today, Bill is talking about two things at the meeting. The first is a new health insurance plan for the employees. The second is vacation schedules. The meeting has been going on for twenty minutes. Bill has just finished explaining the insurance plan.

Bill: "Okay, so that's the insurance plan. Any questions?"

Anna: "Yes, I . . ."

Margie: (Margie interrupts Anna.) "Bill, where do I sign up for this insurance?"

Anna: (Anna thinks to herself, "What did Margie ask? I couldn't hear the question." Anna does not speak.)

Bill:	"See John in the Personnel office." (Then Bill looks at Anna.)
Anna:	"Personnel office?"
Bill:	"You don't know where the Personnel office is?"
Anna:	(Anna thinks to herself, "No, that's not my question. I want to know what Margie asked you." Anna is not sure what to say, so she says nothing.)
Bill:	"Margie, after the meeting will you show Anna where the Personnel office is?"
Margie:	"Okay."
Bill:	"Any other questions?"
Anna:	(Anna thinks to herself, "Yes, I have a question about the insurance, and I still don't know what Margie's question was. What did they mean about the 'Personnel office'? How can I interrupt?" Anna looks confused, but says nothing.)
Bill:	(No one asks a question, so he continues speaking quickly.) "Okay, let's move on then. Have you all turned in your vacation schedules for this year?"
Anna:	(Anna thinks to herself, "What does he mean, 'turned in'? I'm not going to ask since everyone else probably understands.")

QUESTIONS AND DISCUSSION

Comprehension

Write T (true) or F (false) in the space provided.

1. _____ Margie needs to see John in the Personnel office to sign up for insurance.
2. _____ Anna wants to know where the Personnel office is.
3. _____ Anna asks Margie to show her where the Personnel office is.
4. _____ Anna does not ask the question that she wanted to ask before Margie interrupted.

Analysis: Can You Explain?

1. Bill looks at Anna after he answers Margie's question. Why do you think he does this?
2. Anna thinks to herself, "No, that's not my question." Why doesn't she say this, aloud, to Bill?
3. Bill asks Margie to show Anna where the Personnel office is, even though this was not Anna's question. Why do you think Bill did this?

TALK ABOUT YOUR OWN LANGUAGE AND CULTURE

1. Is the style of communication in the meeting in Cross-Cultural Interaction 7A typical of one that might take place in your language and culture? If it is not, what are the differences?
2. Do you think that people who lead meetings in your culture would take the time to speak slowly and explain difficult words to non-native speakers of your language? Explain your answer.

Summary of Cross-Cultural Interaction 7A

This is a difficult meeting for Anna. Margie interrupts her. Then Anna doesn't hear Margie's question. Anna tries to ask a question, but Bill misunderstands her. Bill asks, "Any questions?" but continues talking before Anna has a chance to say anything. Then Bill uses a phrase that Anna does not understand. Anna feels more and more lost. She cannot participate in the group meeting.

Many cultural differences can be seen in the way people interact in groups, particularly in the classroom and at meetings. A person who can participate easily in a group conversation in his or her own culture may not be able to participate in a similar conversation in another culture.

CROSS-CULTURAL INTERACTION 7B

In the following interaction, Anna does not get lost as she did in Cross-Cultural Interaction 7A. Read the skills listed below and then read the dialogue. Identify the skill that is being used and fill in the blanks in the "What Is Happening" column. The first one is done for you.

- Gives feedback (1 example)
- Interrupts (2 examples)
- Checks bits of information (1 example)
- Asks for focused repetition (1 example)
- Asks for focused explanation or more information (1 example)
- Holds her turn (2 examples, one is marked for you)

Dialogue		What Is Happening
Bill:	"Okay, so that's the insurance plan. Any questions?"	
Anna:	Yes, uh . . . can you tell me . . ."	*holds her turn*
Margie:	(She interrupts Anna.) "Bill, where do I sign up for this insurance?"	
Bill:	"See John in the Personnel office." (Bill looks at Anna.)	
Anna:	"Excuse me, Bill, what was Margie's question?"	_____
Bill:	"Uh . . . Margie asked where to sign up for the insurance."	
Anna:	"I see, thank you. We can sign up in the Personnel office?"	_____
Bill:	"That's right. Uh, now . . let's *move on* . . ."	
Anna:	"Before you move on, I've got another question."	_____
Bill:	"Oh, yes. What was it?"	

move on—continue

	Dialogue	*What Is Happening*
Anna:	"I'm not sure I understand about the dental insurance. Is it for my children too?"	_____
Bill:	"Let me check the pamphlet that I gave you."	
Anna:	"Oh, thank you. Um . . . I can read it and then ask you later if I still have any questions."	_____
Bill:	"Okay. Fine." (He is speaking more slowly.) "Are there any more questions before I go on to vacation schedules?" (Bill pauses and makes eye contact around the room.)	

(Answers are given at the end of the chapter.)

Summary of Cross-Cultural Interaction 7B

Anna was able to "stay in" the group interaction by using interaction skills effectively. As a result, she didn't get lost or embarrassed. She made sure that Margie and Bill included her and helped her understand.

In both interactions, Margie interrupted Anna. Is Margie rude by American standards? She is not necessarily being rude in the context of an informal meeting. Margie probably expects Anna to ask her question again later in the conversation. Anna is not being rude when she reminds Bill, "I had a question earlier."

FOCUS ON U.S. CULTURE
Cultural Notes, Exercises, and Skill Practice

HOW MUCH DO YOU ALREADY KNOW ABOUT U.S. CULTURE?

Write T (true) or F (false) in the space provided.

1. _____ If two people are speaking and a third would like to speak, he or she should never interrupt the two speakers.

2. _____ In a group conversation or discussion, it is rude to talk again about a topic people already talked about earlier.

3. _____ Americans will usually give non-native speakers of English extra thinking time and extra time to translate from their own language to English.

4. _____ Americans generally think that it is good to speak up in meetings rather than be silent.

5. _____ Americans are expected to bring up new ideas and suggestions in most meetings.

SECTION 1. GETTING INTO THE CONVERSATION

Margie:	"Bill, where do I sign up for this insurance?"
Bill:	"See John in the Personnel office."
Anna:	"Excuse me, Bill. What was Margie's question?"

Bill: "Let's move on."

Anna: "Before you move on, I've got another question."

Using the skills of holding your turn and interrupting can be very important in a group interaction, especially if you are the only non-native speaker of English. When two or more native speakers are talking together, it can be hard to get into, or join, the conversation. Sometimes it is necessary to interrupt quickly before the topic of conversation changes. You may have to do this even before you have decided exactly what to say. You may sometimes need to interrupt and hold your turn for a few seconds before you speak.

Phrases and Expressions for Getting into a Group Conversation

When you want to get into, or break into, a group conversation, you have to wait for a pause and then interrupt quickly. You could use the interruption phrases presented earlier:

"Excuse me. I have something to add here."

"Uhm . . . I have a question about that."

"Could I ask a question?"

"Could I interrupt for a quick second?"

"Just a quick interruption . . ."

You could interrupt, hold your turn, and then say what you want to say:

"Um . . ."

"So . . . this is what we need to do."

"Do you mean, uh . . . ?"

"Uh . . . I'd like to know . . ."

"Can you tell me . . . ?"

"I can add something here . . ."

"Ah . . . you know . . ."

"Well. . . you know . . ."

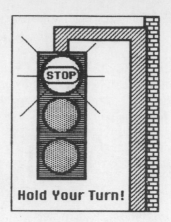

When you hold your turn, it is as if you are putting up a stop light. You are telling others that you want to say something and you don't want anyone else to speak until after you speak.

Skill Practice: Getting into the Group Conversation

Use the phrases above to interrupt quickly and hold your turn. Then ask for focused repetition or explanation when you don't understand something. When you want to add something, get into the conversation.

Topics for a Group Discussion:

- Your instructor discusses students' goals and his own goals for the class.
- You and the other students list the problems of speaking a second language and discuss solutions to those problems.
- Compare a typical school or work day in your native country with that of other students.
- Your choice of topics

Cross-Cultural Exercise: Getting into the Conversation

With two other people who speak your language, demonstrate for the class how you would break into a conversation in your language.

- See if the class can identify any "interruption sounds" you use. (In English, "Uh" and "Uhm" are interruption sounds.)
- Translate into English the phrases and expressions that you used to break into the conversation.

CROSS-CULTURAL NOTE

An Ethiopian man who worked in a hotel restaurant talked about a frustrating experience: "When the kitchen staff have a meeting, I never ask any questions or say anything. Sometimes I want to, but by the time I decide how to say what I want to say, it's too late. They're already talking about something else."

Phrases and Expressions for Going Back to Earlier Topics

If you miss the chance to say what you want to say, you can often go back to it later in the conversation. Repeat the following after your teacher:

"Going back to what we were talking about earlier . . ."
"Could we go back to [state the topic] that we were discussing earlier?"
"I had a question earlier about [state the topic]."
"I wanted to add something to what we were saying earlier."

Skill Practice: Going Back to Topics

Choose a topic to discuss with several other people. If you lose the chance to say something, go back to the topic later in the discussion. Use the phrases listed above. Have your teacher listen to you and tell you if you are using the phrases correctly.

Topics:

Experiences in a second culture   Customs in your country

Learning a second language   Your choice of topics

SECTION 2. PARTICIPATING IN DISCUSSIONS AND MEETINGS

It is not always possible to follow the conversation in a group discussion or meeting. You can be more prepared if you know certain phrases to get into a conversation and if you try to use them. You can also remind people, both directly and indirectly, that you are a non-native speaker of English and that group discussions or meetings are sometimes difficult to follow. The following list includes ways to help you participate in and understand meetings and group discussions:

1. Find a person who can help you understand a meeting or group discussion while it is going on and after it has ended.
2. Tape record meetings and discussions whenever possible.

3. If it is a meeting at work, for example, have your supervisor show you the *agenda* before the meeting starts.

4. Know and use phrases for getting into conversations.

5. Be willing to participate even if you are not used to speaking up in a group.

U.S. CULTURE NOTE

Sometimes in meetings or in group discussions, Americans will forget to give you thinking time and translation time. This is especially true if they have never learned to speak another language or if they have never lived in another country. You may need to explain to them that you sometimes need to think of responses in your language, translate them to English, and then say them out loud. If you are able to speak fairly quickly and communicate your ideas well, it may even be harder for you. People may forget that you sometimes still need extra time for thinking and translating.

Active Participation

Leaders and *active participants* in group discussions or meetings do the following:

Initiate	Begin discussion, bring up new ideas and topics, and make suggestions.
Ask	Ask people for opinions, information, and explanations.
Offer	Offer opinions and give information when needed.
Repeat	Repeat ideas, information, and explanations for the rest of the group when something has not been understood.
Summarize	Summarize information to make sure that something has been understood.
Encourage	Encourage people to speak by being cooperative and by accepting different *points of view*.

agenda—list of topics to be discussed at a meeting
active participants—people who talk (make suggestions, ask questions, etc.) in meetings and discussions
points of view—opinions; viewpoints

Following are some examples of each:

Initiate

"I have an idea about how we could solve the problem."

"May I make a suggestion?"

"One solution to the problem might be to talk to Mr. Jones about it."

"Perhaps we could begin by discussing our problem."

"Could I suggest that we get everyone's opinion on that?"

Ask

"Ms. Smith, could you tell us what you think?"

"I'm not clear about this. Could someone explain it to me?"

"I missed the explanation. Would you mind repeating it?"

"Mr. Walter, would you mind telling us a little bit more about your experiences with this type of problem?"

"Does anyone know some more about this?"

Offer

"I believe that there isn't much more we can do."

"In my opinion there are only two choices."

"It seems to me that the only solution is to lower the prices."

"My feeling is that we should go ahead and buy the product."

"I can show you the numbers, if that will help."

Repeat

"Can I repeat that for anyone?"

"I'm not sure if everyone heard. Let me repeat that."

Summarize

"So you'd like us to discuss this at the next meeting?"

"You mean we all need to meet one more time before we can decide?"

"If I can summarize what we've been talking about. . . ."

"Let me see if I understand. . . ."

"To summarize, we all agree that it is best to wait until we have more information."

Encourage

"Do you have the same opinion, Adam?"

"I think some people here probably disagree with this. I'd like to hear what they have to say."

"I know Sara has a different point of view. I'd be interested in hearing it."

"I hope we can all talk about this, even though some of us may disagree."

"Maybe we can figure out a way to make everyone happy, even though we disagree on the subject."

"Noga, you haven't had a chance to give your thoughts on this. What do you think?"

Phrases and Expressions for Participating in Meetings and Discussions _____

Initiate	*Ask*
"I have an idea about . . . "	"What do you think?"
"May I make a suggestion?"	"Could you explain . . . ?"
"One solution might be . . . "	"Would you repeat that?"
"Perhaps we could begin by . . . "	"Could you tell us more about . . . ?"
"Could I suggest that . . .?"	

Offer	*Summarize*
"I believe that . . . "	"So. . . . "
"In my opinion . . . "	"You mean . . . ?"
"It seems to me that . . . "	"Let me see if I understand."
"My feeling is that . . . "	"To summarize . . . "
"I can show/tell you . . . "	

Encourage

"Do you have an opinion?"
"What do you think?"
"Do you agree?"
"Can you tell us about . . . ?"

Skill Practice: Participating in Discussions and Meetings

Choose a meeting or discussion topic. If you choose a topic for a meeting, think of something that has to be done or decided. If you choose a topic for a discussion, think of something that people don't agree on. For either the meeting or the discussion, choose a topic that will encourage discussion.

Directions:

1. Five to ten people will participate in the discussion or meeting. The rest of the class will observe the discussion.
2. The discussion participants can sit in a circle in the middle of the room while the observers sit in a larger circle around them.
3. Using the observation form on the next page, the observers will note how often the discussion participants *initiate, ask, offer, repeat, summarize,* and *encourage.* (*Variation:* If the group is small enough, the teacher can observe all of the discussion participants.)*
4. After the first meeting or discussion, the observers will change places with the discussion participants.
5. Read the instructions on the observation form. If necessary, review the definitions of *initiate, ask, offer, repeat, summarize* and *encourage* given earlier in this section.

*Note to the teacher: It is not necessary for students to compare their total number of points with each other, but for each to realize their patterns of participation. This activity should be done several times so that students have the opportunity to increase their participation (both the amount of participation and the type of participation).

OBSERVATION FORM

Instructions: Write in the names of the discussion or meeting participants. Every time each participant speaks, mark an X in the box under the name and next to the verb (initiate, ask, offer, etc.) that best describes the type of participation. When the discussion is over, total the number of times each member participated.

	1	2	3	4	5
Name of Participant					
1. Initiate					
2. Ask					
3. Offer					
4. Repeat					
5. Summarize					
6. Encourage					
Total Number of Times Participating					

	6	7	8	9	10
Name of Participant					
1. Initiate					
2. Ask					
3. Offer					
4. Repeat					
5. Summarize					
6. Encourage					
Total Number of Times Participating					

CHAPTER SUMMARY

This chapter presented ways of getting into a group conversation. They include:

- Interrupting
- Holding Your Turn

In addition, you can get into a group conversation by going back to a topic. Phrases that you can use are:

"Going back to what we were talking about earlier . . ."
"Could we go back to the topic that we were discussing earlier?"
"I had a question earlier about [state the topic]."
"I wanted to add something to what we were saying earlier."

This chapter also presented skills for active participation in meetings and group discussions:

1. *Initiate* discussion, bring up new ideas, and make suggestions.
2. *Ask* for opinions, information, and explanations.
3. *Offer* your opinions and give information when needed.
4. *Repeat* ideas, information, and explanations if people have not understood.
5. *Summarize* information to make sure that you and others have understood.
6. *Encourage* others to participate by being cooperative and by accepting different points of view.

Answers to Cross-Cultural Interaction 7B

	Dialogue	*What Is Happening*
Bill:	"Okay, so that's the insurance plan. Any questions?"	
Anna:	"Yes, uh . . . can you tell me . . ."	Anna tries to **hold her turn** (Notice that Anna is not successful in holding her turn because Margie interrupts her. Anna "gets her turn back" later when she interrupts Bill to ask her question.)
Margie:	"Bill, where do I sign up for this insurance?"	
Bill:	"See John in the Personnel office." (Bill looks at Anna.)	
Anna:	"Excuse me, Bill, what was Margie's question?"	Anna **interrupts** to **ask a focused repetition question.**
Bill:	"Uh . . . Margie asked where to sign up for the insurance."	
Anna:	"I see, thank you. We can sign up in the Personnel office?"	Anna **gives feedback** and **checks information**
Bill:	"That's right. Uh, now . . let's move on . . ."	

Anna:	"Before you move on, I've got another question."	Anna **interrupts.**
Bill:	"Oh, yes. What was it?"	
Anna:	"I'm not sure I understand about the dental insurance. Is it for my children too?"	Anna **asks for focused explanation.**
Bill:	"Let me check the pamphlet that I gave you."	
Anna:	"Oh, thank you. Um . . . I can read it and then ask you later if I still have any questions."	Anna **holds her turn.**
Bill:	"Okay. Fine. Are there any more questions before I go on to vacation schedules?"	

Reading Text and Activities

Contents:

READING TEXT: INTERACTING IN ENGLISH
Reading Preview Activities

Reading Outline   Read the outline of the text and discuss the questions following it.

Part I. What Is Interaction?*

A. An example: A telephone conversation
B. Feedback is an important part of interaction in English.
C. In two-way communication, what one person says or does influences what the other person says or does.

To the teacher: The words "interaction" and "feedback" are common terms in the field of cross-cultural communication. Most other ways of describing these two concepts are wordy and roundabout. Explain to the students that these words are used in this chapter with a particular meaning in mind, but that they have other meanings as well. In this text, the following definitions are used: *interaction*—communication back and forth; two-way communication, both verbal and nonverbal; *feedback*—response; answer; ways to show "I'm listening," "I understand," or "I don't understand."

Part II. Interaction and U.S. Culture

    A. The U.S. is a verbal culture.

    B. Americans are uncomfortable with a lack of feedback.

    C. A good speaker lets others take turns in speaking.

    D. There are cultural differences in the ways people interact.

Part III. Your Own Language and Culture

    A. What you already know will help you communicate in English.

    B. Recognize similarities and differences between communicating in English and in your own language.

Part IV. Interacting in New Ways

    A. An example: What does "Uh-huh" mean?

    B. When you learn new skills for interaction, you are adding to what you already know.

OUTLINE QUESTIONS

Based on the outline and your own experiences, answer the following questions:

1. In the first part of the reading, the authors write, "In two-way communication, what one person says or does influences what the other person says or does." Can you give examples of this?

2. In the second part of the reading, the authors write, "The U.S. is a verbal culture." What do you think this means?

3. In the third part of the reading, the importance of recognizing similarities and differences is discussed. How is interaction in your language similar to English? How is it different?

4. The fourth part of the reading gives examples of how an immigrant in the U.S. learned new ways of interacting. Can you give some examples of things that you do differently when you interact in English?

VOCABULARY

Following is a list of vocabulary from the reading in Unit II, *Interacting in English*. To help you with pronunciation, each word is divided into syllables. The stressed syllable is marked with an accent mark. The words are grouped by part of speech (nouns, verbs, etc.) in the order in which they appear in the reading. *Practice saying these words after your teacher says them.* Each word is glossed (defined) at the bottom of the page the first time it appears in the reading. The definition gives the meaning of the word *as it is used in the reading*. These words also appear in the post-reading activities.

PART I

Nouns
RISING INTONATION   ris'-ing in-to-na'-tion
AREA CODE   ar'-e-a code
FALLING INTONATION   fall'-ing in-to-na'-tion
RECEPTIONIST   re-cep'-tion-ist
FEEDBACK   feed'-back

Verbs
INTERACTING   in'-ter-act'-ing
RESPONDING   re-spond'-ing
REASSURES   re-a-ssures'

Adjectives
FRUSTRATED   frus'-tra-ted

Adverbs
IN TURN   in turn'

Idioms
AS WELL AS   as well' as

Exclamations/Sounds
UH-HUH   uh-huh'
UHM-HMM   uhm-hmm'

PART II

Nouns
CONTRAST   con'-trast
PARTICIPATION   par-ti-ci-pa'-tion
CONFLICT   con'-flict
EXPRESSIONS   ex-pres'-sions (verb: EXPRESS)

Verbs
CRITICIZE   crit'-i-cize

Adjectives
SPOKEN   spo'-ken

Adverbs
SOMEWHAT   some'-what'

Conjunctions
YET   yet

Two-Word Verbs/Idioms
GET RID OF   get rid' of
TALK THINGS OUT   talk' things out'
GET IT OUT IN THE OPEN   get' it out' in the o'-pen
GET IT OFF YOUR CHEST   get' it off' your chest'
TAKE TURNS   take' turns'
HOGS THE CONVERSATION   hogs' the con-ver-sa'-tion
GET A WORD IN   get' a word' in
ON THE ONE HAND   on the one' hand
ON THE OTHER HAND   on the oth'-er hand
DUE TO   due' to
IN ORDER TO   in or'-der to
LESS OF A CONCERN   less' of a con-cern'
DEPENDS ON   de-pends' on

PART III

Verbs
RECOGNIZE   rec'-og-nize
ACCEPT   ac-cept'

Adverbs
RATHER THAN   rath'-er than

PART IV

Nouns
FILIPINA   Fi-li-pi'-na

Verbs
JUDGE   judge
HESITATE   hes'-i-tate
GAINING   gain'-ing
RUDE   rude

Idioms
AT LEAST   at least'
GET USED TO   get used' to

Reading Preview Suggestions

Before you begin reading the text, *Interacting In English,* do the following:

1. Read the titles of each part (Parts I, II, III, and IV).
2. Read the subheadings within each part of the reading.
3. Read the sentences in the margins.
4. Read the first sentence of each paragraph.
5. Read the key concepts at the end of each part.
6. Read the glosses (definitions) at the bottom of each page.

READING TEXT: INTERACTING IN ENGLISH

Part I: What Is Interaction?

Example: A telephone conversation

Caller   *Receptionist*

 May I speak to Claudine?

 I'm sorry, but she's not here at the moment.

 Could you ask her to call Bill Johnson, please?

 All right. Does she have your number?

 I'm not sure. Let me give it to you.

 Okay. [said with *rising intonation*, meaning, "I'm ready, go ahead."]

 It's *area code* 1–2–3

 *uh-huh*

rising intonation—the voice goes up, making a higher sound
area code—three numbers you must dial if you are calling long distance; for example, (*415*) 555-7991
uh-huh—yes, I'm listening. (In this sentence, "please continue.")

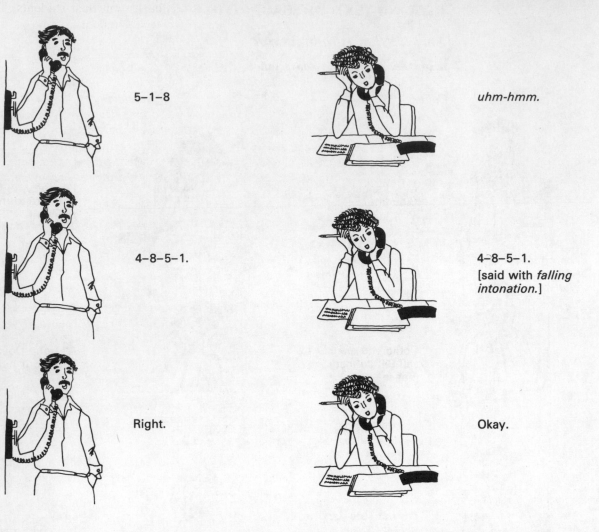

5-1-8   uhm-hmm.

4-8-5-1.   4-8-5-1.
                                                   [said with *falling
                                                   intonation*.]

Right.   Okay.

Interaction is two-way communication.

1. In this conversation, the caller gives his number. How does he know that the *receptionist* has correctly understood it? The receptionist says, "Uh-huh" and "Uhm-hmm" and repeats the last part of the number, "4–8–5–1." The receptionist is *interacting* with the caller. She is *responding* to him so that there is two-way communication. Through the receptionist's interaction with him, the caller knows that he has been understood.

Feedback shows: "I'm listening," "I understand," or "I don't understand."

2. **Feedback.** The receptionist in this example gives *feedback* to the caller. Feedback can be defined as: ways in which a person tells or shows a speaker, "I'm listening," "I understand you," or "I don't understand you." The receptionist, through feedback, tells the caller that she is listening and that she understands him.

3. Feedback is an important part of interaction. Many Americans give *as well as* expect a lot of feedback when they are talking. For example, in the

uhm-hmm—uh-huh (note also: "*uhn-unh*" = "no")
falling intonation—the voice goes down, making a lower sound
receptionist—a person who answers the phone and receives visitors in an office
interacting—communicating back and forth; two-way communication, both verbal and nonverbal
responding—answering (noun: *response*)
feedback—answer; response; ways to show "I'm listening," "I understand," or "I don't understand."
as well as—and; also

classroom, American teachers expect feedback from their students. This is shown by one American teacher's reaction to his students:

> I always ask, "Are there any questions?" Sometimes I get no response from my students. Then I don't know if they understand me or not. So I feel *frustrated* and I try to get them to say something!

Feedback can be verbal or nonverbal.

4. Feedback from students creates two-way communication in the classroom. This interaction makes American teachers feel comfortable. The feedback can be verbal, such as saying "yes" or asking a question. It can also be nonverbal, such as nodding your head "yes" or shaking your head "no." This kind of feedback *reassures* teachers that students are listening and shows what the students understand or don't understand. When there is no feedback, teachers may feel uncomfortable. They may then try harder to make their students say something. This may, *in turn,* make the students feel uncomfortable.

In communication, each person influences the other.

5. **Communication as influence.**   In two-way communication, what one person says or does influences what the other person says or does. This happened between the caller and the receptionist, as well as between the teacher and his students. Similarly, every time you interact with another person, you influence what that person says or does, and he or she influences you.

Key Concepts in PART I

Feedback: Many Americans give feedback as well as expect feedback when they are talking.

Feedback from students: When American teachers don't get feedback from students in the classroom, they may feel uncomfortable.

Influence: When two people interact, each has an influence on what the other says or does.

Part II. Interaction and U.S. Culture

The U.S. is a verbal culture.

6. The United States is a verbal culture. In *contrast* to people from some cultures, Americans see communication as a verbal activity more than a nonverbal one. For most Americans, interacting with someone means speaking with that person. For example, Americans believe that *participation* in a classroom or in a business meeting means speaking. If someone does not speak, then he or she is not participating.

7. A second example shows the importance of talking—of *spoken* interaction—in U.S. culture. Many Americans believe that talking together is the best way to *get rid of* misunderstanding or *conflict*. This belief can be seen in everyday *expressions* such as:

"Let's *talk things out.*"

frustrated—upset or annoyed because you can't do something
reassures—makes someone feel more confident
in turn—as a result
contrast—comparison to show differences
participation—being part of an activity, usually by speaking (verb: to *participate*)
spoken—with words or talking; verbal
get rid of—make something go away
conflict—argument, disagreement
expressions—phrases, sentences
talk things out—to talk about a problem and decide what to do

"It's best to *get it out in the open*."

"*Get it off your chest*."

While not all Americans are comfortable with this, the general cultural belief is to "talk things out."

Most Americans expect immediate feedback.

8. **Immediate feedback.**   Most Americans expect immediate feedback. That is, they expect feedback at the time they are speaking with someone. They want to be reassured that the person is listening and has understood. For example, if a supervisor gives instructions to an employee, the supervisor wants to know, at that moment, "Do you understand? Do you have any questions?" If the employee comes back a day or two later and tells the supervisor that he or she did not really understand, the supervisor may be *somewhat* upset. The supervisor might tell the employee, "If you didn't understand, why didn't you tell me? Why did you wait?"

Silence makes Americans uncomfortable.

9. With a need for immediate feedback, most Americans are uncomfortable with silence in an interaction. For example, one American businessman complained about a meeting with a group of businessmen from another country: "They didn't say anything. I don't know if they understood me or not!" If there is too much silence, Americans will often fill it by talking— even if they have nothing important to say.

10. **Taking turns.**   Many Americans believe that a good speaker is one who lets others *take turns* in speaking. Someone who does not let others speak is often seen as talking too much. Americans use several expressions to *criticize* someone who does not take turns:

"She talks non-stop."

get it out in the open—to talk about a problem, and share it, not hide it inside yourself
get it off your chest—to talk about a problem and feel better
somewhat—a little, not very
take turns—let each person have a chance to speak
criticize—complain, list the bad points about someone

"He always *hogs the conversation*."

"I couldn't *get a word in*."

There are cultural differences in the way people take turns in speaking.

11. People differ culturally in the way they take turns in speaking. This can be seen in English-as-a-Second-Language (ESL) classrooms in the United States, in which the students come from all over the world. Especially in the early weeks of class, some students talk much more than other students do. *On the one hand,* these talkative students see their own behavior as "natural" or "normal," because of their own cultural backgrounds. *On the other hand,* students who do not participate much in class see their own behavior as "normal." In addition, they may want to participate more, but may have difficulty getting a turn to speak, *due to* cultural differences in the classroom.

Taking turns can cause difficulties in cross-cultural communication.

12. Some Americans, when they feel that someone is talking too much, may try to interrupt *in order to* take a turn in speaking. They feel that the other person should give them a turn to speak. In some cultures, however, people expect others to interrupt in order to speak. Giving others a turn to speak is *less of a concern.* This is true for many Americans as well. As you can see, taking turns in conversation can cause difficulties in communication across cultures.

There are no "right" or "wrong" ways of interacting.

13. **An awareness of interaction.** The examples above do not mean that there are "right" or "wrong" ways of interacting. Rather, they show cultural differences. The examples also show that interacting with Americans can be difficult at times. Whether you feel that someone is talking too much, or not enough, partly *depends on* your cultural background. *Yet* how can you know, from a different cultural point of view, whether you are talking too much, talking too little, or giving enough feedback? An awareness of how you interact with Americans will help you here. This means seeing how you, with your own cultural background, influence Americans and how Americans influence you in an interaction. It takes both experience and careful observation to develop this kind of awareness.

Key Concepts in PART II _____

Verbal communication: Americans see communication as a verbal activity more than a nonverbal one.

Silence: Americans are uncomfortable with too much silence in an interaction. They will often fill silence by talking.

Normal or natural: Cultural differences are differences in what people see as "normal" or "natural" behavior. One example is how people take turns in speaking.

Awareness: It takes both experience and careful observation in order to become aware of what people in different cultures see as "normal" or "natural" behavior.

_____

hogs the conversation—does all the talking, so no one else can speak
(couldn't) get a word in—couldn't speak because someone else was talking too much
on the one hand—from one point of view, looking at one side of a question
on the other hand—from the other point of view, looking at the other side of the question
due to—because of
in order to—so that he can (speak), because he wants to (speak)
less of a concern—not as important a problem
depends on—is strongly related to; is the result of something
yet—but

Part III. Your Own Language and Culture

Some differences are easily seen; others are not.

14. A good way to become aware of interaction in another culture is to think about how you interact with people in your own language and culture. This will help you to *recognize* differences as well as similarities between your culture and U.S. culture. Some differences are quite easily seen. For example, in the United States, you quickly learn how to address people. You learn how to use "Mr.," "Ms.," "Mrs.," and "Miss." You learn that people often use their first names *rather than* their family names when talking. On the other hand, some differences are more difficult to see. For example, how do you compliment someone in your own culture, and how are compliments *accepted?* Is it similar to or different than giving and accepting compliments in American culture? Perhaps the types of expressions used to give compliments are different. Also, it may be that compliments are given more often (or less often) in the U.S. than in your own culture.

How do you interact with people in your own language and culture?

15. How do you interact with people in your own culture? How do you show, "I'm listening," "I understand you," or "I don't understand you"? What do you say or do in order to give feedback? How do you take turns when speaking? In comparing your own culture to American culture, you may find both similarities and differences in these important areas of interaction. Where there are similarities, you will probably be able to interact with Americans in ways which are already familiar to you. Where there are differences, you may need to learn new ways of interacting. If you now live in the United States, you may already be aware of many cultural differences and similarities. If you do not live in the U.S., you may not know how Americans interact. Even so, with your own knowledge and experience, you can try to answer:

    How do I interact with people in my own language and culture?

    With Americans, what can I continue to do in a similar way?

    With Americans, what will I need to do differently?

Key Concepts in PART III

Your own language and culture: An awareness of how you interact with people in your own language and culture will help you to interact in English with Americans.

Similarities and differences: Your challenge is to recognize similarities and differences across cultures. Sometimes these are obvious; sometimes they are not.

Part IV. Interacting in New Ways

16. When there are cultural differences, people often need to learn new ways of interacting in order to reach two-way communication. As you learn to communicate in English with Americans, you will be learning new skills for interaction. That is, you will be adding to what you already know how to do in your own language and culture. The following is an example of this. A *Filipina* woman left the Philippines and came to the United States. When she spoke with Americans, she noticed that they often said, "Uh-huh." She was quite bothered by this. One day, after having been in the U.S. for about five

---

recognize—see and understand
rather than—instead of; preferring one choice, not the other
accepted—received
Filipina—a woman from the Philippines

months, she decided to talk about this with an American. She told him, "You always say, 'uh-huh, uh-huh.' That's *rude*." Without being aware of it, the woman was *judging* Americans from her own cultural point of view. "Well," asked the man, "What do you say in the Philippines?" She replied, "We say, 'yes.' " Then the man explained, "That's what 'uh-huh' means. It just means 'yes.' When I listen to someone, I say 'uh-huh,' and that shows I'm listening. But it's not rude—*at least for Americans*. Do you see what I mean?"

17. As she listened to the man's explanation, the woman became aware for the first time that, for Americans, "uh-huh" is not rude. She had felt upset because in her own culture with Filipinos, "uh-huh" would be impolite. So when the man asked, "Do you see what I mean?" she thought for a moment, smiled and replied, "Uh-huh." She was learning the skill of recognizing cultural differences. She was also learning to accept different ways of interacting.

18. **Gaining new skills.** For this woman, accepting a different way of using "uh-huh" was not too difficult. It is not always this easy, however, to accept a different way of interacting. Acceptance can take a long time—much longer than it took the Filipina woman. In interacting with Americans, you may find it hard to *get used to* differences such as in feedback or taking turns in conversation. You may at first *hesitate* to speak in class or in a business meeting. Yet, as you learn to recognize cultural similarities and differences, you will also develop new skills for interaction. You will not forget how to communicate in your own language and culture. Instead, you will be adding to what you already know. You will be *gaining* new skills for communicating across cultures.

Key Concepts in PART IV

New skills: When you use new skills in English, you will be adding to your own cultural ways of interacting.

Judgment: Without being aware of it, people sometimes make judgments about each other from their own cultural points of view.

Acceptance: Acceptance of culturally different ways of interacting can take a long time.

Gain: When you use interaction skills in English, you will be adding to what you already know.

POST-READING ACTIVITIES

READING COMPREHENSION EXCERCISES

True/False

Read each statement. Then, according to the reading, decide whether the statement is true or false. Write T (true) or F (false) in the space provided.

rude—not polite
judge—forming an idea or opinion; deciding that something is good or bad
at least for Americans—for Americans, and maybe for other people too
get used to—become comfortable or familiar with
hesitate—not do something right away, not feel confident
gaining—adding, learning

1. _____ Americans expect little verbal feedback. (Part I)
2. _____ Feedback can be verbal or nonverbal. (Part I)
3. _____ Nodding your head "yes" is a kind of feedback. (Part I)
4. _____ Americans, in general, don't feel that they need words to express themselves. (Part II)
5. _____ "Let's talk it out" means to settle a disagreement by talking about it. (Part II)
6. _____ When there is silence in a conversation, Americans will often become silent themselves. (Part II)
7. _____ "She talks non-stop" is a compliment in U.S. culture. (Part II)
8. _____ Taking turns in speaking is the same all over the world. (Part II)
9. _____ The skills you use to communicate in your own language will not help you when you speak English. (Part III)
10. _____ "Uh-huh" is a polite expression in the Philippines. (Part IV)

Multiple Choice

Circle the letter next to the one best answer. Try to answer each question without looking at the reading. Then, if you cannot answer the question, reread the paragraph indicated.

1. How does the caller in the telephone example know that the receptionist correctly understood his number? (Paragraph 1)
   a) The receptionist repeats the whole number, "518–4851."
   b) The receptionist is a friend and already knows his number.
   c) The receptionist says, "Uh-huh," "Uhm-hmm," and "4–8–5–1."
2. Which of the following best describes the example of the American teacher and his students? (Paragraph 3)
   a) When the teacher gets no response and no feedback, he feels frustrated.
   b) The teacher doesn't expect any questions because he teaches so well.
   c) American students never give feedback to teachers in class.
3. In the same example, how does the teacher influence his students? (Paragraph 3)
   a) The teacher, by trying to get the students to say something, may be making the students uncomfortable.
   b) Because the teacher teaches so well, the students don't need to ask questions.
   c) The teacher, by asking, "Are there any questions?" is showing the students that he can't explain well.
4. Which of the following examples shows that people in the U.S. generally prefer speaking to being silent? (Paragraph 6)
   a) Reading is something many Americans like to do in their free time.
   b) Participating actively in meetings and in classrooms is seen as positive in the U.S.
   c) Taking turns in speaking is important to do in conversations.

5. Which sentence shows that many Americans expect immediate feedback? (Paragraph 8)

   a) "Get it off your chest."

   b) "He always hogs the conversation."

   c) "If you didn't understand, why didn't you tell me? Why did you wait?"

6. When a person is talking too much, some Americans may try to: (Paragraph 12)

   a) Interrupt in order to take a turn in speaking.

   b) Say, "You're hogging the conversation!"

   c) Become silent.

7. Why did the man tell the Filipina woman that "uh-huh" is not rude? (Paragraph 16)

   a) He wanted her to feel uncomfortable.

   b) He was embarrassed because he said, "Uh-huh."

   c) He wanted her to understand that, in the U.S., "uh-huh" is not usually considered rude.

VOCABULARY EXERCISES

Matching

Draw a line from each noun in column A to the matching definition in column B. The first one is done for you.

	A	B	
1.	intonation	a.	something you think about, or that worries you.
2.	feedback	b.	the feeling you have when you can't do what you want.
3.	contrast	c.	argument; disagreement
4.	conflict	d.	answer; response
5.	concern	e.	comparison to show differences.
6.	frustration	f.	the way the voice goes up or down.

Word Forms

Choose the correct word in parentheses ( ) and fill in the blanks in the following sentences. The first one is done for you.

1. (interaction/interact)

   a) It is important to understand how people _interact_ in different cultures.

   b) A telephone conversation is one kind of _____.

2. (response/respond)

   a) When you make a telephone call, it is good to know how the other person will probably _____ to you.

   b) If you get a _____ that you didn't expect, you can say "Ummm" while you try to think of what to say next.

3. (participate/participation)

    a) Americans expect students to _____ in discussions.

    b) To Americans, _____ usually means speaking.

4. (express/expressions)

    a) It is important to _____ your ideas and your opinions so that people will know what you think.

    b) In this book you are learning many different _____ to use in English.

5. (criticism/criticize)

    a) People often _____ someone who talks non-stop.

    b) One woman's _____ of Americans was that they use rude expressions like "uh-huh."

6. (accept/accepting/acceptable)

    a) Did he _____ your invitation to dinner?

    b) In some countries, it is not usually _____ to interrupt or disagree with an older person.

    c) _____ expensive gifts from students is sometimes not comfortable for American teachers.

7. (judge/judgment)

    a) When you make a _____, don't forget that what is not acceptable in your culture may be acceptable in another culture.

    b) Americans sometimes _____ silence, or a lack of feedback, negatively.

8. (hesitate/hesitating)

    a) People sometimes _____ to interrupt a meeting or group discussion.

    b) When you hold your turn, you are pausing or _____ while you decide what you want to say.

Choose the Best Explanation

Each sentence below contains a word or phrase from the reading. Read each sentence and the three possible explanations. Choose the one explanation that best matches the meaning of the sentence. Circle the letter next to that explanation. The first one is done for you.

1. When an American does not receive feedback, he may talk more to fill the uncomfortable silence. This, *in turn,* may make the other person more uncomfortable.

    a) The American may turn and walk away, and this will make the other person uncomfortable.

    b) As a result, the other person may feel more uncomfortable.

    c) From the opposite point of view, the other person may feel more uncomfortable.

2. People give nonverbal *as well as* verbal feedback.

    a) People give nonverbal feedback, and also verbal feedback.

    b) Their nonverbal feedback is better than their verbal feedback.

    c) Their nonverbal feedback is equal to their verbal feedback.

3. How fast someone can learn to speak English partly *depends on* what

their native language is.

a) It makes no difference what their native language is.

b) There is a relationship between what their native language is and how fast they can learn English.

c) They can learn English quickly if they can speak their own native language well.

4. Many Americans believe that if they talk out their problems, they can *get rid of* them.

a) They can really understand their problems.

b) They will become more angry.

c) They can make their problems go away.

5. People who never let other people *take turns* speaking are considered rude.

a) They interrupt other people, and never let them finish.

b) They talk and talk, and no one else has a chance to speak.

c) They never let anyone else use the telephone.

6. Some women like to shake hands. *On the other hand,* some people feel that only men should shake hands.

a) If a woman is holding something in one hand, she can offer to shake hands with the other hand.

b) When women shake hands, they like to take your hand, and then cover it with their other hand.

c) The other point of view is that women should not shake hands.

7. Sometimes it is helpful to say, "Let me see . . ." *in order to* give yourself time to think before you answer.

a) Some people say, "Let me see" so that they can think about what to say.

b) When you are ordering food in a restaurant, you need to give yourself time to think.

c) You can say "Let me see" while you decide what question to answer first.

8. It is often better to repeat just the word that you don't understand, *rather than* saying "I don't understand."

a) You should repeat the word that you don't understand, and then say, "I don't understand."

b) You should say, "I don't understand," and then repeat the word that you didn't understand.

c) You should repeat only the word that you don't understand, and not say, "I don't understand."

9. Before you say, "I don't like that food," you should *at least* try to eat some of it.

a) You should try to eat it last, when you are not hungry.

b) You should not eat foods you don't like.

c) You should try to eat a small piece of the food.

10. It is hard to *get used to* driving on the right side of the road.

a) It is difficult to become comfortable with driving on the right side of the road.

b) It is difficult to get a chance to drive on the right side of the road.

c) It is difficult to drive on American freeways.

GOING BEYOND THE READING

Each group of questions is based on a quote from the reading text. Read the questions and then discuss them in small groups or with the entire class. After the questions have been discussed, choose a topic related to one of the questions and write a composition.*

1. *"Many Americans give as well as expect a lot of feedback when they are talking."* (Paragraph 3)

   a) Do you feel that people who speak your language also expect a lot of verbal feedback?

   b) In your native language, do listeners use sounds such as "uh-huh" and "uhm-hmm" when listening? If so, what are these sounds?

2. *"Many Americans believe that talking together is the best way to get rid of misunderstanding or conflict."* (Paragraph 7)

   a) Do you feel that "talking things out" is the best way to solve problems or take care of misunderstandings? Can you think of any examples of problems or conflicts that are better solved by *not* talking?

   b) In your culture, is there a general belief or attitude about how to get rid of misunderstanding or conflict? For example, is silence thought of as a good way to deal with problems? Explain your answer.

   c) Can you say whether your culture is more of a verbal culture or more of a nonverbal culture? That is, do people mainly depend on words to express themselves or do they expect others to understand them even when they don't express themselves verbally? Explain your answer.

3. *". . . how can you know, from a different cultural point of view, whether you are talking too much, talking too little, or giving enough feedback?"* (Paragraph 13)

   a) When talking with people from other cultures, have you ever had the feeling that you were talking too little or talking too much? Describe the situation.

4. *"It is not always easy, however, to accept a different way of interacting."* (Paragraph 18)

   a) Do you have difficulty accepting different ways of interacting in English with Americans? That is, are there things that Americans do when they communicate in English that are hard for you to accept? Explain.

   b) Do you feel that Americans would have difficulty communicating in your language with people of your cultural background? What, if anything, would they find difficult about the interaction?

   c) How would you prepare them for interaction in your language and culture?

Note to the teacher: Some students may prefer to write out answers to questions that they feel are personal ones. In this case, you may want to use this exercise as a writing exercise.

Making Contact in Another Culture

UNIT III FOUNDATIONS

- Getting to know people from a different culture is not always as easy as getting to know people from one's own culture.
- It takes time and effort to develop cross-cultural relationships.
- In some countries, foreigners are treated like guests. This is not always true everywhere. If you want to make contact with people in the U.S., you may have to "make the first move."

UNIT III CONTENTS

Chapter 9. "Keeping the Conversation Moving" covers:

- greetings and openings
- discussing a topic
- closings and farewells

Chapter 10. "Choosing Conversation Topics" discusses cultural differences in the areas of:

- avoiding certain topics
- discussing common topics

Chapter 11. "Making the First Move" presents information about:

- meeting and getting to know others
- extending invitations
- visiting

Chapter 12. "Reading Text and Activities" contains:

- reading text, "Making Contact in Another Culture"
- comprehension, vocabulary, and discussion questions.

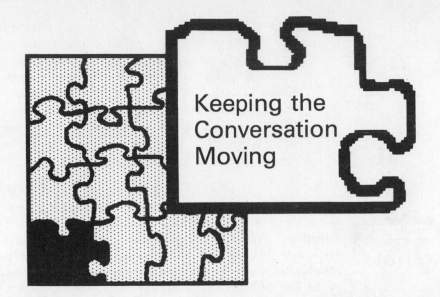

chapter 9

Keeping the
Conversation
Moving

Introduction   Contact with people usually begins with a conversation. If two people enjoy their first conversation or first few conversations, there is a good chance that they will want to have more contact. What makes a conversation comfortable and enjoyable? The answer isn't always the same for people from different cultures. There are culturally different styles of conversations which influence the way people talk to each other. In American English, for example, people often ask a lot of questions *to keep a conversation moving*. To people from different cultures, so many questions may seem rude. This chapter presents information on American style conversations and gives you the opportunity to practice keeping the conversation moving.

to keep a conversation moving—to maintain a conversation; to prevent a conversation from stopping; to prevent silences in a conversation

119

CULTURE LEARNING QUESTIONS

1. In your native language, do you ever have difficulty trying to keep a conversation moving? Explain your answer.

2. Are you comfortable with silences in conversations? Talk about what you do when there are silences in conversations, both in your language and in English.

3. What are some difficulties in conversations that native speakers of English have with native speakers of your language?

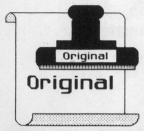

(Revised interaction appears on page 122.)

CROSS-CULTURAL INTERACTION 9A:
Ineffective Communication

Situation: Wan is a college student who is taking several classes. He doesn't know any of the students in his classes so he decides to join a *club* at his college. He chooses the ping-pong club since he really enjoys the game. At the beginning of the first club meeting, a student named George begins talking to him.

George: "Hi. *How ya doin'?*"

Wan: "Uh, fine."

George: "*Ya been here before?*"

Wan: "No."

George: "*Ya play a lot of ping-pong?*"

Wan: "Yes."

George: "Well, this is the place to come."

Wan: (No response. He is silent.)

George: "Uh, what classes are you taking?"

Wan: "Electronics, Computer 1A . . ." (George interrupts.)

George: "I'm taking Computer 1A, too. Are you in the class that meets on Mondays and Wednesdays at 10 a.m.?"

Wan: "Yes."

George: "Hmm. I haven't seen you before. Do you like the class?"

Wan: "Yes, I do." (Long silence.)

George: "Um, uh, do you belong to any other clubs?"

Wan: "No."

George: "I'm in a couple of others." (Long pause.)

Wan: (He says nothing.)

George: (Looking at the ping-pong tables.) "I see they're starting to play. *You gonna* play a game?"

Wan: "Yes."

George: "Okay. *Talk to you later.*" (George walks away.)

club—a group of people who meet to share an interest or activity (example: music club, dance club, chess club)
How ya doin'?—How are you doing? (very informal American English, usually not written)
Ya been here before?—Have you been here before? (informal)
Ya play a lot of ping-pong?—Do you play a lot of ping-pong? (informal)
You gonna . . . ?—Are you going to . . . ?
Talk to you later.—I'll talk to you later.

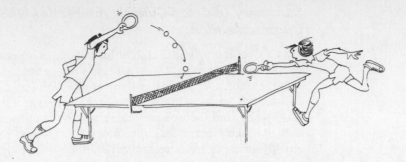

QUESTIONS AND DISCUSSION

Comprehension

Write T (true) or F (false) in the space provided.

1. _____ It is not Wan's first time at the ping-pong club.
2. _____ Wan does not play a lot of ping-pong.
3. _____ George and Wan are in the same job skills class.
4. _____ George belongs to two other clubs besides the ping-pong club.
5. _____ George asks Wan to play a game of ping-pong with him.
6. _____ George and Wan decide to talk after the ping-pong game.

Analysis: Can You Explain?

1. Why are George and Wan having difficulties talking to each other?
2. Do you think that Wan is interested in talking to George? Explain your answer.
3. There is a lot of silence in the conversation. How do you think each person feels when there is silence?
4. What could George do differently so that Wan would talk more?
5. What could Wan do differently?
6. When does George want to end the conversation? (At which sentence?)
7. George says, "Talk to you later." Do you think George is really planning to talk to Wan later? What does this phrase mean?

TALK ABOUT YOUR OWN LANGUAGE AND CULTURE

Español 中
日本語
ف ی 文

1. Wan joins a ping-pong club because he likes playing ping-pong and because he wants to meet people at his school. In your culture, is it common for people to join clubs in order to meet people? What are some ways that people meet and get to know each other?
2. Wan and George are strangers, but George tries to be friendly with Wan. In your culture, is it common for strangers to be friendly with each other? Is it common for strangers to have conversations with each other, for example, in parks, in stores, or on buses? Explain your answer.
3. Do you think it is easier or more difficult to meet people in a country other than your native country? Explain your answer.

Summary of Cross-Cultural Interaction 9A: Ineffective Communication

Wan's decision to join a club at his college is a good one because he has not met people in his classes. (This sometimes happens in classes in the U.S., particularly in large ones.) At the first club meeting, Wan has a chance to get to know George a little, but he doesn't give George the *impression* that he wants to talk. Wan may just be shy, but George may think that he is unfriendly. Wan's short answers and silence make George feel uncomfortable. George probably asks a lot of questions quickly because he is uncomfortable. Wan feels more and more uncomfortable with all of George's questions. George keeps changing *subjects* and doesn't give Wan enough time to answer questions. Wan needs to answer questions more fully, that is, to give more information in his answers. He also needs to ask questions of George so that the conversation is more interactive, that is, more of a *two-way conversation*.

CROSS-CULTURAL INTERACTION 9B

In Cross-Cultural Interaction 9A, the conversation between George and Wan didn't go anywhere; that is, it just stopped. The following is another conversation between Wan and George, but it is a more successful one. Read the dialogue and then the explanations in the "What Is Happening" column.

Dialogue	*What Is Happening*
George: "Hi, how ya doin'?"	George opens the conversation.
Wan: "Fine. How about you?"	Wan **responds** and **asks** George a question, making the conversation two-way.
George: "Great. I'm really ready for a game of ping-pong." (pause) "Ya been here before?"	George **answers** Wan's questions and gives more information. He **begins a new topic** of conversation by asking a question.
Wan: "No, this is my first time. How about you?"	Wan **answers** and **gives more information.** He repeats George's question (using, "How about you?") which shows that he is interested in getting to know George. George now has the feeling that Wan is friendly.
George: "Oh, no. I've been coming here for about a year."	George **answers** by giving more than a "No" answer.
Wan: You probably know a lot of people in the club."	Wan **comments** on George's answer and **opens up a new topic** of conversation. His comment can also be an indirect way of asking George to introduce some people to him.

impression—feeling or idea
subjects—topics of conversation, that is, what they are talking about
two-way conversation—a conversation in which both speakers are talking, not just one

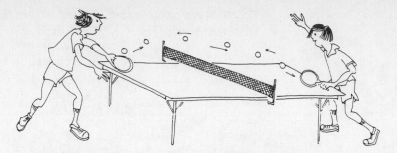

Dialogue	What Is Happening
George: "I do. I know everybody. Do you want me to introduce you to some people after the games?"	George understands Wan's indirect way of asking him to introduce people to Wan.
Wan: "Sure. That'd be great."	Wan **answers** in a way that **shows that he is very interested** in meeting others. He uses informal language: "Sure." "Great."
George: "O.K. No problem. You play a lot of ping-pong?"	George **responds** to Wan in an informal and friendly way. He asks another question to bring up a new topic of conversation.
Wan: "Yes. It's my favorite game. How about you?"	Wan **answers the question** with more than "Yes." He asks, "How about you?" making the conversation **interactive** or two-way.
George: "I play all the time. How about a game right now?"	George **answers the question** and extends an invitation. The invitation shows that George thinks Wan is friendly.
Wan: "Sure. Let's play."	Wan says, "Sure" which is a friendly way of saying, "Yes."

FOCUS ON U.S. CULTURE
Cultural Notes, Exercises, and Skill Practice

HOW MUCH DO YOU ALREADY KNOW ABOUT U.S. CULTURE?

Write T (true) or F (false) in the space provided.

1. _____ It is not polite to use informal, "reduced" speech (example: "He's *gonna* go now") in daily conversations.
2. _____ When people ask, "How are you?" they usually don't expect a detailed or truthful answer.

3. _____ It is impolite to ask questions of someone you have just met for the first time.

4. _____ When a person asks a question such as, "Do you like your job?" it is enough to answer "Yes" or "No."

5. _____ When a person tells another some bad or sad news, it is better to say something (such as, "I'm sorry to hear that") rather than to be silent.

Conversations in English

A good conversation in English is like a ping-pong game. One person has the ball and then hits it to the other side of the table. The other player hits the ball back and the game continues. If one person doesn't hit the ball back, then the conversation stops. Each part of the conversation is like this: the greeting and opening, the discussion of a topic and the closing and farewell. One person says something and the other person responds right away. For example:

Greetings and Openings

Sara: "Hi. *How've* you been?"

Brent: "Pretty good. How about you?"

Sara: "Oh just fine."

Discussion of a Topic

Sara: "Work's been slow. *Not much to do here.* What about you? *Anything interesting going on?*"

Brent: "Yeah. My boss gave me something interesting to do. I have to interview the *hourly employees* here."

Sara: "That sounds interesting. What are you going to ask them in the interviews?"

Brent: "I'm supposed to ask them about their jobs. The boss wants to know if they're happy on the job. Should be interesting."

Closing and Farewell

Sara: (continuing from above) "*Well . . . listen,* I'd better be getting back to work."

Brent: "Yeah. *I'll let you go.* See you later."

Sara: "O.K. Nice talking to you."

Brent: "You too. Bye."

Sara: "Bye."

How've—How have . . . ?
Not much to do here.—There is not much to do here. (Informal speech often leaves out words.)
Anything interesting going on?—Is anything interesting happening?
hourly employees—employees who get paid by the hour
Well . . . listen—used as a way to end the conversation
Yeah—yes
I'll let you go—a way of ending conversations

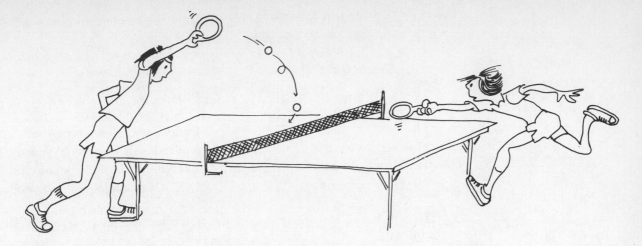

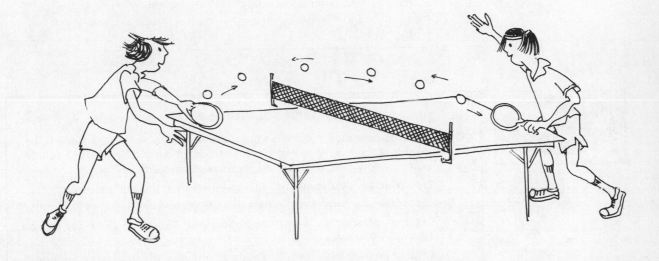

CROSS-CULTURAL NOTE

Not all conversations in every language are like ping-pong games, with the speakers going back and forth and taking turns to speak. In some languages, it is usual for one person to speak for a long time or to speak more than the other person. For example, a boss, teacher, or older person might talk and not expect the other person to say anything.

SECTION 1. GREETINGS AND OPENINGS

There are many ways to greet someone and to open (begin) a conversation. The following common openings and responses are informal, spoken English.

Phrases for Greeting and Responding to Greetings _____

Say these with the teacher or another student:

Greetings and Openings	*Responses*
"Hi (or Hello). How are you?"*	"Fine. And you?"
"Hi. How ya doin'?"	"O.K. How about you?"
"Hi. How's it goin'?"	"Pretty good. How about you?"
"How've you been?"	"Not too bad. How about yourself?"
"Hi. How goes it?" (very informal)	"Everything's O.K. How you doin'?"
"Hi. How are things?"	"O.K. Can't complain." (very informal)
"Hi. What's happening?" (very informal)	"Oh, not much. How about with you?"
"Hi. What's new?"	"Not a whole lot." (very informal) "How about with you?"
"Hi. *What've* you been up to lately? (Often reduced to "Wha-chu been up to lately?")	"Not too much. *How 'bout you?*"

CROSS-CULTURAL NOTE

Greetings and openings in most languages really mean almost the same thing, but sometimes their word-for-word translations are very different. The following all mean "How are you?" but are expressed differently.

"Hi. What are you doing?" (Tagalog—spoken in the Philippines)

"Hi. Have you eaten yet?" (Chinese/Vietnamese)

"Peace" (this is the word for "Hello" and "Goodbye.") *"What can be heard*?" (Hebrew)

"Peace be with you." (or just *Peace* as above). *"How is your condition*?" (Arabic)

CROSS-CULTURAL NOTE

"This was the first day I worked in my factory. I could not speak English. I only said 'Hello' and then I smiled to show that I wanted to make friends. During the break, I sat with my co-workers and we talked a little. When I saw some people I liked I said 'Hello.' They told me not to just say 'Hello' because they have names. They said I should use their names. The next day I said, 'Good morning, Mary. How are you?' She answered, "Very well. Thank you.' It was just a simple conversation, but it was contact. Later we became very friendly with each other."

—Vietnamese man living in the U.S.

*Most of the time when people ask, "How are you?" they are not asking about your health and they do not expect a detailed answer. They are simply greeting you and opening a conversation.

What've—What have
How 'bout you?—How about you?

Cross-Cultural Exercise: Greetings and Openings

Give a few examples of ways you begin conversations in your native language. Say them first in your language and then translate them to English. How do they sound in English? Can you translate them word for word?

Skill Practice: Responding to Greetings and Openings

Respond to the words and questions on the left using one of the responses you learned earlier. Respond with an answer and a question.

For example:

"Hi. How's it going?"	"Not bad." (answer)
	"How are things with you?" (question)

1. "Hi. How's it going?"   _____
    _____

2. "Hi. [name]. I haven't seen   _____
    you in awhile. How've you
    been doing?"   _____

3. "Hi. [name]. Good to see   _____
    you. How are you doing?"   _____

4. "Hi [name]. What've you   _____
    been up to lately?"   _____

5. "Hi. How are things?"   _____
    _____

6. "Hi. How are things going?"   _____
    _____

SECTION 2. DISCUSSING A TOPIC

After the greeting and opening, one or both of the speakers should ask questions in order to find something to talk about. For the conversation to keep going, speakers have to give information and respond to information. This section includes:

A. Finding a Topic by Asking Questions
B. Asking Open-Ended Questions
C. Giving Information
D. Responding to Information

A. Finding a Topic by Asking Questions

Read the following dialogue and note how many questions the speakers ask of each other before they find a topic to discuss.

Situation: Michael and Diane are both students. It is the beginning of December, just before the *winter break*. Michael and Diane run into each other at the cafeteria.

winter break—winter vacation

Michael:	"Hi. Diane. How are your classes going?"
Diane:	"Not too bad, but I have a lot of work. I'm getting pretty tired of writing papers."
Michael:	"It sounds like you're ready for the winter break."
Diane:	"I sure am."
Michael:	"What are you planning to do?"
Diane:	"I'm not sure yet. I'm still *making up my mind*. How about you?"
Michael:	"I'm going to *Lake Tahoe* with friends."
Diane:	"Are you planning to ski?"
Michael:	"That's why I'm going. Do you ski?"
Diane:	"Yeah, I do, and I've been to Lake Tahoe *quite a few* times. Will this be your first time there?"
Michael:	"No, I've been there a few times. I like it, but it's always so crowded."
Diane:	"I know what you mean." (The two continue to talk about skiing.)

Questions:

* How many questions were asked until the speakers found a topic to discuss?
* How many questions were asked throughout the dialogue?

B. Asking "Open-Ended" Questions

Open-ended questions can keep a conversation moving better than close-ended or yes/no questions. You can get much more information by asking open-ended questions. Read the following examples and then ask the questions of your teacher or another student. Compare the answers to each type of question.

Examples:

"Yes/No" Questions	"Open-Ended" Questions"
"Do you like sports?"	"What sports do you like?"
"Do you have a job after school?"	"What do you do after school?
"Do you like your job?"	"How's your job going?"
"Is everything O.K. with your boss?"	"How are things with you and your boss?"
"Did you like your class?"	"What did you think of your class?"

Note: Open-ended questions use such words as *what, when, where, why* and *how*.

making up my mind—deciding
Lake Tahoe—a mountainous area in Northern California
quite a few—many

Skill Practice: Asking Open-Ended Questions

Change the following yes/no questions to open-ended ones.

	Yes/No Questions	*Open-Ended Questions*
1.	"Did you like the movie last night?"	_____ _____
2.	"Do you like this country?"	_____ _____
3.	"Do you like American food?"	_____ _____
4.	"Do you like your job?"	_____ _____
5.	"Have you been in this country for a long time?"	_____ _____
6.	"Do your children like living here?"	_____ _____
7.	"Have you travelled to other countries?"	_____ _____

Some open-ended questions which can encourage conversation are: *"How about you?"* or *"What about you?"* or *"What do you think?"* or *"What do you think of. . . ."* With these questions, the speaker sends the "ball" back to the other person's side and the conversation continues.
   For example:

(Two employees are talking:)

Deena: *"What do you think of* our new office?"

Piper: "I like it, but I still think we need more room for our classes. *How about you?"*

Skill Practice: Asking Open-Ended Questions

Read the following sentences to another student and then ask his or her opinion by using one of these open-ended questions:

"What do you think?"
"How about you?"
"What about you?"

Take turns asking and answering questions.

Example:

Student 1: "At work, *management* is making a new rule saying that people can't smoke in the buildings. I don't really like this rule. <u>What do you think?</u>"

Student 2: (Student gives an answer.), "<u>I think it's a good rule. If you're not a smoker, it's not *pleasant* breathing in other people's smoke.</u>"

1. *Student 1:* "I think people in restaurants should stop smoking. It's not fair to people who want to enjoy their food. _____?"
    Student 2: _____

2. *Student 1:* "It doesn't seem fair to me. When we do business with Americans, we have to do it in English even when they're in our country. They should learn our language. _____."
    Student 2: _____

3. *Student 1:* "I think when a person goes to another country, he or she should do exactly what the people of that country do. You know, 'When in Rome, do as the Romans do.' _____?"
    Student 2: _____

4. *Student 1:* "English is a very easy language. That's my opinion. _____?"
    Student 2: _____

5. Your choice of topics.

C. Giving Information

When speakers in a conversation answer only "Yes" or "No," or give short answers to questions, the conversation will probably not "go anywhere"; that is, the conversation will stop. The person who gives only "Yes/No" or very short answers gives the impression that he is not friendly or that he does not want to talk. Compare the following two answers:

1. *Question:*   "How do you like American food."
    Answer: "I like it."
2. *Question:*   "How do you like American food?"
    Answer: "It's O.K. I'm used to spicier food, so some American food tastes *bland* to me. Is there an American food that's spicy?"

Note: The person answering the second question wants to share information and keep the conversation going. The question at the end of the second answer gives the "ball" back to the first person so that the conversation will continue.

---

management—the people who run a company or business and who make the rules
pleasant—nice
bland—not spicy, plain

Skill Practice: Asking Questions and Giving Information

In the following dialogue, only one of the speakers is helping to keep the conversation going. Rewrite the conversation so that both speakers ask questions. Change the short answers to longer ones to show that both speakers are interested in the conversation. *Note:* You will have to change some of the original sentences to go with your new sentences.

Situation: Two students are standing near the door to a classroom. It is almost time for class to start.

Lily:	"Hi. Are you in this class?"
Mara:	"Yes."
Lily:	"My name is Lily. You are . . .?"
Mara:	"Mara."
Lily:	"Where are you from?"
Mara:	"India."
Lily:	"Did you come to this country to study?"
Mara:	"Yes."
Lily:	"What are you studying?"
Mara:	"Engineering."
Lily:	"How long do you plan to stay here?"
Mara:	"I'm not sure yet."
Lily:	"When did you come here?"
Mara:	"Three months ago."

Now rewrite the dialogue according to the instructions above:

Lily:	_____
Mara:	_____
Lily:	_____
Mara:	_____
Lily:	_____
Mara:	_____
Lily:	_____
Mara:	_____
Lily:	_____
Mara:	_____
Lily:	_____
Mara:	_____
Lily:	_____
Mara:	_____

Skill Practice: Giving Information

Instructions: Make a list of "typical" questions that people ask you in the United States (or that Americans ask you when you are in your own country). Ask and answer these questions with another student. Make the answers interesting. Try to encourage a two-way conversation. For example:

Question: "Where are you from?"

Answer: "I'm from Brazil, the only non-Spanish-speaking country in South America. Have you ever been there or do you know anyone from there?"

Other "typical" questions include:

"How long have you been here?"
"Do you like it here?"
"How do you like the food?"

D. Responding to Information

If a listener does not respond verbally to what a speaker says, the speaker may think that the listener is not interested or concerned. When this happens, a conversation can stop or become uncomfortable. Yet, when people speak another language, they don't always know how to respond to information. The list below and the skill practice after the next cross-cultural note will help you learn phrases and short answers that you can use to respond to information.

Phrases and Expressions for Responding to Information _____

Say these with the teacher or another student.

If someone says:	*You could respond:*
"I'm not feeling too well today."	"Oh, that's too bad. What's the matter?"
"I just had an operation."	"You did? How are you feeling now?"
"I'm just getting over the flu."	"Good. I hope you're feeling a lot better now."
"I'm sorry that I won't be able to come to the party tonight."	"That's too bad. I hope you'll be able to come to the next one."
"I'm sorry that I didn't phone you earlier. I've been busy."	"No problem. Don't worry about it."
"I didn't do very well on the test."	"That's too bad. What do you think the problem was?"
"Do you have a minute to talk? I'm having some problems that I'd like to talk to you about."	"Sure. Go ahead."
"Did I tell you what happened to me the other day?"	"No, you didn't. What happened?"
"I've got some good news."	"You do? What is it?"
"My wife had a baby!"	"Congratulations! A boy or a girl?"
"We're getting married!"	"Congratulations! When's the big event?"
"I finally got the job I wanted!"	"Congratulations! When do you start?"
"Things have been so busy around here. I'll never get things done."	"I know what you mean. It's the same with me."

I'm just getting over the flu—I had the flu, but I'm almost all better.

CROSS-CULTURAL NOTE

An American woman lived in France for about a year. Although she had studied the language for many years and could speak it well, she had one major problem. She said that she didn't know how to respond to what people said. For example, she said, "When someone told me about some good news or something nice, I'd always say (in French), 'That's nice' or 'That's good.' I wouldn't know how to respond in different ways. Or when people told me about some bad news, I'd always say, 'That's too bad.' But I had the feeling that they wanted me to say more than 'That's good' or 'That's too bad,' and I wanted to say more than that, but I didn't know what to say."

Skill Practice: Responding to Information

Respond to the sentences on the left in a way that shows that you are interested in what the speaker is saying. First write your responses and then practice saying them with a teacher or student.

For example:

"That was a difficult test."   "I know what you mean. I had a hard time, too."

If someone says: *You could respond:*

"I've just gotten some bad news."   _____

"I finally got the job I was waiting for."   _____

"I heard some great news today."   _____

"Could I talk to you a minute? I have a problem that I think you could help me with."   _____

"My children are both sick with the stomach flu."   _____

"I really don't understand the lesson we're studying."   _____

"My sister just had a baby."   _____

"I feel really angry at the boss today."   _____

"Did I tell you the good news?"   _____

SECTION 3. CLOSINGS AND FAREWELLS

CROSS-CULTURAL NOTE

"See you later" is a way of saying "goodbye" in American English and it often does *not* mean "I'll see you later." An American woman said "See you later" to a new immigrant in the U.S., who understood it *literally*. The American said "See you later" to her friend as they were leaving an office building. The American went one way, but the immigrant friend stayed in front of the building for twenty minutes! Later she told her friend about this and was very embarrassed about the misunderstanding. This is how she remembers her first week in the U.S.

literally—word for word

Phrases and Expressions for Ending a Conversation _____

Say these with the teacher or another student

Closings	*Responses*
"O.K. Nice to talk to you."	"You too. See you later."
"Well, I *gotta* be going."	"Talk to you later. Bye bye."
"Well, gotta get back to work."	"Same here. See you."
"Hope to see you again soon."	"Me too. Take care."
"Good seeing you."	"You too. Hope to see you soon."
"I've got to *run*."	"I do too. I'll see you later."

Skill Practice: Responding to Closings

In pairs or with the teacher, respond to the following closings. Try to vary your responses.

For example:

"Nice talking to you."   "You too. See you later. Bye." _____

1. "Good to talk to you."   _____
2. "Well, I've got to run."   _____
3. "I've enjoyed talking to you." _____
4. "O.K. I'd better be going now." _____
5. "Hope to see you soon."   _____

U.S. CULTURE NOTE

Sometimes Americans have trouble ending conversations with each other. This may be because there is no one way of ending a conversation. In some other cultures, there are specific ways to end the conversation, such as bowing or shaking hands. After the bow or the handshake, the conversation stops. In the U.S., people sometimes take several minutes to say "Goodbye" and, as they do, you can see them backing away from each other. By the time they are about fifteen or twenty feet apart, they've often said their last "Goodbye."

E. Ending Telephone Conversations

On the telephone, people sometimes have difficulty ending or closing a conversation. If the person to whom you are talking says the following, it means that he or she is ready to hang up!

"Thanks for calling."
"It's been good (or nice) talking to you."
"I'm really glad you called. Let's keep in touch."
"I've enjoyed talking to you."
"Sorry I have to cut this short, but I have to go now."

gotta—(reduced form of "got to" or "have got to") have to; must
run (in this case)—go

"I'd better let you go now."
"I know you're busy, so I'll let you go."

Note: The last two sentences are often said when the *speaker* wants to end the conversation!

CHAPTER SUMMARY

In this chapter you looked at cultural differences in the area of:

- keeping conversations moving

You practiced language and communication skills in the areas of:

- greeting people and opening conversations
- discussing topics
     finding a topic by asking questions
     asking "open-ended" questions
     giving information
     responding to information
- closing a conversation

Note: Answers to exercises in this chapter can be found in the separate Answer Key.

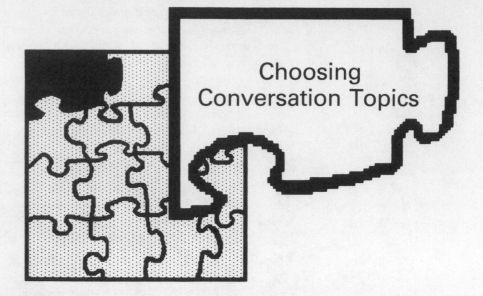

chapter 10

Choosing
Conversation Topics

Introduction "I have found, in my experience with Americans, that they are friendly and that they seem to talk easily with each other. When I talk to them, I often wonder what to talk about. I say, "Hello" and "How are you?" After that, I don't know what to say."

—Immigrant, ten years in the U.S.

Two people from the *same* culture can have this feeling. However, if two people have not grown up in the same culture, they have less shared experience than two people who have grown up together. Shared culture is shared experience. With shared experience, conversation is easier. In situations of cross-cultural communication, people sometimes have to try harder to make conversation. Chapter 10 gives examples and explanations of topics that Americans commonly discuss. It also gives information about topics or questions which are considered *personal* or not appropriate to *bring up*.

CULTURE LEARNING QUESTIONS

1. When people meet each other for the first time, what kinds of things do they talk about? (Talk about your own language and culture.)
2. What topics or questions do people usually avoid when they first meet each other?
3. Are there topics of conversation that Americans frequently talk about with people from your culture? If so, give examples.

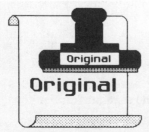

CROSS-CULTURAL INTERACTION 10A:
Cultural Differences

Situation: It is the weekend and Pali is doing some work in his front yard. His next-door neighbor, Joe, is also doing some yard work. Joe stops working for a few minutes to talk to Pali.

(Revised interaction appears on page 138.)

personal—private (a question or topic you feel shouldn't be asked)
bring up—talk about; ask about

Joe: "Hi, Pali. How's it going?"

Pali: "O.K. How are things with you?"

Joe: "Not too bad. In fact, pretty good! Did I tell you that I got a new job?"

Pali: "No, you didn't. That's good news!"

Joe: "Well, you knew that I was *laid off* last month. I heard about a job opening in another company. I applied and had an interview. Three days later, someone called to tell me that I got the job."

Pali: "That's great. How much money do you make now?"

Joe: (Looking surprised) "Uh, uhm . . . well, let's just say that I can pay my bills and put food on the table."

Pali: (Not really understanding the answer.) "Oh." (Waiting for Joe to answer the question.)

Joe: "Well, listen. I have to get back to work. There's a lot to do."

Pali: "Uh, O.K." (Not knowing why the conversation stops.)

Joe: "See you."

Pali: "Bye."

QUESTIONS AND DISCUSSION

Comprehension

Write T (true) or F (false) in the space provided:

1. _____ Joe had to get a new job because he was *fired* from his other job.

2. _____ It took a long time (after the interview) for Joe to know if he got the job.

3. _____ Joe doesn't understand Pali's question, so he doesn't answer it.

4. _____ Pali wants Joe to tell him exactly how much money he makes.

5. _____ When Joe says, "I can pay my bills and put food on the table," he means that he makes a lot of money (that is, he is rich).

6. _____ The conversation stops because Joe and Pali have a lot of work to do.

Analysis: Can You Explain?

1. Why does Joe look surprised when Pali asks, "How much money do you make now?"

2. Pali doesn't understand Joe's answer (". . . I can pay my bills and put food on the table"), but he only says, "Oh" and waits for Joe to answer the question. If you were Pali, what would you say?

3. Who wants to end the conversation? What is said to show that this person wants to stop talking?

laid off—lost one's job because of not enough work
fired—lost one's job because of something inappropriate that the employee did

TALK ABOUT YOUR OWN LANGUAGE AND CULTURE

1. In your culture, do people commonly talk about their salaries and other things that are related to money (for example, the price of things)? Is it acceptable to ask someone, "How much money do you make?"
2. If someone asked you a question that you felt was too personal, what would you say?

Summary of Cross-Cultural Interaction 9A: Cultural Differences

Pali's question, "How much money do you make?", is considered to be a very personal question in the United States. The question makes Joe uncomfortable, but Joe doesn't stop to think that maybe, in Pali's culture, it is acceptable to ask this question. Instead, he wants to end the conversation as soon as possible. He shows that he wants to end it when he says, "Well, listen. I have to get back to work." Pali doesn't understand why the conversation stops so suddenly. For him, the question is a normal or usual question. He would be surprised to know that, in the U.S., even close friends do not often tell each other how much money they make.

CROSS-CULTURAL INTERACTION 10B

Read the following cross-cultural interaction, which shows more successful communication between Pali and Joe.

Joe: "Hi, Pali. How's it going?"

Pali: "O.K. How are things with you?"

Joe: "Not too bad. In fact, pretty good! Did I tell you that I got a new job?"

Pali: "No, you didn't. That's good news!"

Joe: "Well, you knew that I was laid off last month. I heard about a job opening in another company. I applied and had an interview. Three days later, someone called to tell me that I got the job."

Pali: "That's great. How do you like the job?"

Joe: "I like it." The salary's a bit higher than on my last job and the *benefits* are very good."

Pali: "I'm glad to hear that."

Joe: "Yeah. The other job was really starting to *get me down*. There was never enough work. Also I can get a good raise in six months if I do well."

Pali: "Sounds good. *How long does it take you to get to your new job?*"

(Joe and Pali continue talking.)

Summary of Cross-Cultural Interaction 10B

In this interaction, Pali asks about the job, but doesn't ask about the pay. Joe answers the question and offers information about the pay, but he isn't specific.

benefits—in addition to salaries, employers give benefits to full-time employees which include: vacation, sick leave, insurance, etc.

get me down—make me feel sad or depressed

How long does it take you to get to your new job?—How long does it take to drive to your new place of work?

He says, "The salary's a bit higher than on my last job and the benefits are very good.", Joe's answer is indirect and typical of American responses about money. Joe does not tell the exact amount of money he makes. Notice how Joe does not continue talking about the salary, but changes the subject: "The other job was really starting to get me down." This time, the interaction is comfortable for both Joe and Pali because Pali is aware of cultural differences in asking personal questions.

FOCUS ON U.S. CULTURE
Cultural Notes, Exercises, and Skill Practice

HOW MUCH DO YOU ALREADY KNOW ABOUT U.S. CULTURE?

Write T (true) or F (false) in the space provided.

1. _____ One of the most common questions that people ask each other when they first meet is, "What do you do?" which means, "What job do you have?"

2. _____ It is usually acceptable to ask people, "How old are you?"

3. _____ Many people think that religion is a personal subject and so they usually don't talk about it when they first meet each other.

4. _____ It is not polite for people to talk about themselves when they first meet other people.

5. _____ The question, "How much do you weigh?" is an acceptable one to ask most Americans.

6. _____ It is acceptable to ask a married couple, "When are you going to have children?"

7. _____ It is acceptable to ask a single woman, "When are you going to get married?"

SECTION 1. AVOIDING CERTAIN TOPICS

The following is a list of topics and questions that people usually avoid when they do not know each other well or if they are not very close friends:

1. **Money**   Although some people will tell you how much money they paid for something, many do not like to be asked such questions as:

    "How much did your house cost?"

    "What did you pay for your car?"

    "How much did that dress cost?"

    "How much money do you make?"

CROSS-CULTURAL NOTE

In some cultures, there are certain times when you can talk about money and other times when you can't. Sometimes families have rules about this. One man from France said that he had always been told that people shouldn't talk about money while they are eating.

2. **Age**   Some people will answer questions about age, but many people would feel uncomfortable answering them. It is, however, a common question to ask of a child.

3. **Religion**   This is considered a personal question. Most people don't ask, "What is your religion?" when they first meet someone. The subject usually is not discussed until people know each other better.

4. **Physical Appearance**   People often compliment each other's physical appearance, for example, "Your hair looks nice," or "I like your blouse." However, they usually do not ask questions about this topic. For example, many Americans would *not* like to be asked:

    "How much do you weigh?"

    "Have you gained weight lately?" ("Have you lost weight?" is usually acceptable, especially if you know that the person wants to lose weight.)

    "Is that your natural hair color?"

5. **Certain Information about Marriage**   There are some questions that are common and acceptable in other cultures about marriage that are not considered polite in the U.S. They include:

    "When are you going to get married?"

    "Why aren't you married?"

    "When are you going to have children?" (although sometimes it is acceptable to ask, "Are you planning to have children?")

    "Why don't you have children?"

    Also, people usually don't like to be told:

    "You should get married soon."

    "You should have children (or another child)."

6. **Politics** When people first meet each other, they sometimes avoid the subject of politics. If they don't know each other well, they probably won't ask, for example, "Who are you going to vote for?" This, however, can differ from person to person. Some people like to talk about politics and get into "heated discussions" (arguments or discussions in which people strongly disagree). Other people like to avoid arguments and won't talk about politics. Still others are not at all interested in politics.

CROSS-CULTURAL NOTE

In some cultures, people really enjoy having heated discussions. For example, a man from Spain said that a conversation is always more interesting if people disagree about something and then discuss their reasons. A man from Israel said that heated discussions are very common in his country. He said, "If I go to a party and nobody is arguing about politics, there's something wrong with the party!"

Phrases and Expressions for Asking Personal Questions _____

Repeat these after your teacher says them.

When you're not sure if a question is personal, you could say:

"I have a question to ask you, but I'm not sure if it's a personal one for you."

"I'd like to ask you a question, but I'm not sure if it's considered personal in your culture."

If you've already asked the question, you can say:

"If I've asked you a personal question, I'm sorry. In my culture, people ask this question all the time."

"Please tell me if I'm asking any questions that are too personal."

"I hope you don't mind that I asked you that question."

If you know someone well, you might be able to ask personal questions. You could say:

"Would you mind if I asked you a personal question?"

"I hope you don't mind if I ask you this question." (then ask your question.)

"I have a question to ask you, but please don't answer it if you don't want to."

CULTURE PUZZLE

Read the situation and choose the appropriate answer or answers.

What would you do if someone asked you a question that you felt was too personal?

a) You could say directly, "I don't want to answer that question."

b) You could answer the question in a general way and then change the subject.

c) You could explain that, in your culture, people usually don't ask that question and that you'd feel uncomfortable answering it.

Do you have any other suggestions?

(Answers are given at the end of the chapter.)

Phrases and Expressions for Avoiding Answers _____

Repeat these after your teacher says them.

If someone asks you a question that you don't want to answer, there are polite ways of saying so:

"I'm sorry. I prefer not to answer that question."
"I'm sorry. That's a hard question for me to answer."
"I'm sorry. I'd feel uncomfortable answering that question."
"If you don't mind, I'd rather not answer that."

If you want to change the topic of conversation, you could say:

"By the way, did you hear about . . . ?"
"By the way, did I tell you . . . ?"
"I've been meaning to tell you . . ."
"On another subject . . ."
"Speaking of [state new topic] I wanted to tell you about . . ." (use a word or phrase that has been mentioned before in the conversation.)

SECTION 2. DISCUSSING COMMON TOPICS

In every culture, there are certain topics that people commonly talk about. These topics may not be the same across cultures or, if they are, they may be discussed differently. In English, people have conversations or *small talk* about a variety of subjects. When people make small talk, they talk about things like the weather, sports, their weekend, and so on. The topic may be unimportant, but small talk itself is important for the following reasons:

- Small talk helps people decide if they want to get to know each other better.
- Some people think that if a person doesn't make small talk, then he or she is not friendly. (Friendliness is something that is important for Americans.)
- Small talk helps people feel comfortable with each other, especially at the beginning of a conversation (for example, in a phone conversation).
- Small talk can lead to conversations about more interesting, more serious, and more important topics.

A topic can begin as small talk and then turn into a more serious topic for conversation. Some common topics of small talk and conversation are:

1. **Job, Work** One of the first questions that people ask when they first meet is, "What do you do?" which means, "What is your job?" or "What line of work are you in?" The next question may be, "Where do you work?" or "Do you like your job?" Be prepared to talk about what you do *without going into a lot of detail*.

2. **School** Students are always asked these questions:
   "What are you studying?"
   "What classes are you taking?"
   "What is your major?"
   "How do you like your classes (or teachers)?"
   "What do you plan to do after you finish school?"

3. **Weekend and Vacation Activities** On Fridays, people at work and at school often ask each other about plans for the weekend (Friday night, Saturday, and Sunday).
   "What are you going to do this weekend?"
   "Do you have any interesting plans for the weekend?"

   On Mondays, people often ask about the weekend:
   "How was your weekend?"
   "How'd your weekend go?"
   "Did you do anything exciting over the weekend?"

4. **Family** People often ask married couples, "Do you have children?" (*not* "When are you going to have children?"). If the answer is "Yes," then there are many questions that can be asked:
   "How many children do you have?"
   "What are their names?"
   "How old are they?"
   "Are they in school?"

small talk—light conversation about common, everyday things
without going into a lot of detail—without explaining too much; without giving unnecessary information

People also ask questions about each other's *spouses*:
  "What does your husband/wife do?"
  "Where does your husband/wife work?"
People usually like to talk about their spouses. If they don't want to, they will probably give short answers to questions about them.

5. **Weather** The weather is a common topic of conversation, especially when there isn't much else to talk about. Strangers often talk about the weather for brief periods of time. For example:

    (As two people [strangers] are leaving a store:)
    A: "Nice weather we're having."
    B: "Sure is. I hope it stays this way."
    A: "Beautiful day, isn't it?"
    B: "Oh, yes. It's gorgeous."
    A: "What awful weather we're having!"
    B: "I know. When's it going to end?"

6. **Money matters** Men seem to talk more about money (except their own salaries) than women. Money matters include things like investments, stock, etc.

spouses—husbands and wives

CROSS-CULTURAL NOTE

An American observed a difference between Saudi Arabians and Americans in the way conversations begin. She said that every time her Saudi friends called her on the phone, they always asked, "How's your husband?" "How are your children?" and those who knew her parents asked, "How are your parents?" She said that she sometimes felt that it took too long to get to the point of the conversation.

7. **Possessions, Things**   Again, men seem to talk more than women about things they own or would like to own: computers, stereo equipment, televisions, cars, cameras, etc.

8. **Sports**   Many men and some women like to talk about sports such as baseball (during spring and summer), football (during fall and winter), and basketball (all year round).

9. **Themselves**   People enjoy hearing other people talk about themselves, as long as one person doesn't do all the talking! You probably have had many experiences that Americans have not had. If you feel comfortable talking about yourself, then the person you are talking to will probably also talk about himself or herself. Also, many Americans are interested in hearing about your experiences in the new culture.

Skill Practice: Making Small Talk

With another student, role-play one or more of the following situations. Take turns starting the conversation. Try to keep the conversation going for about three minutes.

1.   You are at work taking a break. You have only three minutes left. You see a co-worker who is standing by the coffee machine.

2. It is the first day of your English class. You and one other student have arrived early. You are standing in front of the classroom waiting for the teacher and the other students to come.

3. You are at work and one of your co-workers is ready to leave. It is 2:30 p.m. (employees usually leave at 5 p.m.) on a Friday afternoon.

4. Your choice of situations (think of situations you may have been in before).

Skill Practice: Keeping the Conversation Moving

Start a conversation with your teacher or another student. Ask open-ended questions, answer questions with more than "yes/no" or short answers, and respond to information. Choose topics from the following list or think of your own. Try to keep the conversation going for at least five minutes.

- Tell something about your culture.
- Talk about family, jobs, work or school.
- Give an opinion on a topic.
- Your choice of topics.

CHAPTER SUMMARY

This chapter discussed cultural differences in the areas of personal questions and topics and commonly discussed topics. Many Americans consider the following to be personal:

- money
- age (particularly older people)
- religion
- physical appearance (example: questions about weight)
- certain information about marriage
- politics (however, some people enjoy discussing politics)

Many Americans commonly discuss (or make small talk about) the following topics:

- job, work
- school
- weekend and vacation activities
- family
- weather
- certain money matters
- possessions, things
- sports
- themselves

This chapter also gave you the opportunity to:

- make small talk
- keep a conversation moving

ANSWERS TO CULTURE PUZZLE IN CHAPTER 10

a) No. This is a rude answer and would not encourage the other speaker to continue talking. It's possible that the person asking the question does not think it is personal. There are other more polite ways to say that you don't want to answer a question.

b) Possibly, but the person might ask you the question again. For example, Someone could ask, "What do you think of the government in your country?" A general answer could be, "I think all governments have their problems. I let them take care of their problems and I take care of mine." If you give an answer like this, you are responding to the question, but you aren't really answering it. The person who has asked you the question may ask again.

c) Yes. If the question is clearly one that is personal in one culture, but not in another, this is valuable information. If you said, "It's hard for me to answer that question because people in my country usually don't ask it," then you are teaching something about your culture. This will probably be interesting information for the other person, and he or she will not feel offended by your not answering the question.

Note: Answers to other exercises can be found in the separate Answer Key.

chapter 11

Making
the First
Move

Introduction   A foreign student who had lived in the U.S. for three years said that his advice to all newcomers would be, "*Make the first move.* Don't wait for people to come to you. Go to them and begin conversations. Introduce yourself, ask them questions, and, if you like them, extend invitations." He continued to say, "Don't expect to be treated like a guest in the U.S. *You* have to make sure that people get to know you. This is easier to do if you make the first move." This chapter explains ways of making the first move in order to meet and get to know people. It also explains American style invitations and visits.

CULTURE LEARNING QUESTIONS

1. How are foreigners treated in your culture? Are they treated like guests or do they have to make the first move in order to make contact with people?
2. Have you had any experience inviting Americans to your home (or being invited by Americans)? Were there any cultural differences in the way they accepted your invitation or in the way they invited you? Explain your answer.
3. If you have visited Americans' homes or have had American visitors in your home, what, if any, cultural differences did you observe? Have you had any other cross-cultural experiences with visiting (that is, with people other than Americans)?

CROSS-CULTURAL INTERACTION 11A:
Ineffective Communication

The following interaction could easily take place between two Americans. Here, however, it takes place between people from two cultures, Judy and Carmen. (Carmen is not from the U.S.) In this interaction, neither person really makes the

(Revised interaction appears on page 151.)

make the first move—take the first step; be the first one to do something (for example, start a conversation, introduce yourself)

first move to develop a friendship. Read it and explain what else they should do to make *further* contact with each other.

Situation: Two mothers, Carmen and Judy, are talking to each other at a park while their children are playing. They have a friendly relationship, but are not close friends.

Carmen: "Hi, Judy. (Judy and Carmen's children begin playing together in the sand.)

Judy: "Hi, Carmen. How are you?"

Carmen: "Fine. I'm glad to see that our children like to play together."

Judy: "Yeah, *me too*. I remember just a month ago they weren't sharing their toys."

Carmen: "Now it looks like they're enjoying each other."

Judy: "Finally! Maybe we could get together at each other's houses sometime. I'm sure the *kids* would enjoy that."

Carmen: "Sure. *That'd* be nice."

Judy: "Well, let's do it soon."

Carmen: "O.K." (Judy and Carmen continue to talk while their children play.)

Two weeks later at the park:

Judy: "Hi, Carmen."

Carmen: "Hi, Judy. How are you?"

Judy: "Fine, how about you?"

Carmen: "Pretty good."

further—more
me too—I am too
kids—children
that'd—that would

Judy: "I've been so busy lately, but I still want to get together soon. I know our kids would enjoy that."

Carmen.   "Yes. They would."

Judy: "Let's do it soon."

Carmen: "O.K. That sounds like a good idea." (Judy and Carmen continue to talk for a few minutes.)

Judy: "I can't stay long. I promised my kids that I would take them to the library across the street."

Carmen: "Yeah. I have to go too." (Carmen and her children begin to get ready to leave.)

Judy: "Let's get together soon. I'll give you a call."

Carmen: "O.K. That sounds good. Bye."

Judy: "Bye."

QUESTIONS AND DISCUSSION

Comprehension

Write T (true) or F (false) in the space provided.

1. _____ Judy thought it would be nice to get together with Carmen and the children sometime.

2. _____ Judy invited Carmen to come and visit her house.

3. _____ Judy invited Carmen to her house a second time when she saw her two weeks later.

4. _____ Carmen and Judy chose a day during the month to meet.

5. _____ When the two women left each other, they knew that they would see each other soon.

Analysis: Can You Explain?

1. Why do you think that Judy and Carmen didn't get together after they talked about getting together?
2. Do you think that Judy and Carmen really want to get together? Why or why not?
3. In both interactions, Judy is the one who suggests getting together. If Judy were from your culture, should she be the one to suggest a time and place to meet? Should Carmen suggest a time and date? What do you think they should do to make the invitation definite and specific?

TALK ABOUT YOUR OWN LANGUAGE AND CULTURE

1. In Cross-Cultural Interaction 11A, Judy showed some interest in getting together with Carmen, but she didn't extend a definite invitation (that is, she didn't mention a time and a place). Do people from your culture extend this kind of invitation to each other? If so, how do people respond?
2. Is extending invitations to a person's home a way to develop friendships? Explain your answer. What other ways do people develop friendships in your culture?
3. What would you say to an American if he or she asked you, "What is the best way to make contact with people from your culture?

Summary of Cross-Cultural Interaction 11A: Ineffective Communication

Americans may say something at the end of a conversation that sounds like an invitation, but it doesn't always result in people getting together. "Let's get together sometime," or "I hope I see you soon," are ways of telling another person that the conversation was enjoyable, but they are not always real invitations. In the case of Judy, she seemed interested in getting together with Carmen, yet her suggestions to meet were indefinite because she did not mention a time and place to meet. If Carmen wants to get together with Judy, she should make the first move and say something like, "How about getting together this Friday morning?" She shouldn't wait for Judy not to be busy if she's interested in making further contact with her.

CROSS-CULTURAL INTERACTION 11B

The following interaction shows Carmen making the first move so that she can make further contact with Judy. Read this interaction and discuss the differences in the interaction between Judy and Carmen.

Situation: Judy and Carmen are at the park talking while their children are playing.

Judy: "Maybe we could get together at each other's houses sometime. I'm sure the kids would enjoy that."

Carmen: "Sure. That'd be nice."

Judy: "Yeah. Let's do it soon."

Carmen:	"How about this Friday morning? Are you free?"
Judy:	"I'm not sure. I have to check my calendar."
Carmen:	"Okay. If that day's not good for you, maybe we could meet Monday morning."
Judy:	"Okay. I'll give you a call."
Carmen:	"Or I can call you. Let's exchange phone numbers."
	(Carmen and Judy give each other their phone numbers and continue to talk.)

Summary of Cross-Cultural Interaction 11B

In this interaction, Carmen makes the first move after Judy suggests getting together. Instead of waiting for Judy to extend a definite invitation, Carmen suggests a time to meet and offers to call Judy to decide on a day to meet. Instead of waiting for Judy to make further contact with Carmen, Carmen makes the effort to develop their relationship. By doing this, she shows Judy that she is interested in getting to know her better.

FOCUS ON U.S. CULTURE
Cultural Notes, Exercises, and Skill Practice

HOW MUCH DO YOU ALREADY KNOW ABOUT U.S. CULTURE?

Write T (true) or F (false) in the space provided.

1. _____ If someone wants to meet another person, he or she always waits for a third person to make the introduction.

2. _____ People do not invite others to their homes until they know them very well.

3. _____ People don't usually invite others to their homes; instead they invite them to restaurants.

4. _____ When people *decline* an invitation, they usually explain why they can't accept.

5. _____ At the end of a conversation, sometimes people say things like, "We really should get together soon." This means that the two people will definitely see each other soon.

6. _____ People usually prefer to know that someone is coming to visit rather than having a visitor come *unannounced*.

SECTION 1. MEETING AND GETTING TO KNOW OTHERS

If you asked Americans, "What are some ways to meet and get to know others?" you would probably get an answer based on their cultural beliefs. You might hear, for example, that you should smile when you first meet people and you should call them by their first name. These are not *universally accepted* ways of meeting people and, in fact, in some countries these ways would be considered

---

decline—not accept
unannounced—without telling the person
universally accepted—accepted or "correct" all around the world

offensive or rude. The list below is based on some American ideas about how to meet people and improve conversations and relationships.

Read the following information and indicate whether the behavior would be common and acceptable in your culture. Notice that many of the suggestions have to do with making the first move. Discuss your answers.

		Common in my culture? *YES/NO*
	Meeting and Getting to Know Others	
1.	Don't wait for the other person to say "Hello" first.	_____
2.	Introduce yourself to others; don't wait for another person to introduce you.	_____
3.	Reintroduce yourself to someone who has forgotten your name.	_____
4.	Look people in the eye and smile when you first meet them.	_____
5.	Start conversations with people.	_____
6.	Use the person's name at the beginning and end of the conversation.	_____
7.	Don't give only short answers or say only "Yes" or "No" to questions. Give more information in your answers.	_____

8. Express your opinions and feelings so that people will know how you think and feel.   _____

9. Ask for other people's opinions and accept differences in their thinking.   _____

10. Try not to talk too much in conversations but don't be silent, either. Participate in conversations.   _____

11. Compliment others on what they do and what they say.   _____

12. Always give feedback on what people say. That is, show that you are listening; react and respond to their words.   _____

13. Tell people that you are interested in getting together with them.   _____

14. Once you've met someone with whom you would like to be friends, invite him or her to an activity, a meal, or to your home.   _____

15. Take the time to be friendly with your co-workers and neighbors.   _____

Cross-Cultural Exercise: Making Contact in Your Culture

Write a list similar to the one above, telling what you need to do in your own culture to meet and get to know people.

CROSS-CULTURAL NOTE

"My first real contact with an American was with a guy at work. At first, I felt nervous talking to him, but then I told him that he could help me with my English by correcting my mistakes. He was happy to do it. We became friendly and I asked him for his phone number. I called him one evening and asked him if he wanted to come over for dinner. He accepted and since then, we have been friends. I thought it would be harder to make friends, but it wasn't. It took me four years to make the contact."

—Vietnamese man

Contact Assignment

The following is a list of places where people can go (in U.S. cities) in order to find out where and how to make contact with others.

- Chamber of Commerce
- Community Centers
- Public Libraries
- Community Colleges
- Adult Schools
- Religious Institutions (churches, synagogues)

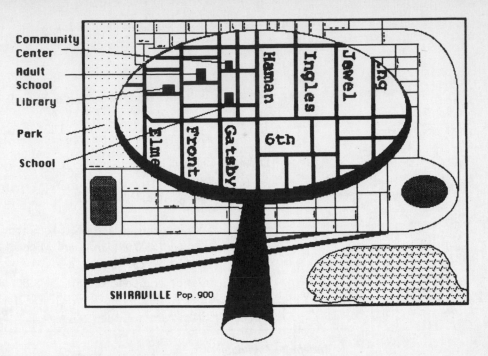

1. Find out if the city or town in which you live has the places listed above.

2. Go to as many of these places as you can (or groups of students can go to different places) and find out what is available in your city or town. Make a list of local:
   • activities
   • clubs
   • organizations
   • adult school classes
   • volunteer organizations
   • newcomer clubs

3. Report back to the class and compile a list of ways to make contact in your community.

4. Are these common ways of making contact in your own country? Explain your answer.

SECTION 2. EXTENDING INVITATIONS*

One way to make the first move is to extend invitations. There are different ways of extending invitations; some ways are *more effective* than others. In the next few pages, you will read examples of different types of invitations that Americans extend. Two main types of invitations are **definite** and **indefinite** invitations.

more effective—better; more successful

*The authors wish to thank Nessa Wolfson for her paper entitled, "Let's Have Lunch Together Sometime: Perceptions of Insincerity" (presented at TESOL conference, Boston 1979) from which these examples were adapted.

Definite Invitations

These include a time or date, a place and a yes/no question asking if a person can come. For example:

1. Deena: "Jim, are you and Claudine free on Saturday night? We'd like to have you over for dinner."

   Jim: "Yes. I think we're free. That sounds nice. Let me check with Claudine."

   Deena: "If you can, let's make it for 8:00 or 8:30 after the kids are asleep."

   Jim: "Good idea."

2. Piper: "We're going to a concert tomorrow night and there are still tickets left. Would you and Michael like to join us?"

   Deena: "We'd love to."

   Piper: "Good. The concert starts at 8:00, so why don't we pick you up at 7:30?"

   Deena: "Okay. See you then. Thanks."

Indefinite Invitations

These do not include a specific time and place and may not include a yes/no question. When people extend indefinite invitations, they do not really know when and if they will get together with the other person. For example:

1. Rebeccah: "Hi, Belle."

   Belle: "Hi, Rebeccah."

   Rebeccah: "We really should get together sometime."

   Belle: "Yeah. We really should."

   Rebeccah: "You know my number. Just give me a call."

   Belle: "Okay."

2. Shira: "Listen. I have a lot to talk to you about. I think we should try to have lunch together sometime soon."

   Adam: "Okay."

   Shira: "I'll call you."

   Adam: "Sounds good."

3. Brent: "Okay. Good talking to you. Let's get together sometime."

   Char: "Sounds good."

   Brent: "I'll call you one of these days and we'll set up a time that's good for both of us."

   Char: "Great. Talk to you soon."

   Brent: "See you soon."

   Char: "Talk to you later."

Exercise: Recognizing Definite and Indefinite Invitations

Read each of the short conversations below and circle either DEFINITE or INDEFINITE. Remember that when an invitation is definite, it includes a yes/no question and a specific time or date. For example:

Jon: It's been a long time since we've gotten together." "Let's get together soon."

Noga: "I'd like that, but February is impossible and March is pretty busy too."

Jon: "Well, let's decide in April!"
DEFINITE (INDEFINITE)

1. Michael: "Hi, Mel. Did I tell you that we're having a party Friday night? Do you think you can come?"

   Mel: "I'll check with Belle and let you know."
   DEFINITE   INDEFINITE

2. Judi: "I hope we can get together before I go to Texas next month. Give me a call and we'll try to figure out a date."

   Sarah: "Okay. You'll be hearing from me."
   DEFINITE   INDEFINITE

3. Benji: "Are you free to come over to our house for dinner next Tuesday night? I want you to see our new house."

   Ilana: "Sure. What time would you like us to come?"
   DEFINITE   INDEFINITE

4. Kenzo: "Let's have lunch sometime soon."

   Jim: "You choose a day."

   Kenzo: "Okay. I'll let you know."
   DEFINITE   INDEFINITE

Phrases and Expressions for Definite and Indefinite Invitations
Definite	*Indefinite*
"Can you come to my house for dinner Friday night?"	"Let's get together sometime."
"Would you like to go out to dinner and the movies?"	"We really should have lunch soon."
"Are you and your family free to come over Sunday morning?"	"Why don't we get together one of these days?"
"Would you like to spend the weekend with us in the mountains?"	"Let's go out some weekend."

Skill Practice: Changing Indefinite Invitations to Definite Invitations

It is possible to make indefinite invitations definite if you want to get together with another person. Read the following conversation between two businessmen and note how the invitation becomes definite.

Jim: "Let's get together soon."
Taka: "I'd like that."
Jim: "Good. I'll give you a call and we'll find a day that's good for both of us."
Taka: "I've got my datebook with me. How about if we set a date now?"

Jim: "Uh, sure. I'm free any day next week at noon."

Taka: "I've got meetings every day but Wednesday. Let's make it next Wednesday."

Jim: "Sounds fine. Next Wednesday at noon."

Taka: "See you then."

Question: Who makes the invitation definite?

Now, in pairs, have conversations in which you make small talk and extend invitations. For each situation, one student will extend an indefinite invitation. The second student will change it to a definite one.

- Two friends in the cafeteria at work
- A man and a woman at a party
- An English teacher and one of his or her students
- Your choice.

U.S. CULTURE NOTE

Sometimes people extend indefinite invitations and don't really want them to become definite. They may say at the end of a conversation, "I've got to go now. Let's get together soon." For some people, this simply means, "I've enjoyed the conversation with you. I hope we can talk again." If this is the case, the person is probably not interested in making the invitation definite. It isn't always easy to know when it is worth trying to change an indefinite invitation to a definite one. To get an idea of how sincere the person is, you could ask, "Do you want to set a date now or would you rather wait to do that?" If the person is too busy to be able to plan a time to get together, then it may be that he or she is really not interested in extending a definite invitation.

CULTURE PUZZLE #1

Read the situation and choose the appropriate explanation or explanations. There may be more than one possible answer.

Situation: An American, Diane, invited her Japanese friend, Michiko, to come to her house one afternoon. Michiko couldn't come and said, "No, I can't come. Please invite me again to your house." Diane was surprised by what Michiko said.

Why do you think Diane was surprised?

a) Diane thought that Michiko didn't want to come to her house because of the way she said, "No, I can't come." She couldn't understand why Michiko added, "invite me again" when it seemed that she didn't want to visit her.

b) When Michiko said that she couldn't come, Diane thought Michiko would invite her to her house. She was waiting for Michiko to say, "Why don't you come to my house in a couple of days?"

c) Diane thought Michiko was rude not to explain why she couldn't come and to invite herself so directly for another visit.

(Answers are given at the end of the chapter.)

U.S. CULTURE NOTE

When Americans respond to invitations, they usually say either, "Yes I can come," or "I'm sorry, I won't be able to *make it*." If a person doesn't know, he or she might say, "I'll let you know as soon as I can." When a person accepts an invitation, to a party, for example, then it means that he or she will go to the party. If a person says, "Yes, I will come," but doesn't come, many Americans would be confused and possibly even angry. Most Americans would prefer to hear directly, "No, I'm sorry, I won't be able to make it because. . . ."

CROSS-CULTURAL NOTE

In many cultures, it is rude to say directly, "No, I can't come." Even if a person knows that he or she cannot accept an invitation, the response might be, "Yes, I'll come." An American might think that the person was not telling the truth. There are many cultures where people do not say "No" directly to another person.

Phrases and Expressions for Responding to Invitations ————————————

1. *Accepting Invitations*

   "Yes, I'd really like to come. Thanks for inviting me."

   "That sounds nice. I'd be happy to come."

   "Sure. I can come." (informal)

   "Great. I'll be there." (very informal)

   "Sounds good. I'll see you then." (informal)

2. *Declining Invitations* (but showing interest in accepting another time)

   "I'm afraid I can't make it that day. Can we make it another time?"

   "I'm really sorry. We already have plans for that night. I hope we'll be able to make it another time."

   "Wednesday? [for example] That's too bad. I have to go to a meeting that night. Let's try to plan for another day."

   "I'd really like to, but that's the day that my brother's going to be in town. Would it be possible to make it another day?"

3. *Declining Invitations* (and not showing interest in accepting another time)

   "No. I'm sorry. I'm busy that night."

   "Thanks. I already have plans."

   "No, I'm not free then. Sorry."

   "I can't make it then."

4. *Delaying an Answer*

   "I'm not sure about that day yet. Let me go home and check my calendar. I'll let you know as soon as I can."

   "The twenty-fifth? [for example] I think I may have something that day, but I'm not sure. I'll call you tonight and let you know."

   "I won't know if I'll be sure then until I talk to my cousins who are going to be in town [for example]. Let me call you after I talk to them."

—————————————————————————————————————

make it—come

```
┌─────────────────────────────────────────────────────────────┐
│                      U.S. CULTURE NOTE                         │
│                                                                │
│  If you can't accept an invitation right away, most Americans  │
│  would expect you to give a reason for not being able to       │
│  respond. If you don't give a reason, it can seem like you     │
│  are not interested in getting together with the person who    │
│  invited you.                                                  │
└─────────────────────────────────────────────────────────────┘
```

Skill Practice: Responding to Invitations

In pairs, take turns making definite invitations using one or more of the situations below. Make some small talk before you invite the other person. For each situation, practice accepting, not accepting, and delaying a response to the situations.

- A student invites a teacher to his/her home for dinner.
- A man invites a woman on a date.
- A woman invites a man on a date.
- An employee invites his boss to his house for a Sunday *brunch*.

SECTION 3. VISITING

Before you visit someone from your own culture, do you let them know that you're coming or do you just *drop by?* Do you tell them that you're coming, or do you ask them if it is okay to come? How long do you usually stay?

CULTURE PUZZLE #2

This culture puzzle describes a situation involving Jim, from the U.S., and Magid, from an Arab country. As you discuss the situations and answers, give your own reactions and compare cross-cultural similarities and differences. Read the situation and choose the appropriate explanation or explanations. There may be more than one possible answer.

Situation: After a busy week, Jim was looking forward to spending Saturday reading and relaxing by himself. He had been very busy at work during the week and had worked overtime hours. Saturday came and Jim had just sat down in his most comfortable chair. Just as he started to read, the doorbell rang. He answered the door and to his surprise, his *former co-worker,* Magid, was standing at the door. They had been good friends at work, but had lost contact after Magid left. It had been several months since they saw each other.

How do you think Jim felt?

a) Jim probably had *mixed feelings* when he saw Magid. He was happy to see him, but disappointed that he couldn't spend the time alone.

b) Jim was a little bit upset at Magid for dropping by.

c) Jim was so happy to see Magid that he forgot about wanting to spend the day by himself.

brunch—breakfast and lunch combined, usually served at about 10:30 or 11 a.m.
drop by—visit without calling first
former co-worker—someone he used to work with
mixed feelings—two emotions at the same time

Now read the situation from Magid's point of view:

Situation: One Saturday morning, Magid was home and didn't have much to do. He had been thinking about his friend, Jim, who he used to work with. It had been a long time since they had seen each other and Magid felt bad about this. He had told Jim that he would come and visit him, but several months had passed and he just hadn't found the time. He remembered that Jim had told him, "Come and visit when you get the chance. I want to *stay in touch* with you." So this Saturday morning seemed like a good time to visit. He went to Jim's house and rang the doorbell. When Jim first answered the door, he didn't look completely happy to see Magid. Then, after a few seconds, he smiled and said, "Hi, Magid. Come on in."

How do you think Magid felt?

stay in touch—continue to see or talk to someone, especially after they have changed jobs or moved away

a) Magid was probably offended.

b) Magid understood that Jim wanted to be by himself that day.

c) Magid understood that Jim was a little bit upset that he had just dropped by without calling first.

Now continue reading about what happened during the visit:

Situation: Jim asked Magid to come into his home. The two of them drank coffee and talked about what they had been doing since Magid left the company. Magid stayed about three hours and then said, "I'd better go now." Jim got up and walked Magid to the door. They said goodbye to each other and Jim thanked Magid for coming. As they left each other, they both felt a little uncomfortable.

Why do you think Magid was a little uncomfortable?

a) Magid thought that Jim should have asked him to stay longer.

b) Magid thought that he didn't stay long enough.

c) Magid couldn't understand why Jim thanked him for coming.

Why do you think Jim was uncomfortable?

a) Jim thought that Magid should have stayed longer. Three hours was too short a visit.

b) Jim thought that Magid should have apologized for visiting without calling first.

c) Jim thought that Magid had stayed too long and that he should have said something like, "Let me know if you're busy or if I'm interrupting your plans."

(Answers are given at the end of the chapter.)

U.S. CULTURE NOTE

In the U.S., it is usually not acceptable to invite yourself to someone's house. You can make a suggestion to get together, but you usually do not say, "Can I come to your house?" "When can I visit you?" or "I'm planning to come this weekend."

CROSS-CULTURAL NOTE

Some students from Argentina said that they never call each other before visiting. An American asked them, "What happens if you're busy when your friends come and visit?" They all agreed that they would stop what they were doing and would spend time with their friends. The American asked, "Would you tell them that you have things to do and can only spend an hour (for example) with them?" One of the Argentinians answered, "Oh, no. That would be rude. I would spend as much time with my friends as they wanted to spend with me."

Phrases and Expressions for Visiting ——————————————————

Repeat these sentences after your teacher says them.

Letting another person know that you'd like to get together for a visit:

"I'd like to get together with you sometime. When is a good time for you?" [Wait for an answer] "Would you like to come to my house or should we meet somewhere else?"

"Are you free any time in the next couple of weeks to get together? We could meet at my house, if you want."

"Are you interested in getting together for a visit sometime soon?"

Dropping by, explaining, apologizing:

"Excuse me for dropping by without calling first. I happened to be in your neighborhood. I'll only stay a few minutes."

"I know I should have called first. Please let me know if I'm interrupting anything. I won't stay long."

"I just dropped by to say a quick 'Hi.' I know you're busy, but I was in the neighborhood. Don't let me interrupt what you're doing."

Knowing when to leave:

"Please let me know what your plans are for the rest of the day. I don't want to *overstay my welcome*."

"Let me know when you would like us to leave. We don't want to interrupt your plans." (This can be said to someone you know fairly well.)

"There are probably cultural differences as to how long visits are. How long do people here usually stay during visits like these?"

Note: You can also ask *before* you visit, "How long do people in this culture usually stay for visits?"

CHAPTER SUMMARY

This chapter presented information on American ideas about how to meet and get to know people. The following list includes some of the most important points:

- Make the first move; don't wait for others to approach you first.
- Look people in the eye and smile when you first meet.
- Begin conversations with people.
- When answering questions, give full answers; don't answer with only "yes" or "no" or short answers.
- Express your opinions and feelings.
- Give feedback on what people say.
- Take the time to be friendly.

overstay my welcome—stay too long

The chapter also included information on:

- *Definite invitations.* Invitations that mention a specific time and place, assuring that people *will* get together.
- *Indefinite invitations.* Invitations that do not mention a time or place; this type of invitation ("Let's get together sometime") may only be a way of ending conversations or a way of saying, "I've enjoyed the conversation."
- *Visits.* (announced, unannounced, length of visits, cross-cultural differences).

You practiced language and communication skills for:

- extending, accepting and declining invitations
- asking about getting together

ANSWERS TO CULTURE PUZZLES IN CHAPTER 11

Culture Puzzle #1

a) No. Diane doesn't have any reason to think that Michiko didn't want to visit. Just because a person says that he or she can't come doesn't mean that he or she doesn't *want* to come.

b) No. The person who cannot accept an invitation for a particular day does not have to invite the other person.

c) Yes. Diane thought that the way Michiko asked to be invited again was rude. However, Diane should have understood that Michiko didn't know exactly how to respond in English. Michiko did not mean to be rude. She simply didn't know the American English way of telling Diane that she was interested in getting together. She also didn't realize that people usually give an explanation when they decline an invitation.

Culture Puzzle #2

How do you think Jim felt?

a) Yes. Many Americans do like to spend time by themselves and will often plan time that is not shared with others. On the other hand, he was happy to see Magid.

b) Yes. Most of the time Americans prefer to know that someone is coming to visit, especially if they didn't invite the person for a particular day.

c) Probably not. Since he had planned a day for himself, he probably didn't forget about it so quickly.

How do you think Magid felt?

a) Yes. Magid probably was offended because he considered Jim his friend. In Magid's culture, friends would always welcome each other happily into their homes. Jim's reaction was insulting to him. Hospitality (making guests feel comfortable and happy) is a very important part of Arab culture.

b) No. Magid had no way of knowing this. In addition, Magid comes from a culture where it might be considered strange for a person to want to be by himself all day long.

c) Probably not. If Magid had known, he probably would have called first.

Why do you think Magid was a little uncomfortable?

a) Yes. He thought that Jim wanted him to leave because Jim didn't say anything like, "Please stay. You haven't been here very long." In Magid's culture, people often invite the guest to stay longer when the guest says that he wants to leave.

b) Yes. Magid thought that he *didn't* stay long enough. For him, three hours was not a long visit.

c) No. In Magid's culture, it is usual for people to thank guests for their visit.

Why do you think Jim was uncomfortable?

a) No. Three hours was too long for a visit that was unannounced. Jim probably expected Magid to stay about an hour, or an hour and a half at the most.

b) Yes. Occasionally Americans visit each other without saying that they are coming, but they usually apologize by saying something like, "I'm sorry if I'm disturbing you" or "I'm sorry if I'm coming at a bad time."

c) Yes. See a.

Note: Answers to other exercises can be found in the separate Answer Key.

chapter 12

Reading Text and Activities

Contents:

Reading Preview Activities
Reading Outline
Outline Questions
Vocabulary
Reading Preview Suggestions
Reading Test

Post-Reading Activities
Reading Comprehension
Vocabulary Exercises
Going Beyond the Reading

READING TEXT: MAKING CONTACT IN ANOTHER CULTURE
Reading Preview Activities

Reading Outline   Read the outline of the text and discuss the questions following it.

Part I. A Comparison (of making contact in your own culture and in another culture)

A. In your own culture, you usually don't have to figure out ways to meet people.
B. In a new culture, speaking another language requires effort; it's difficult to relax when speaking a new language.
C. Many newcomers may want to avoid cross-cultural contact.
D. Happiness in another culture, in large part, depends on how comfortable a newcomer feels with the people of that culture.

Part II. Making Contact in the U.S.

A. Making contact with people doesn't happen by itself.
B. A foreign student's advice to newcomers is to "make the first move."

1. Initiate contact.
2. Begin conversation.
3. Extend invitations.

Part III. Different Kinds of Contact

A. Strangers often have friendly conversations with each other, but this kind of contact usually doesn't lead to friendships.
B. All conversations in English can serve a purpose; they are opportunities to practice the language and learn about American interaction.
C. When some Americans move to a different city or state, they become involved in community affairs in order to meet people.
D. Newcomers to the U.S. can initiate contact in a number of ways.

Part IV. Cross-Cultural Contact

A. Don't be discouraged if some of your efforts to make contact are not successful.
B. You'll find a variety of types of Americans in the United States; some are interested in cross-cultural contact.
C. You might have to actively seek out the type of person who wants to meet people from different cultures.
D. Without some cross-cultural contact, a person may never even begin to feel integrated into another culture.

OUTLINE QUESTIONS

Based on the outline and your own experience, answer the following questions:

1. In the first part of the reading, there is a comparison between making contact in a person's own culture and making contact in a new culture. How easy (or difficult) is it to meet and get to know people in your own culture?
2. In the second part of the reading, a foreign student gives advice to newcomers in the U.S. He says, "Make the first move." What other advice would you give people who want to meet Americans?
3. In the third part of the reading, the authors write about conversations with strangers. In your experience with Americans, have you found strangers to be friendly and talkative? Describe your experiences.

VOCABULARY

Following is a list of vocabulary from the reading text in Unit III, *Making Contact in Another Culture*. To help you with pronunciation, each word is divided into syllables. The stressed syllable is marked with an accent mark (´). The words are grouped by part of speech (nouns, verbs, etc.) in the order in which they appear in the reading. *Practice saying these words after your teacher says them.* Each word is glossed (defined) at the bottom of the page the first time it appears in the reading. The definition gives the meaning of the word *as it is used in the reading*. These words also appear in the post-reading activities.

PART I

Nouns
EFFORT   ef'-fort
FATIGUE   fa-ti'gue
ASPECTS   as'-pects

Verbs
STRAIN   strain
AVOID   a-void'

Adjectives
INTEGRATED   in'-te-gra-ted

Adverbs
ADMITTEDLY   ad-mit'-ted-ly

Two word Verbs/Idioms
FIGURE OUT   fig'-ure out'
FOCUS ON   fo'-cus on
FEEL AT EASE   feel' at ease'

PART II

Nouns
MIDST   midst

Verbs
REQUIRES   re-quires'
INITIATE   in-i'-ti-ate

Adjectives
WORTH   worth

Adverbs
EVEN THOUGH   e'-ven though'

Idioms
HAPPEN TO BE   hap'-pen to be
GO OUT OF (their) WAY   go out' of (their) way'
MAKE THE FIRST MOVE   make' the first' move'

Adjectives
MINIMAL   min'-i-mal
RELIGIOUS   re-li'-gious
UNIQUE   u-nique'

Adverbs
AWHILE   a-while'

Two-Word Verbs/Idioms/Compound Nouns
LEAD TO   lead' to
SERVE A PURPOSE   serve' a pur'-pose
BECOME INVOLVED IN   be-come in-volved' in
VOLUNTEER WORK   vo-lun-teer' work
NEWCOMER CLUBS   new'-com-er clubs'
INFORMAL VISIT   in-for'k-mal vis'it
NIGHT CLASSES   night' class'-es

PART III

Nouns
SMALL TALK   small' talk
OPPORTUNITIES   op-por-tu'-ni-ties
ACQUAINTANCES   ac-quain'-tan-ces
INSTITUTIONS   in'-sti-tu'-tions
SYNAGOGUES   syn'-a-gogues
AFFAIRS   af-fairs'
INVENTIONS   in-ven'-tions
CAFETERIA   caf'-e-te'-ri-a

Verbs
PROVIDE   pro-vide'
RELOCATING   re-lo'-cat-ing
APPROACH   ap-proach'
EXTEND   ex-tend'

PART IV

Nouns
ATTEMPTS   at-tempts'
TUTORING   tu'-tor-ing
POT LUCK   pot' luck

Verbs
WIDEN   wi'-den
APPEAR   ap-pear'
ENCOURAGE   en-cour'-age

Adjectives
DISCOURAGED   dis-cour'-aged

Adverbs
UNDOUBTEDLY   un-doubt'-ed-ly

Two-word Verbs
SEEK OUT   seek' out'

Reading Preview Suggestions

Before you begin to read the text, *Making Contact in Another Culture,* do the following:

1. Read the titles of each part (Parts I, II, III, and IV).
2. Read the subheadings within each part of the reading.
3. Read the sentences in the margin.

4. Read the first sentence of each paragraph.
5. Read the key concepts at the end of each part.
6. Read the glosses (definitions) at the bottom of the page.

READING TEXT: MAKING CONTACT IN ANOTHER CULTURE

Part I. A Comparison

It is often easier to meet people in your own culture than in another culture.

1. In your native language and culture, it is often easier to meet and get to know people than it is in another language and culture. In your own country, you may have lived in the same neighborhood all your life and you know almost everybody. Maybe in your own country you meet people through your family or through people you've always known. You usually don't have to *figure out* ways to meet people—they're just there! You have a community because you've grown up in a place with a lot of people that you already know.

You are yourself when you speak your own language.

2. You share a language with people from the same culture. When you talk, you don't have trouble expressing yourself. In your own language, you can usually *focus on* what you're saying and not on the way you're saying it. You don't have to worry about saying something incorrectly or not finding the right word. You share a common background, so it isn't difficult to think of things to talk about. You're comfortable in your own language. Let's just say that you are yourself when you speak your own language.

It is tiring to speak another language.

3. **Effort in another language and culture.** This changes in another country when the language and people are different. First of all, it takes more *effort* to speak a second (or foreign) language than to speak your own. In a new language, you use different muscles from those you are used to using. That's tiring. Anyone who has spent a few hours speaking a new language knows that headaches are common. It's hard to search for words when you're talking, or to *strain* to understand when someone is talking too quickly. In addition to the *fatigue*, adults learning a new language have other complaints.

    "I feel like a child when I speak the new langauge."

    "I don't sound like myself."

    "It's hard for others to get to know who I really am."

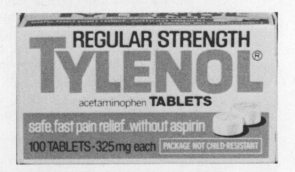

figure out—understand; know what to do
focus on—think only about
effort—trying; working hard
strain—have difficulty; have to try hard
fatigue—very tired feeling

These are all frustrating feelings for adults who know how to express themselves well in their native language, but not in the new language. It's not surprising that it's difficult to relax when speaking a new language.

It is a natural feeling to want familiar contact.

4. **Avoiding cross-cultural contact.** For all of these reasons, many travelers and immigrants may choose to *avoid* cross-cultural contact. They may spend most of their time with relatives and friends from their own culture. It is a natural and understandable feeling to want that familiar contact. Without it, one might feel lost. At the same time, without cross-cultural contact, a newcomer may have a hard time feeling part of the new culture. Some newcomers may never feel totally *integrated,* but it is possible for them to become comfortable with at least some *aspects* of the new culture.

If newcomers avoid contact with others, they probably won't become comfortable, in the new culture.

5. What does it mean to become comfortable in another culture? Whether or not a person is comfortable depends, in large part, on how the person feels with the people from the new culture. If newcomers or travelers avoid contact with others, then they probably won't learn to *feel at ease.* Admittedly, it's not always easy to make contact with people whose beliefs and customs are very different from yours. This is not to say that people always have an easy time making contact in their own cultures. However, at least in a person's own culture, he or she probably knows what to do in order to make contact and to get to know people.

Key Concepts in PART I _____

In your own culture: When you grow up in a place, you have a community. You don't have to figure out ways to meet people.

Shared language and culture: In your own language, you focus on what you are saying and not on the *way* you are saying it. It usually isn't difficult to think of things to talk about.

Cross-cultural contact: Without it, newcomers may have a hard time feeling part of the new culture.

_____

Part II. Making Contact in the U.S.

One way not to make contact is to wait for it to happen.

6. Making contact with people doesn't just happen by itself. You have to put yourself in places where there are people around. This is done more easily when you can simply walk to a nearby cafe, neighborhood park, or town plaza where a lot of people *happen to be.* Unfortunately, that's not the way most American cities and towns are built. Distances are great, and people can't usually walk a short distance and find themselves in the *midst* of groups of people. It *requires* effort and time to make contact. One way not to make contact is to wait for it to happen.

7. **Advice to newcomers.** In some countries, the newcomer (the visitor, the immigrant, the foreign student) is often invited places by others and meets people quickly. In the United States, this is not always what happens. *Even*

avoid—try not to do something; keep away from something
integrated—being part of or a member of a group
aspects—parts; characteristics
feel at ease—feel comfortable
admittedly—"To be honest"; "To tell the truth"
happen to be—be somewhere by accident or without planning
midst—middle
requires—needs

Making contact with people may require you to make the first move.

though you may be the newcomer, you may find that people don't *go out of their way* to meet you. What advice can be given to people who come to the U.S.? A foreign student from the Middle East said that the most important advice he could give would be:

> "Don't be shy with people. *Make the first move.* If you want to be invited to people's homes, invite them first. When you see someone you'd like to meet, talk to them. Begin conversations."

Your attempts to *initiate* contact may not always be successful, but it's *worth* the effort to make the first move.

Key Concepts in PART II _____

Meeting people in the U.S.: Making contact with people doesn't happen by itself.
Advice to newcomers: Initiate conversation and contact with people. Sometimes people won't come to you; you have to go to them if you want to meet them.

_____

Part III. Different Kinds of Contact

8. How do you make contact? Contact often begins with a conversation. Many conversations may never *lead to* anything, but without them, it is unlikely that any contact would ever develop.

even though you may be the newcomer—you may be the newcomer, *but . . .*
go out of (their) way—make a special effort
make the first move—start conversations and extend invitations
initiate—start; begin (adverb: *initially*—in the beginning)
worth—has value; is not a waste of time
lead to—become

It is very common for strangers to have friendly conversations with each other.

9. **Conversations with strangers.** In the United States it is common and acceptable to have conversations with strangers. Quite often, you see strangers having friendly conversations with each other. In many cases, the contact that you have with strangers will be *minimal,* even if they seem friendly and warm toward you. It might even happen, for example, that a stranger will tell you some very personal things in the ten minutes that you're waiting for the bus together. It may seem that this person wants to become friends. That probably won't happen. People can be very friendly without wanting real friendship. A French woman who lived in the U.S. said that she was surprised when strangers such as store clerks and bank tellers would smile at her and talk to her as if they were her closest friends. After *awhile,* she learned how to respond to *small talk* and began enjoying the conversations.

Every conversation can be seen as an opportunity to practice English.

10. **Conversation as language practice.** A newcomer shouldn't avoid this kind of conversation with strangers. All conversations in English can *serve a purpose.* They are *opportunities* to practice and interact in English. Although a conversation may not mean much, it can *provide* minimal contact with people and be one more way to learn the language and learn how people interact.

11. **Places to make contact.** It isn't easy, especially for adults, to develop a new circle of friends and *acquaintances.* Many Americans have a difficult time beginning new friendships when they move from city to city, even within a state. Of course, it is much easier to move within one's own country than to move to another country, but *relocating* anywhere, even to a nearby city, can be difficult. When Americans move within the country, they often need at least six months to begin to feel settled and to make contact with people. Many people who have moved say that they only begin to feel at home in a new place after two or three years.

Relocating anywhere, even within one's own country, can be difficult.

12. **Where Americans make contact.** What, specifically, do some Americans do to make contact when they move? Some join *religious institutions* such as churches and *synagogues.* Some *become involved in* community *affairs,* joining groups, associations, and organizations or doing *volunteer work.* Others join clubs where they know they'll meet people with whom they have interests in common. Some of these ways of making contact may be unfamiliar to people who are visiting the U.S. or who are immigrating from other countries. In many countries, for example, volunteer organizations don't exist. *"Newcomer clubs"* and agencies that arrange for people to meet may be *unique* American *inventions.* Still, you do not have to be born in the U.S. to

minimal—very little; almost none
awhile—some time
small talk—light conversation about common, everyday things
serve a purpose—be useful; be helpful
opportunities—chances
provide—to give or offer
acquaintances—people you know a little, but who are not friends
relocating—moving your job, home, and family
religious—about religion
institutions—organizations
synagogues—buildings where Jewish people meet to practice their religion
become involved in—start doing something; become part of a group (noun: *involvement*)
affairs—activities; things that need work or help
volunteer work—work that people do without pay; volunteer work often benefits old people, refugees, immigrants, and political causes. Churches and synagogues often have volunteer organizations.
newcomer clubs—many cities in the U.S. have clubs for people who have just moved to that city to give them a chance to meet other newcomers and acquaint them with the city.
unique—special; only in one place
inventions—things that are new, made or created by someone for the first time

try some of these ways of making contact. Of course, there are the more usual places to make contact, and these places may provide a more comfortable way of meeting people.

A friendly first conversation with people at work, school or in your neighborhood could turn into something more.

13. Where are the places to make contact? Your neighborhood is a place to start, but remember that *you* may have to be the one to *approach* your neighbor first. If one of your neighbors seems friendly but you've only exchanged greetings, try starting a conversation. Once you've had several conversations, *extend* an invitation. Have that person come into your home for an *informal visit*. If you work in the day and don't have much of a chance to talk to neighbors in the day, take a *night class* in a subject or activity that interests you. Talk to people before class and during the breaks. Remember they may not come to you first. It's like this at work or at school. You probably see the same people in the *cafeteria* or by the coffee machines. Start talking to them. Some may not respond very much; others will respond in a way that tells you that they would enjoy talking to you again. If you have children, go to the same park a few times a week. You'll start seeing the same people. Which people seem approachable? Start conversations with them. A friendly first conversation could lead to something more.

Key Concepts in PART III

Friendliness: People, including strangers, may be friendly, but may not be interested in real friendship. However, even conversations with strangers can be opportunities to practice and interact in English.

Involvement: One way of making contact is to become involved in clubs or organizations or to do volunteer work.

Places to make contact: Start conversations with people in the neighborhood, at school, at work, or in parks. A friendly conversation could lead to more contact.

Part IV. Cross-Cultural Contact

Don't be discouraged if some of your attempts to make contact are not successful.

14. Don't be *discouraged* if some of your efforts to make contact are not successful. You can't always know who will and who won't be responsive to your *attempts* to make contact. Some Americans feel too busy to *widen their circle of friends* and may simply not want to develop a friendship. Some native-born Americans have only had contact with other Americans and may *appear* shy and inexperienced with people from different cultures. And, unfortunately, there are always some people who do not want to get to know others from different cultures. You can probably find this type of person in every culture.

There are many different types of Americans.

15. **Types of Americans.**   In the United States, you'll find a variety of "types." Many Americans enjoy meeting people from different cultures, but you have to know where to find them. If you're a student and your school has an international student club, you will *undoubtedly* find Americans who are

approach—try to talk to someone (adjective: *approachable*—easy to begin to talk to; friendly)
extend—offer
informal visit—casual visit; for a short time, generally not for a meal
night class—a class in an adult school or community college
cafeteria—eating place or restaurant, often in a company or school
discouraged—disappointed, not wanting to try again
attempts—efforts, (verb: *attempt*—try)
widen (their) circle of friends—make new friends
appear (shy)—look as if he is (shy), seem to be (shy)
undoubtedly—no question, certainly

interested in cross-cultural contact. Maybe you know a neighbor or a fellow employee who has travelled to different countries and who would like to know more about the country you're from.

16. **Finding people to meet.** You might have to actively *seek out* the type of person that wants to meet people from different cultures. For example, at work or at school, you could post a sign offering *tutoring* in your language (in exchange for English lessons, for example). You could organize a *pot-luck dinner* for people you work with and in this way, you will probably *encourage* interest in your culture. (Remember, too, that food provides a good topic of conversation and helps people feel comfortable!) Involvement with people who are interested in your background can lead to contact and interesting relationships. It will probably take awhile to make contact, and especially to make friends, in a new culture. Sometimes it is easier to get to know other newcomers or foreigners than people from that culture. The easiest type of contact, of course, is the familiar contact with people from one's own culture. It is important to have this familiarity when everything else is different. However, without some cross-cultural contact, a person may never even begin to feel integrated into another culture.

Key Concepts in PART IV

Types of Americans: Many Americans have never had contact with people from different cultures. Some avoid this kind of contact; others enjoy meeting people from different cultures.

Cross-cultural contact: Contact with people from one's own culture is important. However, some cross-cultural contact is needed in order to become integrated into the new culture.

seek out—look for
tutoring—private classes for only one student at a time
pot-luck dinner—a party where each person brings some food to share
encourage (interest in something)—help people to become (more interested in something)

POST-READING ACTIVITIES

READING COMPREHENSION

True/False

Read each statement. Then, according to the reading, decide whether the statement is true or false. Write T(true) or F(false) in the space provided.

1. _____ It is often easier to meet people in your own culture than in another culture. (Part I)

2. _____ In your own language, you usually focus on the way you're saying something and not on what you're saying. (Part I)

3. _____ Newcomers sometimes avoid cross-cultural contact because they are more comfortable with relatives and family. (Part I)

4. _____ In most U.S. cities, people can't walk to parks and cafes because distances are great. (Part II)

5. _____ If a person is very friendly, it always means that he or she wants to be friends. (Part III)

6. _____ It may take as long as two or three years for Americans to feel settled in a new city within the U.S. (Part III)

7. _____ Newcomer clubs and volunteer work organizations are common all over the world. (Part III)

8. _____ Newcomers will feel more integrated in a culture if they end their relationship with people from their own culture. (Part IV)

Multiple Choice

Circle the letter next to the one best answer. Try to answer each question without looking at the reading. Then, if you cannot answer the question, reread the paragraph indicated.

1. In your native language and culture, it is often easier to meet and get to know people than in another culture. Which of the following reasons for this is *not* talked about? (Paragraphs 1 and 2)

   a) In your own culture, you already have a community because you've grown up in a particular place.

   b) In your own culture, you know people who can introduce you to others.

   c) In your own culture, you share a common background with people.

2. "You are yourself when you speak your own language." This means: (Paragraph 2)

   a) Only you can speak your own language.

   b) You can express the "real" you because you are comfortable speaking your own language.

   c) You are usually by yourself when you speak your own language.

3. What can happen if newcomers completely avoid contact with people from the new culture? (Paragraph 4)

   a) They will probably not feel part of the new culture.

   b) They will become completely comfortable in the new culture.

   c) They will feel lost without the familiar contact.

4. Which of the following points is *not* made in Paragraph 5 of the reading?

   a) A person's comfort in another culture depends on how he or she feels with people in the new culture.

   b) Some people have difficulty making contact in their own cultures.

   c) People do not know what to do in order to make contact in their own culture.

5. Why is making contact in the U.S. particularly difficult? (Paragraph 6)

   a) In American cities and towns, people can't usually get to places easily and quickly where there are a lot of people around.

   b) The distance between neighborhood parks and town centers is so great that people cannot walk from one to the other.

   c) Most people don't live near cafes.

6. Why does the foreign student from the Middle East give the advice, "Make the first move."? (Paragraph 7)

   a) In the U.S., people don't move out of the way when they meet newcomers.

   b) In the U.S., people don't always approach newcomers first.

   c) In the U.S., in order to be invited to people's homes, it is always necessary to extend an invitation first.

7. Which of the following ideas is mentioned in Paragraph 11?

   a) It is easier to move from country to country than to move within one's own country.

   b) It is difficult to move from city to city within one's own state.

   c) It is not as difficult to move to another country as it is to move within one's own country.

8. There are several things you can do to make contact with people in a new culture. Which of the following is not talked about in Paragraph 13?

   a) Start conversations and extend invitations.

   b) Invite people to restaurants.

   c) Go to the same park often, as you are likely to see the same people.

VOCABULARY EXERCISES

Matching

Draw a line from each noun in column A to the matching definition in column B. The first one is done for you.

A	B
1. attempt	a. some time
2. aspect	b. organization
3. awhile	c. try
4. acquaintance	d. person you know a little bit, but who is not a friend
5. institution	e. part, characteristic

Word Forms

Choose the correct word in parentheses ( ) and fill in the blanks. The first one is done for you.

1. (avoiding/avoid)
    a) Sometimes people feel like _avoiding_ interaction with people from other cultures.
    b) People who _____ asking questions may make serious mistakes (for example, on the job).

2. (integration/integrating/integrated)
    a) Sometimes people prefer not to be totally _____ into a new culture. They like to keep some of the behaviors of their own native culture.
    b) Racial _____ is a goal in the U.S.
    c) Some people adapt to a new culture by _____ parts of their own culture with the new culture.

3. (initially/initiate/initial)
    a) The first letter of a name is an _____.
    b) When you "make the first move," you _____ a conversation.
    c) Many people feel uncomfortable in a new culture _____, but after awhile they feel more integrated.

4. (became involved/involved/involvement)
    a) As soon as he moved to the new city, he _____ in a church group and a hiking club.
    b) For many years, immigrating to the U.S. _____ waiting for weeks or months at an immigration center like Ellis Island in New York or Angel Island in San Francisco.
    c) He got to know the people in his town through his _____ in community affairs.

Fill In the Blanks

From the list of verbs below, choose the correct word and fill in the blanks. Use each word only once.

focus on	encourage	requires	appear
strain	approach	provide	

1. Sometimes someone will _____ to be rude, when really he is just being informal and friendly.
2. When you are speaking in a second language, you sometimes have to _____ to understand people's speech.
3. Language learners should _____ using correct intonation, so that they will be understood.
4. It _____ a lot of time and understanding to learn to work and live comfortably in a new culture.
5. Joining a club or doing volunteer work can _____ you with the opportunity to make friends and learn about the culture.
6. If you _____ people in a friendly way, they will probably respond in a friendly way.
7. In American culture, good teachers _____ their students to ask questions.

Choose the Best Explanation

Each sentence below contains an italicized word or phrase from the reading. Read each sentence and the three possible explanations. Choose the one explanation that best matches the meaning of the sentence. Circle the letter next to that explanation. The first one is done for you.

1. In a social situation, eating can help people to *feel at ease.*
   a) People feel more comfortable if they can eat while they talk to new acquaintances.
   b) People feel better when they are not hungry.
   c) Food that is easy to eat is the best thing to serve guests.

2. *Even though* some of the food that she offered was strange to me, I was glad she invited me to dinner.
   a) I like all the food she served.
   b) I am sorry I went to her house for dinner. I did not have a good time.
   c) I did not like some of the food, but I had a good time.

3. I *happened to be* waiting for the elevator, so when he came to wait for the elevator too, I decided to start a conversation.
   a) I waited by the elevator because I wanted to talk to him.
   b) I did not plan to talk to him.
   c) I was very happy to see him.

4. Sometimes an unplanned, accidental meeting can *lead to* a friendship.
   a) It is not a good way to start a friendship.
   b) It can end a friendship.
   c) It can be the beginning of a friendship.

5. All conversations in English can *serve a purpose.* They are opportunities to practice and interact in English.
   a) English conversation provides many opportunities for cross-cultural communication.
   b) Every conversation in English can give you the chance to practice the language and communicate in English.
   c) English conversations are only useful if the language learner practices every day.

GOING BEYOND THE READING

Each group of questions is based on a quote from the reading. Read the questions and then discuss them in small groups or with the entire class. After the questions have been discussed, choose a topic related to one of the questions and write a composition.*

1. "*. . . you are yourself when you speak your own language.*"
   (Paragraph 2)
   a) Do you feel like another person when you speak English? That is, do you feel that your personality changes? Explain.

Note to the teacher: Some students may prefer to write out answers to questions that they feel are personal ones. In this case, you may want to use this exercise as a writing exercise.

2. *"I feel like a child when I speak the new language."* (Paragraph 3)

   a) Do you have this feeling when you speak English? Explain.

   b) Do you feel that others react to you in this way? If so, what do they do that gives you this feeling?

3. *"Some newcomers may never feel totally integrated, but it is possible for them to feel comfortable with at least some aspects of the new culture."* (Paragraph 4)

   a) How easy or difficult is it for newcomers to feel integrated in your own culture (whether in a community in the U.S. or in your native country)?

   b) What would a newcomer have to do to feel integrated in your culture?

   c) Is it possible for newcomers to feel totally integrated in another culture? What is your experience? Explain.

4. *"In some countries, the newcomer . . . is often invited places by others and meets people quickly."* (Paragraph 7)

   a) How are newcomers treated when they first come to your country? Are there differences between the way tourists, immigrants, foreign students, and business people are treated? Explain your answer.

   b) Talk (or write about) your own experiences when you first came to the U.S. Did you expect to be received by Americans in a certain way? If so, were you received in that way? Explain your answer.

5. *". . . unfortunately, there are always some people who do not want to get to know others from different cultures."* (Paragraph 14)

   a) Why do you think certain people do not want to have contact with others from different cultures? What are some of the reasons?

   b) Are the reasons the same for people in the U.S. as for people in your culture? Explain your answer.

CULTURE LEARNING

UNIV IV FOUNDATIONS

- There are ways to "learn culture," just as there are ways to learn language.
- People can't always accept everything that is different in another culture. They must decide, however, what is needed for successful communication.
- Often people begin to understand their own cultures only after they have begun interacting with someone from another culture.

UNIT IV CONTENTS

Chapter 13. "Exchanging Cultural Viewpoints" presents:

- culture learning questions
- learning from miscommunication

Chapter 14. "Understanding Cultural Differences" shows how to appreciate cultural differences by:

- observing cultural behavior
- asking without judging
- looking at your own experiences

Chapter 15. "Reading Text and Activities" contains:

- reading text, "Culture Learning"
- comprehension, vocabulary, and discussion questions.

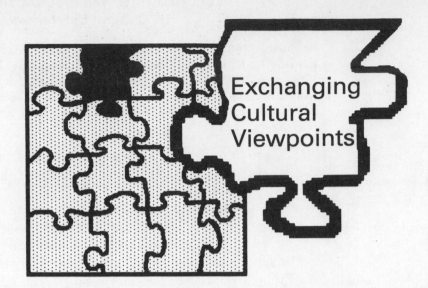

chapter 13

Exchanging
Cultural
Viewpoints

Introduction   When we meet people from other cultures, we cannot see all the ways that their cultures have influenced them. This is because culture is like an iceberg; the only part of the iceberg you see is the tip. You don't see the rest because it is submerged below the water. Most of the iceberg is deep within the ocean just as much of culture is deep within people. We can more easily understand a person from another culture if we try to understand the hidden parts of culture. To do this, it is necessary to know how a culture is different from one's own and how it has influenced people in ways that are not obvious.

Culture learning goes *hand in hand* with language learning. With language learning, you don't just learn about the language. You learn to speak the language. With culture learning, you don't just learn about a culture. You learn how to *cope with* cultural differences and you learn how to communicate comfortably with people in another culture. This chapter, using many *real-life* examples, presents information on culture learning. The focus is on asking questions and on learning from miscommunication or misunderstandings.

CULTURE LEARNING QUESTIONS

1.   Have you ever had a problem of miscommunication or a misunderstanding because of cultural differences? Describe the situation.

2.   Did you find out the reason for the miscommunication? If so, how? Who did you talk to?

3.   Has anyone ever asked you to explain your cultural point of view in order to understand a cultural conflict or an incident of cross-cultural miscommunication. Describe the situation.

hand in hand—together
cope with—deal with; handle
real life—true; not made up

CROSS-CULTURAL INTERACTION 13A:
Cultural Differences

Situation: Matt, Jeff, and Kam, a foreign businessman, work together in a company in the U.S. Today, Matt and Jeff decide to have lunch together and they ask Kam to join them. They ask Kam to recommend a restaurant that serves food from his country. At the end of the meal, Kam takes the check, and *insists on* paying for everyone. Now Matt, Jeff, and Kam are talking in the restaurant parking lot.

Matt: "Here, take this please." (He offers Kam $20.)

Kam: "No, no." (He holds his hands in the air to avoid taking the money.)

Jeff: "Kam, you shouldn't pay for all of us."

Matt: "I really can't let you pay for all of us. *I* asked you to join *us*." (He offers the money again, and looks upset.)

Kam: "No, no. It's okay. Please don't worry about it."

Matt: (He continues to look upset.)

Kam: "It was my pleasure to introduce you to this restaurant."

Matt: "Yes . . . but please let us pay for ourselves. We invited you to join us, not *the other way around*."

Kam: "No, no, today you are my guests."

Matt: (*Reluctantly*) "Well, okay . . . but next time *it's on me*." (He puts the money back in his wallet.)

Kam: "No, no. You don't have to do that."

(Everyone feels uncomfortable.)

QUESTIONS AND DISCUSSION

Comprehension

Write T (true) or F (false) in the space provided.

1. _____ Kam invited Matt and Jeff to lunch.
2. _____ Matt and Jeff asked Kam to recommend a restaurant.
3. _____ Kam does not have enough money to pay for everyone, so Matt gives him $20.
4. _____ Matt and Jeff do not want Kam to pay for them because the restaurant is very expensive.
5. _____ Kam finally accepts the $20 from Matt.
6. _____ At the end of the conversation, Matt and Jeff feel uncomfortable because they ate too much.

Analysis: Can You Explain?

1. Why do you think Kam wants to pay for Matt and Jeff?
2. How do Matt and Jeff expect to pay the bill?
3. How do you think Kam feels at the end of this conversation?

insists on—says that he must (pay)
the other way around—the opposite ("We invited you, you didn't invite us," in this case)
reluctantly—not willingly, without wanting to
it's on me—I will pay for you

TALK ABOUT YOUR OWN LANGUAGE AND CULTURE

1. If a group of people go to a restaurant together, does one person usually pay for everyone, or does each person pay for his or her own meal?
2. If one person pays in a restaurant and then other people offer to pay him back, what would his response be?

Summary of Cross-Cultural Interaction 13A: Cultural Differences

In this interaction, there is a misunderstanding between Kam and the two Americans. At the end of the conversation, the Americans still feel upset, and probably Kam does, too. The problem is not a language problem, but a difference in expected behavior. Matt and Jeff expect Kam to behave one way, but Kam's *expectations* are different. Each may feel that the other is not very sensitive, or does not know "proper" behavior. What is "proper" depends on the cultural background.

CROSS-CULTURAL INTERACTION 13B*

The following dialogue takes place a few days *after* Kam went out for lunch with Matt and Jeff. Read the dialogue and then the explanations in the "What is Happening" column.

	Dialogue	*What is Happening*
Kam:	"You know when we went to the restaurant the other day?"	
Matt:	"Yes."	
Kam:	"Well, something happened that I don't really understand. Can I ask you about it?"	Kam starts to **talk about the miscommunication.**
Matt:	"Sure."	
Kam:	"At the restaurant, you and Jeff seemed very upset that I tried to pay for both of you."	Kam **describes what he observed.**
Matt:	"Yeah. That really surprised me."	
Kam:	"When you tried to give me the money, I felt that you weren't really serious. That's why I didn't take it at first."	Kam starts to **explain his cultural point of view.**
Matt:	"Oh, I was serious. Didn't I seem serious to you?"	
Kam:	"Well, no. In my culture, you would try to put the money in my hand or my pocket. You wouldn't just offer it to me once or twice. You might insist many times that I take it, but I would still refuse."	Kam **explains his cultural point of view,** and **talks about nonverbal communication.**

expectations—what we expect will happen, based on our own background and experience

*Note: The format varies here. Cross-cultural interaction 13B is *not* a revised version of 13A.

Matt:	"Really? For me, it wouldn't be polite to insist many times."	Matt **explains his point of view.**
Kam:	"I didn't know that. Now I understand what happened."	
Matt:	"I'm glad you asked about it."	

FOCUS ON U.S. CULTURE
Cultural Notes, Exercises, and Skill Practice

HOW MUCH DO YOU ALREADY KNOW ABOUT U.S. CULTURE?

Write T (true) or F (false) in the space provided.

1. _____ Americans like to talk about themselves as a group. For example, they often say, "*We* Americans feel this way. *We* Americans usually do it this way."

2. _____ Americans feel that it is always best to talk directly to a person with whom you've had a problem of miscommunication.

3. _____ If you are having a cultural problem with an American, it can help to explain your own cultural point of view.

4. _____ If a person from another culture acts in a way that is culturally unfamiliar, most Americans will feel that it's okay because he's a foreigner and is not expected to know the customs.

SECTION 1. CULTURE LEARNING QUESTIONS

The following interaction illustrates how you can ask culture learning questions to prepare for a cross-cultural interaction.

Situation: In Cross-Cultural Interaction 13A, Kam, Matt, and Jeff go out to lunch and Kam pays for everyone. Below is a different interaction. Imagine that this interaction took place *before* Kam went out to lunch with Matt and Jeff. Kam decides that he wants to invite some friends out for lunch. Kam has heard that Americans like to pay for themselves when they go out to eat with friends. Kam is not sure what to do, so he decides to ask another American friend, Ron, for advice. Here is Kam's conversation with Ron.

Kam:	"Ron, I have some questions about American customs. *Do you have a minute?*"
Ron:	"Sure."
Kam:	"I'm going to ask some American friends from work to have lunch with me. In my culture, I'd pay for everyone. How about in the U.S.?"
Ron:	"Well, have they taken you out before?"
Kam:	"You mean, have they paid for me before?"
Ron:	"Yeah."

Do you have a minute?—Do you have a few minutes right now to help me with something?

Kam: "No."

Ron: "Well, then they'd probably be more comfortable if each person paid for himself."

Kam: "Oh . . . but . . . if I ask them to have lunch with me, shouldn't I pay?"

Ron: "No, I don't think so. It depends on what you say. If you want to take them you can say, 'Can I take you to lunch?' or 'Let's go to lunch together. It's on me.' But if you just want to eat with them, you can say, 'Do you have any plans for lunch?' "

Kam: " 'Do you have any plans for lunch?' "

Ron: Right. That means, 'Do you want to have lunch with me?' "

Kam: "Okay. Thanks. I'll try that."

Ways To Ask Culture Learning Questions

Say these sentences after your teacher says them:

"Do you have a minute? I'd like to ask you a couple of questions."

"I'm not sure what Americans usually do in this situation. Can you give me your opinion?"

"Can I say, 'Can I take you to lunch?' "

"Is it okay if I say, 'I'd like you to recommend a good restaurant.' "

"Will he/she probably ask me to pick him/her up?"

"What would you say in this situation?"

"Should I pay for everyone?"

"In my culture, I would pay for everyone. *How about in the U.S.?"*

U.S. CULTURE NOTE

An American woman said, "When I was in Japan, my Japanese friends often told me, 'We Japanese do this' or 'We Japanese feel this way.' Then they'd ask, 'How about Americans?' It was very difficult for me to answer these questions. I would say, 'Well, my friends do this' or 'The people I know do that' or 'Many Americans probably think this way.' I think they expected me to say, 'We Americans do this.' I could never say that! I dont know how everyone thinks. You just don't hear people saying 'We Americans.' "

Ways to Explain Your Cultural Point of View

It is often helpful to explain the customs or usual behavior in your culture. This can help people understand why you are uncomfortable with something or why you did something that seemed unusual to them.

"In my culture, people usually/often bow when they greet someone."

"In my culture, people would not kiss in public."

"In my culture, people are expected to disagree with each other openly."

"In my culture, people usually don't hide their feelings."

"In my culture, people feel uncomfortable expressing their feelings."

"In my culture people are not expected to ask questions during class."

Skill Practice: Asking Culture Learning Questions

With a partner, ask as many questions as you can think of about the following situations. Use the sentences from "Ways to Explain Your Cultural Point of View" and "Ways to Ask Culture Learning Questions" given previously.

For example:

You say: "I'd like to ask some American friends from work to have lunch with me."

You ask: "In my culture, I would pay for everyone."
"How about in the U.S.?"
"What if these friends won't let me pay for them?"
"What should I do or say?"

Your partner should try to answer your questions. Ask the teacher his or her advice about each situation.

Situations:

1. You're going to an American's house for dinner.
2. You're going to have a meeting with your supervisor to discuss a problem on the job. Your supervisor thinks that the problem is your fault. You do not think so.
3. You'd like to invite an American friend to your house for a meal.
4. You're going to have a performance review with your supervisor.
5. You'd like to *invite an American on a date.*
6. Your choice of situations (Think of a situation that has already happened or one that you anticipate.)

SECTION 2. LEARNING FROM MISCOMMUNICATION

People often think that what is usual behavior in their own culture is also usual behavior in another culture. In another culture, they may act in a way that they think is "normal." If a misunderstanding or miscommunication occurs because of this, the people involved can try to analyze the problem and learn from it. Learning from miscommunication and from cultural differences can take place when people ask questions and explain their cultural point of view.

CULTURE PUZZLE #1

Read the situation and choose the appropriate explanation or explanations. There may be more than one possible answer.

Situation: An American in the U.S. invited a group of Japanese students over to his house. He and his wife had spent a lot of time preparing food and getting the house ready. They were looking forward to the party and hoped that the Japanese would enjoy themselves. They came at about 8:00 at night and right away seemed to be enjoying themselves. There was a lot of dancing and singing and good conversation. Then, almost suddenly, one of the students said "thank you" to his hosts and said that it was time to go. After that, all of the Japanese began to get

invite (someone) on a date—invite someone (usually of the opposite sex) to do something with you, such as going to a movie, out for dinner, etc.

ready to leave. The American and his wife couldn't understand why this happened. *They felt insulted* that everyone left so early and at the same time.

How can you explain what happened?

    a) The Americans must have done something that bothered the Japanese.
    b) The Japanese really weren't having a good time.
    c) Japanese usually leave people's houses as a group and try not to stay too long, so as not to *offend* their hosts.

(Answers are given at the end of the chapter.)

Discussion: After reading the correct answer at the end of the chapter, discuss:

    1. What, if anything, should be done?
    2. Could this situation have been prevented?

CULTURE PUZZLE #2

Read the situation and choose the appropriate explanation or explanations. There may be more than one possible answer.

Situation: Tom, an American man, was invited to dinner at the home of Abdul, a Saudi Arabian friend. As is the custom in many parts of the U.S., Tom wanted to bring a bottle of wine or something else to eat. He remembered that *Moslems* usually do not drink alcohol, so he brought cookies that he had bought at a bakery. When he gave his friend the cookies, Abdul said "thank you," but he didn't seem very pleased by the gift.

Tom probably thought that:

    a) Abdul did not like cookies.
    b) Abdul was not very polite.
    c) Abdul thought that the gift was too cheap.

Abdul probably thought that:

    a) Tom should have brought wine or beer.
    b) Tom was not polite to bring his own food because he was the guest.
    c) Tom should have brought something for the main part of the meal, such as the salad or a vegetable.

Discussion: In the above culture puzzle, we do not know if Tom is in Saudi Arabia or if Abdul is in the U.S. Would your answers be different if the situation took place in Saudi Arabia or in the U.S.? Explain your answer.

(Answers are given at the end chapter.)

they felt insulted—their feelings were hurt
offend—make angry; cause displeasure
Moslem—a person who practices the religion of Islam

U.S. CULTURE NOTE

If you do something that upsets an American, and then later ask him or her to explain what was upsetting, many Americans will try to explain their feelings. However, other Americans will be very uncomfortable and will not know how to answer you. When this happens, it is easier and more helpful to discuss the situation with a third person.

Ways To Talk About Miscommunication _____

What can you do or say if you feel that you have upset someone from another culture?

1. You can talk directly to the person right away:

    "I'm sorry. Did I say (or do) something to upset you?"

    "I didn't mean to upset you."

    "I think we misunderstood each other."

    "In my culture it's a little different."

    "I think there's been a misunderstanding. Can you tell me if I said something that upset you?"

    "I think I upset you, but I'm not sure why."

2. You can talk directly to the person a few days later:

    "Do you have a few minutes to talk about what happened the other day?"

    "Can I talk to you about something? I've been wondering about what happened a few days ago."

    "I don't quite understand why there was a misunderstanding. Can we talk about it?"

3. You can explain the situation to a third person and ask for advice:

    "Something happened to me the other day that I don't understand. Maybe you can help me understand and tell me what you think I should do."

    "Can I ask you about something that happened with an American? I don't know the culture well enough to understand."

    "Why do you think he said that?"

    "What would you do in this situation?"

    "What would most Americans do in this situation?"

Skill Practice: Learning from Miscommunication

Read the following dialogues with a partner. Discuss the problem or the miscommunication. The student who reads the part labeled "You" will ask questions using "Ways To Talk About Miscommunication." The student who reads the part of the American will try to explain the miscommunication. (The explanations can be found at the end of the chapter.)

Variation: Do this skill practice in groups of three. Describe the situation to the third person. This person can then give advice as to what to do.

Dialogue 1: (between 2 friends)

American: "What movie would you like to see?"
You: "Oh, I don't care. You choose."
American: "No, no, you decide. You'll only be here for one more month. I can go to the movies anytime."
You: "No, no. I really don't care."
American: (looking a little *annoyed*) "Well, okay!"

Dialogue 2:   (between an American teacher and a student)

You: "Are you the teacher of this class?"
American: "Yes. Can I help you?"
You: "Yes. I am registered in this class, but I missed the first week. Can you accept me now?"
American: "What is your name?"
You: "My name is [say your name]."
American: "Oh yes. No, I'm sorry. I *dropped* you when you didn't come by the end of the first day. That's the rule. There were several people on the waiting list, and the class is full now. I'm sorry. You'll have to take it next quarter."
You: "How many people do you have in the class?"
American: "Twenty-seven. That's actually more than I'm supposed to accept. I accepted everyone who came the first day. You can register for the class next semester."
You: "Twenty-seven? What's one more? Can't you accept me?"
American: "No, I'm sorry. The class is full. If you had telephoned the school and left a message on the first day, telling me that you couldn't come, but that you wanted to take the class, I would have held a place for you. But today is the first time I've heard from you."
You: "I was very busy. I didn't have time to call. But I really want to take this class. The students say you are a very good teacher and I really want to take your class. Please accept me."
American: "I'm sorry. The class is full. I have to start class now." (The teacher turns away.)

Dialogue 3:   (between two co-workers)

American: "Did I ever show you pictures of my family?"
You: "No, let me see them."
American: "Okay." (taking out pictures) "Here is my mother and father, and here is my brother and my sister."
You: "That's your brother?"
American: "Yes. That's Tim."
You: (laughing) "He's so *skinny!*"
American: (looking upset) "Well, yeah . . ." (The American puts the photos away.)

annoyed—irritated; upset
dropped—took your name off the class list
skinny—very thin

Dialogue 4:   (in a restaurant between an American waitress or waiter and a foreign student)

> You: (Snapping fingers) "Miss! Miss!"
> American: "Yes? What do you want?" (The waitress seems angry.)
> You: "Could you bring us some more water, please?"
> American: (Still angry) "In a minute."
> You: "Thank you."
> American: (no answer.)

U.S. CULTURE NOTE

If someone does something that is culturally unfamiliar, Americans will *not* usually say, "That's okay, he's a foreigner. He is not expected to know American customs." Although the majority of Americans are European, racially and culturally, Americans include people from *every* race and cultural background. For this reason, a person who has a foreign accent, is not light-skinned, or dresses or acts a little differently from most Americans is usually not given special attention. In fact, because the population in the U.S. includes so many races and cultures, foreign visitors or immigrants are sometimes mistaken for native-born Americans.

Skill Practice: Explaining Your Cultural Point of View

Write (or tell another student) examples from your own culture for each sentence listed below.

For example, an American might explain:

"In my culture, people often accept compliments by saying, "Thank you."

"In my culture, people are expected to interrupt and ask if they don't understand something.

1. In my culture, people usually _____.
2. In my culture, people don't usually _____.
3   In my culture, people are expected to _____.
4. In my culture, people are not expected to _____.
5. In my culture, people feel uncomfortable _____.
6. In my culture, people would _____.

CROSS-CULTURAL NOTE

Mark, an American doctor, was working in a hospital in Arizona where many of the patients and nurses were American Indians. Mark said to one Indian nurse, "We need to get information on the patient in Room 62." When the nurse did not answer, Mark became annoyed and said, "Alright, I'll go get it myself!" Then the Indian nurse realized what had happened. She explained, "The information is on that table. I pointed with my lips. I guess you didn't notice. In our culture, it's okay just to point with your lips."*

---

*Adapted from an anecdote contributed by Judith Smith, in "Little Glimpses," edited by Judy Winn-Bell Olsen, Alemany Community College Center, San Francisco, 1983.

*Skill Practice: Explaining Your Cultural Point of View**

Think of some behavior that you observed recently that seemed strange or different to you. Describe or write about what you observed and explain your own cultural point of view, using the phrases listed above.

For example:

What you observed: "I saw an American teacher leaving his classroom at the end of the class. His wife came to the school to meet him. I saw them give each other a brief kiss in the hallway outside the classroom."

Your own cultural point of view: "In my culture, people usually do not kiss in public, even if they are married. In my culture, the teacher's behavior would be *shocking*."

What you observed: _____

_____

_____

_____

_____

Your own cultural point of view: _____

_____

_____

_____

CHAPTER SUMMARY

This chapter presented ways of exchanging cultural viewpoints and learning from miscommunication. The following are the most important points of the chapter:

- If you are not sure what people in another culture usually do or say in particular situations, it can be helpful to ask culture learning questions. This way, you can find out what will probably happen and you can avoid problems of miscommunication.
- It is often helpful to explain your own cultural point of view, since people don't always realize that certain behavior is cultural.
- You can use experiences of miscommunication to help you understand cultural differences.

The following are ways to exchange cultural viewpoints, along with phrases to help you use this skill.

shocking—very surprising and upsetting

**Note to the Teacher:* If you are teaching this class overseas, and your students have never been in the U.S., ask them to describe behavior they saw in a movie, or read about in a book. It does not have to be American behavior, just behavior from a culture different from their own.

Ask culture learning questions. These kinds of questions will help you prepare for cross-cultural interactions:

"Do you have a minute? I'd like to ask you a couple of questions."
"I'm not sure what Americans usually do in this situation. Can you give me your opinion?"
"Can I say . . . ?"
"Is it okay if I say . . . ?"
"Will he/she probably ask me . . . ?"
"What should you say in this situation?"
"Should I . . . ?"

Explain your cultural point of view. It is helpful to explain usual behavior in your culture. This way people can understand why you might be uncomfortable with culturally different behavior.

"In my culture, people usually/often . . ."
"In my culture, people would . . ."
"In my culture, people are expected to . . ."
"In my culture, people usually don't . . ."
"In my culture, people feel uncomfortable . . ."
"In my culture, people are not expected to . . ."

Learn from miscommunication. You can use every incident of miscommunication as an opportunity to learn about cultural differences and to prevent miscommunication of the same kind in the future.

- You can talk to the person with whom you've had the miscommunication right away.
- You can talk directly to the person a few days later.
- You can explain the situation to a third person and ask for advice.

ANSWERS TO CULTURE PUZZLES AND SKILL PRACTICES

Culture Puzzle #1

How can you explain what happened?

a) No. There is no information that says that the Americans did something wrong.
b) No. The Japanese were enjoying the singing and dancing.
c) Yes. The Japanese culture is a very group-oriented culture. When one person left (and this was probably the leader), the rest felt that they had to leave, even if they didn't want to. Americans don't usually arrive or leave in groups, so this behavior seemed strange to them. The group was trying to be polite and not stay too long at the party. They didn't realize that two hours was too short for the Americans and that the Americans were insulted by the fact that everyone left early.

Culture Puzzle #2

Tom probably thought that:

a) Possibly. Tom may think that Abdul does not like cookies, but this is not the complete answer.
b) Yes. Tom may think that Abdul was not polite. Even if he didn't like cookies, he should not have shown that he didn't like them.

c) Possibly. Tom may wonder if Abdul was expecting something more expensive. Tom doesn't know what (if anything) Saudis bring to people's houses when they are invited for a meal.

Abdul probably thought:

a) No. Abdul wouldn't be expecting wine or beer, since Moslems don't drink alcohol.
b) Yes. In Saudi culture, it is not polite to bring food when you go to someone's home for a meal. If a guest brings food, it can mean that he or she thinks that the host will not have enough food.
c) No. see b).

Skill Practice: Learning from Miscommunication

Below are examples of how an American might explain each of the situations in this Skill Practice.

Dialogue 1: "I really don't know what movie you want to see. I'd feel much better if you told me what you want to see. If I want to see a certain movie, I'd probably suggest it. For me, it sounds rude when you say, 'I don't care.' And if you don't help me choose a movie, you're putting too much responsibility on me to *guess* what you want to see."

Dialogue 2: If you ask for the same favor many times, and you don't have a good reason, you will probably just make the other person annoyed. Most Americans have a very negative reaction to begging. On the other hand, if you give a good reason, or if you apologize for your mistake, then some Americans might be sympathetic and helpful. For example, you might have a better chance of getting into the class if you said, "I'm sorry I didn't call the school and leave a message. That was my mistake. But I would really like to take this class."

Dialogue 3: For Americans, it's not polite to talk about someone that way, even if you are very close friends. Your friend might say something about his own brother, such as, "This is my brother Tim. He's kind of thin." In that case, an American might say something like "Oh, he looks like a very nice person." For most Americans, it is rude to say something like "He's very skinny," or "He's very fat," or "He's not very smart" about someone who is their close friend or relative.

Dialogue 4: For Americans, it is rude to snap your fingers to call someone. You might call a dog that way, but not a person.

Note: Answers to other exercises can be found in the separate Answer Key.

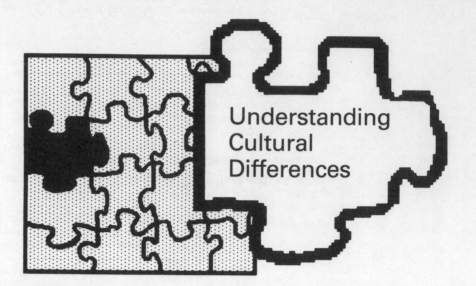

chapter 14

Understanding
Cultural
Differences

Introduction There are different ways to understand cultural differences. One way is to look at them from your own cultural point of view. This way is not always helpful, because then you would be judging the differences as if you were in your native country with people from your own culture. This would prevent you from understanding how people's behavior is, in large part, influenced by culture. When people observe cultural behavior that is different from their own, it is natural to have an opinion about it. It also is natural to make quick judgments about cultural differences. Quick judgments, however, are sometimes based on a lack of cultural information that is necessary for true understanding. This chapter shows how observing and asking about cultural differences in a nonjudgmental way can lead to a better understanding of aspects of culture that are not immediately visible.

CULTURE LEARNING QUESTIONS

1. In your native country, how do people react to immigrants or foreigners who behave differently from the majority of the people? Do people generally accept differences or do they expect foreign people to behave in the same way they do?

2. How do people in your culture react to someone who has changed because of his experiences with people from another culture? For example, if a person has spent a lot of time in another country or with people from another culture and, as a result, acts differently, how might people feel about the person's changes?*

*Note to the teacher: In a multicultural class, this question can lead to interesting discussions. Some of the topics that may come up are: (a) immigrant parents and their native-American born children: how each feels about the others' "Americanization" or resistance to American values and behavior; (b) people who choose to work for a foreign company (such as people who work for a branch or subsidiary of an American company in their own country): how they are viewed by family and friends if they begin to develop different attitudes or behaviors; (c) foreign students who return home and find that they have adopted some American values or behaviors: how they are received; (d) foreign visitors, foreign businessmen, foreign students, immigrants, or members of minority groups: how they are viewed or treated by the majority population in the students' home country.

CROSS-CULTURAL INTERACTION 14A*
Cultural Differences

Situation: Fawzi and Mubarek are students in an English language class in the U.S. They are standing outside of the school building.

Fawzi:	"Look! There's our English teacher, Mrs. McCarthy."
Mubarek:	"Who's that man she's hugging?"
Fawzi:	"That's not her husband! I've seen her husband before. That's a different man!"
Mubarek:	"Oh! How terrible! How can she hug a man in public? And he's not even her husband!"
Fawzi:	"American women *have no morals!*"

*Note: In this interaction, both people are from the same culture and are talking about someone from a different culture.

have no morals—don't care about what is right and wrong behavior

QUESTIONS AND DISCUSSION

Comprehension

Write T (true) or F (false) in the space provided.

1. _____ Fawzi and Mubarek's English teacher is not married.
2. _____ Fawzi and Mubarek are surprised to see a woman hugging a man in public.
3. _____ Mrs. McCarthy met her husband outside the school building.
4. _____ Fawzi and Mubarek like the way American women behave.

Analysis: Can You Explain?

1. Who do you think Mrs. McCarthy could be hugging?
2. Why do you think Fawzi and Mubarek said, "American women have no morals" when they saw Mrs. McCarthy hugging the man?
3. Even without knowing the specific country that the two foreign students are from, how do you think women are expected to behave in their country?

TALK ABOUT YOUR OWN LANGUAGE AND CULTURE

1. In your culture, do women ever have close friends (not including boyfriends, husbands, or relatives) who are men? Explain.
2. If you answered "Yes" to the first question, how would you answer this question? If a woman sees a close friend (a man) for the first time in a long time, how might she greet him?
3. What would you need to explain to Americans to help them understand relationships between men and women in your culture?

Summary of Cross-Cultural Interaction 14A: Cultural Differences

In this interaction, Fawzi and Mubarek are talking about their American teacher from their own cultural point of view. They are not observing her as an American would observe her; they are seeing her as they would observe a woman from their own country (in this case, an Arab country). This is a natural thing to do when in another culture. However, they are *prejudging* her behavior without knowing what is acceptable or "normal" in her culture.

CROSS-CULTURAL INTERACTION 14B*

This dialogue takes place a few days after the dialogue in Interaction 14A. It is between Mubarek and an American student named Jack.

Mubarek: "Jack, something happened the other day that I don't understand. I'd like to ask you about it."

Jack: "Sure, Mubarek. What happened?"

*The format varies here. Cross-Cultural Interaction 14B is *not* a revised version of 14A.

prejudging—judging or giving an opinion before having enough information to fully understand

Mubarek:	"Well, Fawzi and I were coming out of the building and we saw Mrs. McCarthy hugging an American man."
Jack:	"Was it her husband?"
Mubarek:	"That's what I thought, but Fawzi said he knows her husband. He said that man was someone else."
Jack:	"Oh. Well, it must have been an old friend, or maybe her brother."
Mubarek:	"Oh."
Jack:	"Yeah, or maybe he was just a good friend that she hadn't seen in a long time."
Mubarek:	"Is it okay for an American woman to hug a man who is not a relative? In public?"
Jack:	"Well, yes. Sometimes."
Mubarek:	"If she did that in my culture, she would have looked very bad. Lots of people were watching her!"
Jack:	"Well, maybe she should be more careful around foreign students, but what she did is okay in the U.S."
Mubarek:	"I see. Thanks for telling me."
Jack:	"Sure. Anytime."

Summary of Cross-Cultural Interaction 14B

In the interaction above, Mubarek describes his observations to Jack without making a judgment. This way Jack is able to give good cultural information. Mubarek learns that from an American point of view, his teacher's behavior was acceptable. Mubarek may not like the teacher's behavior and he may never accept it, but at least he understands it. He also explains to Jack that in his culture, his teacher's behavior would not be acceptable.

FOCUS ON U.S. CULTURE
Cultural Notes, Exercises, and Skill Practice

HOW MUCH DO YOU ALREADY KNOW ABOUT U.S. CULTURE?*

Write T (true) or F (false) in the space provided.

1. _____ American children have to leave their parents' home at eighteen years of age.

2. _____ It is acceptable for women teachers to wear pants while teaching in many parts of the U.S.

3. _____ When a woman smiles often at a man in a business situation, it means that she is interested in getting to know him outside of work.

4. _____ In the U.S., a president of a company would never serve coffee to a visitor; a secretary would always do it.

5. _____ In many American families, children help the parents make decisions, such as where to go on family vacations.

*Note to the teacher and student: This chapter contains a variety of situations involving cultural differences, rather than one content or skill area. These questions reflect some of the chapter content which illustrates cultural differences.

SECTION 1. OBSERVING CULTURAL BEHAVIOR

Read the following conversation between two Latin American women who now live in the U.S.

Rafaela: "I was talking to my American neighbor yesterday, and she told me that her 20-year-old daughter is moving into her own apartment next month. I asked her why her daughter didn't plan to live at home until she got married, and my neighbor said, 'Oh, no, my daughter's ready to be *on her own*.' I thought my neighbor and her husband really loved their daughter, but I guess maybe they don't. It seems like they want her to leave."

Annalilia: "One of the American women at work told me that her son hasn't lived at home since he graduated from college. She says she and her husband were happy he moved out. She said they miss him, but they also enjoy having some peace and quiet and *leading their own lives*."

Rafaela: "Some things about this country are really terrible. People here don't care about their children very much."

Annalilia: "I feel so sorry for them!"

Exercise: Making Observations

Look at the conversation between Rafaela and Annalilia repeated below. This time, their comments have been separated into two columns. Read the conversation again and discuss the differences between the comments in column A, and the comments in column B.

A	*B*
Rafaela: "I was talking to my American neighbor yesterday, and she told me that her 20-year-old daughter is moving into her own apartment next month. I asked her why her daughter didn't plan to live at home until she got married, and she said, 'Oh, no, my daughter's ready to be on her own.'"	
	"I thought my neighbor and her husband really loved their daughter, but I guess maybe they don't. It seems like they want her to leave."
Annalilia: "One of the American women at work told me that her son hasn't lived at home since he graduated from college. She says she and her husband were happy he moved out. She said they miss him, but they	

on her own—independent, making her own decisions, having a job and paying for her own food, house and clothes

leading their own lives—living independently; not being responsible for others' day-to-day lives

also enjoy having some peace and
quiet and leading their own lives."

Rafaela: "Some things about this
country are really terrible. People
don't care about their children very
much."

(Before you read the following summary, discuss the differences between the
comments in column A and in column B.)

Summary: The comments in Column A are **observations.** The comments in col-
umn B are **judgments.** Observations are things we see, hear, and know to be true.
Judgments are reactions or feelings about what we observe. When we observe
things about another culture, it is easy to make judgments that are incorrect.
Incorrect judgments can lead to cross-cultural miscommunication and *stereotypes.*
Before continuing this summary, read the next U.S. Culture Note, which gives
information that can help explain the American behavior that the two Latin
American women heard about.

U.S. CULTURE NOTE

Americans *value* independence. Most Americans feel that it is very important
for each person to be able to take care of himself. American parents, like
parents anywhere, love their children, but teach them to be independent at a
very early age. Many parents feel that when grown children live on their own,
they learn the independence necessary to become full adults. They also learn
to *take financial responsibility* for themselves. Usually (unless there are money
problems), children move out of the parents' house by age twenty or twenty-
two. At this age, they may begin working full time, they may get married, or
they may go away to school. An adult son or daughter who still lives at home
may be considered *too dependent.* If parents *pressure* their grown children to
continue living at home, people might say that they are not allowing their
children to *grow up.* Many American parents feel that they have raised their
children well when the children become independent.

Rafaela and Annalilia are making their judgments as if the Americans were
living in their own country. In other words, if a child in Latin America left home
at the age of eighteen, this would be considered very bad. There, children tend to
depend on their parents longer than American (U.S.) children do. The two Latin
American women don't realize that American parents miss their children when
they move away, and look forward to seeing their children often. Although sometimes children move to another city or state, many prefer to live in the same town

---

stereotypes—general descriptions of a group of people, often negative, that don't allow for differences
    among individuals
value—feel that something is very good and very important
take financial responsibility—pay one's own bills and earn one's own salary (sometimes grown children
    who live at home pay their parents rent money if they are working)
too dependent—not able to make decisions or take care of oneself
pressure—encourage someone very strongly to do something, make that person feel bad or guilty for
    not doing something
grow up—become mature adults

or near their parents' town, especially when there are grandchildren. Often older parents go to live with or near their children so that the children can help to take care of them in their old age.

Exercise: Observations or Judgments?

Look at the definitions of observations and judgments again. Then read the sentences below. Mark the observations with an (O) and the judgments with a (J). The first one is done for you.

Observations: Things we see, hear, and know to be true. They are not opinions, reactions, or personal feelings.

Judgments: Reactions and feelings about what we observe.

1. __J__   "She has no sense of humor. She doesn't laugh at things that are funny."
2. _____   "He sighed and looked tired."
3. _____   "They are not very polite."
4. _____   "She didn't like my cooking. She didn't ask for a second serving of anything."
5. _____   "I didn't receive a thank-you note."
6. _____   "She is angry because she is talking loudly."
7. _____   "She smiled."
8. _____   "He doesn't want to be friends with me."
9. _____   "They don't know how to behave at a wedding!"
10. _____   "He's *hiding something* because he is not showing his feelings.

(Answers are given at the end of the chapter.)

hiding something—not telling the truth; not telling everything

It is important to separate observations from judgments when you are learning about another culture. If you find yourself making a judgment (and this is very natural), you can ask yourself the following questions:

"Do I have enough information to make a correct judgment about the behavior that I'm observing?"

"Do I really understand the point of view of the people in that culture or am I basing my judgment on my own cultural beliefs?"

Exercise: Observing Nonverbal Behavior

It is very easy to make judgments about other people's nonverbal behavior when it is different from your own. Many incidents of cross-cultural miscommunication are due to people's incorrect judgments of others' nonverbal behavior. The following are statements about nonverbal behavior. Mark the observations with an (O) and the judgments with a (J) as you did in the previous exercise. The first one is done for you.

1. __J__ "That woman is *aggressive* because she always stands very close to men when she is talking to them."
2. _____ "The two men hugged each other when they met at the airport."
3. _____ "The woman stood three feet away from the man."
4. _____ "She is very *superficial.* She smiles too much."
5. _____ "That husband and wife don't love each other anymore because they didn't hug or kiss each other when he left on a business trip."
6. _____ "The two women walked *arm in arm* along the street."
7. _____ "The father does not love his son because he just shook hands with him when saying goodbye instead of hugging him."
8. _____ "She patted the children on the head."

(Answers are given at the end of the chapter.)

Exercise: Observing without Judging

In the first conversation below, Mari and Nabi are observing and judging at the same time. In the second conversation, Mari is talking to an American about what she observed and is not making judgments. Read the two conversations and discuss your reactions to each. Have you heard people making these sorts of observations about Americans?

(Mari and Nabi are students at a university in their own country. Mari is taking an English class taught by a new American teacher.)

Mari: "That American teacher, Miss Hamilton, really makes me uncomfortable!"

Nabi: "I've heard other students talk about her. What does she do?"

Mari: "She talks to us as if we were her close friends. Can you believe she really wants us to call her by her first name? And sometimes she comes to class wearing pants."

aggressive—overly active; pushing; wanting to dominate or be too powerful
superficial—not sincere; not a deep person
arm in arm—one person's arm is bent around the other person's arm while they are walking close
  together

Nabi: "How strange."

Mari: "And she wears her hair loose, like a teenager! I think she's really *unprofessional.*"

Nabi: "Yeah. I wonder why the college hired her?"

In this next conversation, Mari is discussing her observations with an American friend, Helen. The questions in italics are examples of the types of questions one can ask to get information about another person's culture.

Mari: "Miss Hamilton makes me uncomfortable. She wants us to call her by her first name, and she dresses like a student. *Is that what American teachers usually do?*"

Helen: "Well, yes. Some teachers are very casual."

Mari: "Really? *You feel it's okay for her to act that way?*"

Helen: "Sure. Is she young?"

Mari: "Yes. I think she's about 30."

Helen: "Well, a lot of American teachers, especially younger ones, like to have an informal, friendly relationship with their students."

Mari: "In my culture, we don't respect a teacher who acts like that. *How do most Americans feel?*"

Helen: "Well, I guess that older students like a teacher to act more formally. Some teachers always wear suits and are always called 'Mr.' or 'Mrs.' It depends. I feel comfortable with a more informal teacher. I feel I can ask questions more easily. I feel that I can learn more."

---

unprofessional—not acting in a way that is proper on the job

U.S. CULTURE NOTE

Americans are often criticized for being too informal. In many cultures a person who acts informally, especially in business and in teaching relationships, is considered unprofessional or not serious. Many Americans act informally to show that they trust or feel comfortable with the person to whom they are talking. Since trust is important in good business and teaching relationships, many Americans use informal language and dress informally to help everyone feel comfortable quickly. However, what makes people in one culture feel comfortable can make people feel uncomfortable in another culture.

SECTION 2. ASKING WITHOUT JUDGING

If you want to learn something about what you've observed, it is necessary to separate observations from judgments. Then you can decide:

> "Who can best answer my questions?"
> "What kind of questions are best to ask?"

U.S. CULTURE NOTE

Any two Americans may explain cultural behavior differently. For this reason, it is good to ask questions of more than one person. Remember that the Americans you ask may have never thought about your questions before. An American who has spent a lot of time with people from different cultures can often answer questions better than someone who has had little experience with people from different cultures.

In addition to asking questions of the right person, you will get better information if you ask questions in a **nonjudgmental** way. This means that you ask questions without judging the behavior about which you are asking. The following example shows a question asked in a judgmental and nonjudgmental way:

Judgmental question:

"Why don't some American parents want their children to live with them once they are eighteen? Don't they love their children?"

The next question shows how the judgment is taken out of the question. It is a *nonjudgmental* question:

Nonjudgmental question:

"I've heard that some American children leave their parents' home at the age of eighteen. Can you explain the reason for this? Things are different in my country."

CULTURE PUZZLES

Background: Janice, an American businesswoman, and Maya, a businesswoman from Mexico, both work for the same company. Maya has just come to the U.S. to work in the American office of her company. Below are several situations involving Janice and Maya.

In the following culture puzzles, circle the letter next to the nonjudgmental questions that will help Maya get the most helpful answers. After you choose the best question for each situation, read the U.S. Culture Note that explains the American behavior.

Situation 1:* Maya is introduced to Janice. Maya notices that Janice often smiles as she talks to the men and women in the company. In Maya's culture, a woman who smiles frequently when she talks to men is probably *flirting*. Maya asks a co-worker from her own culture:

a) "Janice is not a good woman, is she?"
b) "Why do American women flirt with strange men?"
c) "What does it mean when an American woman smiles at a man?"

U.S. CULTURE NOTE

Americans, especially American women, smile more than people from many other cultures. This smile is usually just a sign of friendliness.

---

*Adapted from Genelle Morain, 'The Cultural Component of the Methods Course,' from *Designs for Foreign Language Teacher Education,* in 'Little Glimpses,' edited by Judy Winn-Bell Olsen, Alemany Community College, 1983.

flirting—acting playful and sexually encouraging.

Situation 2: Maya and Janice are having lunch. Maya cuts her hand while she is opening a soft drink can. She says, "Oh, that hurts!" Janice says, "I'm sorry! Are you all right?" Later Maya says to a friend from her country:

a) "Why do Americans act like any problem is their fault?"
b) "Do Americans feel that it is their fault when someone gets hurt using an American product?"
c) "When I cut my hand, Janice said, 'I'm sorry.' It wasn't *her* fault. Do most Americans apologize when it's not their fault?"

U.S. CULTURE NOTE

Some Americans say, "I'm sorry" if someone tells them sad news or is hurt. The American means, "I'm sorry about what happened. I feel sympathy for you." In this case, "I'm sorry" is not an apology.

Situation 3: Maya sees the president of her company (an American) serve some coffee to a visitor. In her country, a company president would always ask a secretary to do things like that. She asks Janice:

a) "I saw the company president serve coffee to a visitor. For me, that was very unusual. Does that seem unusual to you?"
b) "Don't American secretaries like to take care of their bosses?"
c) "Is the President's secretary sick?"

U.S. CULTURE NOTE

Recently the responsibilities of American secretaries have changed. Now, in some companies, secretaries do not do things such as serving coffee. Instead, they do the work that they are trained to do, such as typing, filing, answering phones, and writing letters.

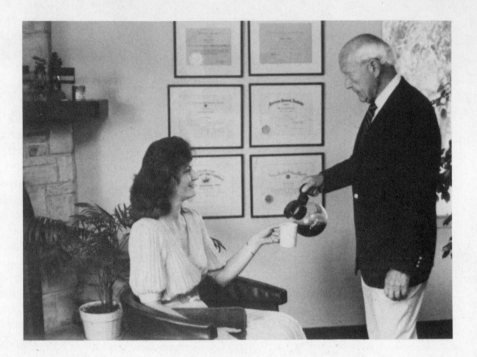

Situation 4:* Maya visits Janice's house one Saturday afternoon. She is listening to a conversation the family is having. Janice, her husband and the children are discussing where to go for their summer holiday. Janice wants to go to New York City, but the children want to go camping instead. Janice listens carefully to the children's reasons. Later, Maya asks another American:

a) "Why do American children have so much power in the American family?"

b) "Why do American parents let their children tell them what to do?"

c) "Do Americans often let their children help decide where the family will go on vacation?"

U.S. CULTURE NOTE

Americans often encourage their children to express and defend their opinions, and to be included in family decisions. Parents feel this helps the children to learn to express their ideas clearly.

*Adapted from Allison Lanier, 'Foreign Nationals in Your Corporate Nest,' *International Business*, 1979. Contributed by V. Lynn Taylor to 'Little Glimpses,' edited by Judy Winn-Bell Olsen, Alemany Community College 1983.

Ways To Ask Nonjudgmental Questions

"Do most Americans feel it's okay if [a woman teacher wears pants to class]?"

"How do most Americans feel about that?"

"How do you feel about what he did?"

"For me, what he/she did was unusual. How about you?"

"What does it mean when [an American teacher sits on a student's desk]?"

"Is that what Americans usually do?"

"Is it okay for someone to do that in the U.S.?"

Skill Practice: Asking Nonjudgmental Questions

Each of the following situations describes how one American acted. Imagine that you observed each situation

1. Read the situations and then, using the preceding list of phrases, ask your teacher questions about them. (The questions should be nonjudgmental and should help the teacher understand the situation.*)
2. After your teacher has answered your questions, work with another student and practice asking and answering questions about these situations.

Situation 1: You were invited to visit an American friend and her new baby. You took a gift for the baby. You were very surprised when your friend opened the gift right away and showed it to her family. You felt embarrassed. In your culture, people say, "Thank you" to a person for bringing a gift, but they do not open the gift right away, as this would be considered rude.

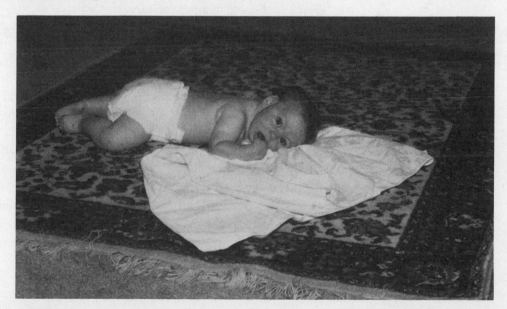

**Note to the teacher:* In this Skill Practice, the description of each situation includes a judgmental reaction. One purpose of the exercise is to see if the students can avoid making these judgmental remarks when they ask questions about these situations. The other purpose of the exercise is to see if students can give enough information about what they saw so that you can give a helpful answer. Try to answer the exact question that the student asks. Don't be *too* helpful. For example, in Situation 1, if a student asks you, "Why do Americans open presents right away?" you might just say, "Why not? What do you mean?" and wait for them to explain more. See the answers at the end of the chapter for a guide to answering your students' questions about each description.

Situation 2: Your boss questioned you in front of some other workers about a mistake you made. You were very embarrassed. You felt he should have been more sensitive.

Situation 3: (Two women) When you went for a walk with your friend, you put your arm through hers the way any two women would do in your culture, as a sign of friendship. She pulled away, and has not been friendly since then.

Situation 4: You invited an American friend to your house for dinner. At the last minute he called and said that he couldn't come. Later you found out that he had gone out on a date with his girlfriend that night.

(A discussion of this Skill Practice is at the end of the chapter.)

SECTION 3. LOOKING AT YOUR OWN EXPERIENCES

When you live in a different country or interact with people from another culture, you may sometimes feel pressure to behave or act in a way that is new for you. Sometimes you will feel comfortable making changes in your behavior or in your style of communicating. Other times you will feel uncomfortable and you may think to yourself, "No, I can't (or don't want to) do this. This is not me." Making decisions about what you can or can't do is part of *adapting* to a new culture. In the process of making these decisions, you may feel many *ups and downs*. You may change your mind a number of times about the way you think you should act in the new culture.

The following questions are to think about, write about, or discuss with other students and the teacher. The questions will help you understand some of your own experiences in a new culture.

1. How do I feel about the people from this culture?
    How did I feel a year ago?
    Do I feel differently now?
    If "yes," what do I feel differently about and why?
2. Do people expect me to behave or communicate in ways that are uncomfortable for me? If "yes," give examples.
    What new ways of communicating or behaving can I accept?
    What new ways *can't* I accept?
3. Do I know someone who I can talk to about the new culture?
    What advice or information has this person given me?
4. Have my feelings about my own culture changed? If so, how?
    What do I understand about my own culture that I didn't understand before?

Cross-Cultural Exercise: Adapting Behavior

The following dialogue is between an older American employee, Sam, and his younger Chinese supervisor, Son. The dialogue takes place in a company in the U.S. Son is unable to act in a way that his employee, Sam, wants him to act. Sam expects Son to treat him as an American supervisor would. Read the dialogue and answer the questions following it. Then read the summary.

---

adapting—changing in order to be able to live in and adjust to a new situation or environment
ups and downs—feelings of happiness and sadness

Sam: "Well, how am I doing?"

Son: (Thinking, "Sam makes a lot of mistakes, but I don't want him to feel discouraged, so I won't tell him.")

"Just fine. You're doing just fine. You learn very quickly."

Sam: (Thinking, "Why is he complimenting me? I don't think I'm doing a very good job.")

"How about this part? Is this okay?"

Son: (Thinking, "It's hard for me to say this! If he thinks he made a mistake, why doesn't he say so?")

"Oh, yes . . well, . . . um, I think maybe you need to work ah . . . a little more slowly . . . ah . . . I'm sorry, I don't mean to criticize . . . "

Sam: (Thinking, "Why is he afraid to criticize me?")

"No, no, I want to know what needs improvement. I didn't do this part correctly, did I?"

Son: (Thinking, "You're right. You did it all wrong.")

"Oh, I didn't mean that. Really your work is fine."

(He wonders, "What does he want me to say?")

Questions:

- What exactly does Sam want Son to do?
- What is Sam doing that makes Son uncomfortable?
- Should Sam or Son adapt his behavior in any way? Explain.

Summary:

In the dialogue above, Sam expects Son to be a typical American supervisor. He expects Son to criticize his work if necessary, and tell him how to do better. Son has lived in the U.S. for a long time. He speaks English very well and has a good job. He likes his job, and the opportunities he has in the U.S. Sometimes, however, he feels, that he just can't be like an American supervisor. He can't criticize or be completely honest when someone's work is not good. He is afraid of hurting people's feelings. Sometimes he thinks, "I just *can't* do what Americans want me to do. It doesn't feel natural to me."

Cross-Cultural Exercise: Looking at Your Own Experiences

Look at the following list of situations. Think about your own experiences in the U.S. or with Americans abroad. For the situations that apply, answer the following questions:

- Have you been in any of the situations listed below?
- If so, did you do exactly what you would with someone from your own culture?
- If you changed your behavior in order to communicate effectively with Americans, what did you do?
- How did you deal with situations in which there was a cultural misunderstanding or miscommunication?

Note: In answering the above questions, either orally or in writing, you will be reviewing much of the cultural information presented in this book. At the same time, you will be looking at and evaluating your own cross-cultural experiences and progress.

Addressing People

1. Your teacher or supervisor at work wanted you to use his or her first name.
2. You didn't know how to address a woman because you weren't sure if she was married or not.
3. You were introduced to a woman and you weren't sure whether you should shake hands or not.
4. You were at a party or with a group of people and nobody introduced you to anyone else.

Complimenting and Showing Appreciation

1. Someone you didn't know very well complimented you.
2. A teacher or supervisor complimented you and you felt embarrassed.
3. You brought a gift to your supervisor who said, "I'm sorry. I'm not allowed to accept gifts from employees."
4. Someone brought you a gift and waited for you to open it right away.

Expressing Emotion

1. You were upset about something and an American asked you, "What's wrong?"
2. An American said or did something that made you very angry.
3. You tried to communicate something nonverbally to an American (for example, facially or with silence), but he or she did not seem to understand.

Showing that You Understand

1. You didn't understand a word that someone was using.
2. You weren't sure that you understood someone's explanation.
3. A teacher or a supervisor asked you in a group, "Do you understand?"

Guiding the Conversation

1. Someone said something that was not correct.
2. Someone interrupted you when you were not finished speaking.
3. You wanted to interrupt someone who was speaking.

Interacting in a Group

1. Two Americans were speaking quickly to each other in front of you and you couldn't understand them.
2. You wanted to say something at a meeting or in a group discussion, but people had already moved on to another topic.
3. You had an idea or a suggestion at a meeting.

Keeping the Conversation Moving

1. You were talking to someone and there was an uncomfortable silence in the conversation.
2. You felt that an American was asking too many questions.
3. Someone you didn't know well wanted to start a conversation with you.
4. You wanted to start a conversation with someone you didn't know well.

Choosing Conversation Topics

1. An American asked you a question about something that you didn't feel comfortable talking about.
2. You asked an American about something that he or she did not want to talk about.

Making the First Move

1. Someone you didn't know very well (who you wanted to get to know) kept talking about getting together with you, but she never really extended a definite invitation.
2. You were in the neighborhood of someone you wanted to visit. You hadn't called ahead of time, but you decided to drop by anyway.
3. An American invited you to a party and you knew you would not be able to go.

Exchanging Viewpoints

1. You did not understand why an American acted in a certain way and you wanted an explanation of the behavior.
2. You thought that you said or did something that an American misunderstood.

Understanding Cultural Differences

1. You saw or heard about something that would be considered very bad in your culture.
2. An American expected you to do something that you didn't want to do.
3. Someone from your own culture criticized you for adapting to certain aspects of American culture and communication style.
4. Someone from your own culture (with little experience with Americans) asked you for advice that would help him understand Americans.

CHAPTER SUMMARY

This chapter, using many specific examples, gave a perspective on understanding cultural differences. Some of the skills, ideas, and phrases that will help you understand cultural differences are listed here.

Observing cultural behavior.   Ask yourself these questions:

> "Do I have enough information to make correct judgments about the behavior I'm observing?"
>
> "Do I really understand the point of view of the people in the different culture, or am I basing my judgments on my own cultural beliefs?"

Asking without judging.   Ask these types of questions:

> "Do most Americans feel it's okay if . . . ?"
>
> "How do you feel about what he/she did?"
>
> "For me, what he did was unusual. How about you?"
>
> "What does it mean when . . . ?"
>
> "Is that what Americans usually do?"
>
> "Is it okay for someone to do that in the U.S.?"

Looking at your own experiences. Evaluate how comfortable you feel with people from the different culture and how you are adapting to another way of communicating. Thinking about the following questions can be helpful:

> "How do I feel about the people from this culture?"
>
> "How did I feel a year ago?"
>
> "Do I feel differently now? If yes, why?"
>
> "Do people expect me to behave or communicate in ways that are uncomfortable for me?"
>
> "What new ways of communicating can I and *can't* I accept?"
>
> "Do I know someone who can give me advice from this culture?"
>
> "How have my feelings about my own culture changed?"

ANSWERS TO EXERCISES, CULTURE PUZZLES AND SKILL PRACTICE IN CHAPTER 14

Exercise: Observations or Judgments?

1.	J	6.	J
2.	O	7.	O
3.	J	8.	J
4.	J	9.	J
5.	O	10.	J

Cross-Cultural Exercise: Observing Nonverbal Behavior

1.	J	5.	J
2.	O	6.	O
3.	O	7.	J
4.	J	8.	O

Culture Puzzles

1. a) and b) No. Both these questions include strong judgments. Also, Maya does not say exactly what behavior caused her to make negative judgments about Janice. Therefore, Maya's friend cannot give Maka a helpful answer.

   c) Yes. This question can help Maya to get a good cultural explanation of Janice's behavior. Maya will probably have to add more information, such as, "The American woman smiled a lot when she was talking to Jack today."

2. a) No. This statement is very judgmental, and Maya's friend will not know what she is referring to.

   b) No. Maya is making a judgment, and she is not describing the particular situation that she observed.

   c) Yes. Maya describes the situation and asks if Janice's behavior is typical.

3. a) Yes. This tells Janice the situation, and explains Maya's point of view.

   b) No. This question does not explain the situation. In addition, Maya has already made a judgment.

   c) No. This question does not explain the situation at all.

4. a) and b) No. Maya is already making a strong judgment based on her own cultural point of view.

   c) Yes. This question does not contain a judgment and asks for information.

Skill Practice: Asking Nonjudgmental Questions

1. Your friend's behavior is customary. Americans usually like to see the reaction of the person who received their gift. An exception is wedding gifts, which may be opened during the wedding reception or party after the ceremony, or may be taken home and opened later. Sometimes guests send or take a gift to the parents' house a few days before the wedding. In most situations, an American will be disappointed if you do *not* immediately open a gift that he or she gives you.

2. Compared to people in some cultures, Americans are not as concerned about being criticized in front of other people. In a situation like this, it is appropriate to say to your boss, "Can we discuss this in private?"

3. For many American women, walking arm in arm is not usual. It is probably best to watch to see what a particular person does with other Americans. It is also okay to ask, "In my country, women who are good friends sometimes walk arm in arm. How about here?"

4. The American man was rude. He should not have cancelled his plans with you unless he was sick, or something else very important had happened. Most Americans would be upset by his behavior. This is an example of a situation which is not really cultural. Sometimes you will observe behavior that is not typical behavior of people from that culture. By asking someone from that culture, you can find out if what you observed was an example of cultural behavior or not.

Note: Answers to other exercises can be found in the separate Answer Key.

Reading Text and Activities

Contents:

Reading Preview Activities
Reading Outline
Outline Questions
Vocabulary
Reading Preview Suggestions
Reading Text

Post-Reading Activities
Reading Comprehension
Vocabulary Exercises
Going Beyond the Reading

READING TEXT: CULTURE LEARNING
Reading Preview Activities

Reading Outline   Read the outline of the reading text and discuss the questions following it.

Part I. U.S. Culture

   A. Culture is knowledge, beliefs, and behavior, shared by a group of people.
   B. There are many races and cultures in America.
   C. We can talk of "mainstream" U.S. culture.
   D. Many people are not fully aware of their own culture and how it influences them.
   E. Learning American culture is a challenge because:
      1. There are many different kinds of people in the U.S.
      2. Culture learning takes time, just as learning language does.

Part II. Learning American Culture

   A. It is difficult to decide what is personal behavior and what is typical American behavior.

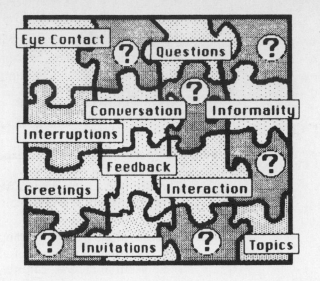

B. Culture clues—examples of behavior—can help you understand what is typical of many Americans.

C. You can use experiences of miscommunication to help you learn about another culture.

Part III. Is This Really American Culture?

A. Some values describe what people *think* their culture is like.

B. How can you learn real American culture?
   1. Ask several people the same questions.
   2. What is true for one group of Americans may not be true for another group.

C. Americans generally do not have a cross-cultural perspective on U.S. culture. That is, they do not know how most Americans interact with people from different cultures.

Part IV. Avoiding Cultural Stereotypes

A. A stereotype, positive or negative, describes a group of people without looking at individual differences between people.

B. Although it is difficult to make generalizations about Americans, it is possible.

Part V. Culture Fatigue

A. Culture learning is hard work, and can lead to culture fatigue.

B. When you are feeling culture fatigue, you may find yourself:
   1. looking for exact answers about what to do and what not to do.
   2. criticizing the new culture.

C. As you adapt to American culture and interaction with Americans, you will probably decide to accept some aspects of the culture and not others.

Conclusion

A. You do not have to change completely to adapt to another culture.

B. Culture learning is:
1. gaining knowledge and skills
2. adapting in a way that is possible for *you* to do.
C. Culture learning is a gain, not a loss.

OUTLINE QUESTIONS

Based on the outline and your own experiences, answer the following questions:

1. The first part of the reading states that it is not possible to say that all Americans share the same culture. What are some of the different cultures in America?
2. The second part of the reading discusses learning from miscommunication. Describe an example of miscommunication that you have had with someone from another culture.
3. The third part of the reading talks about values that people *think* describe their culture. What are some values of your culture that are not always seen in daily behavior?
4. The fourth part of the reading discusses cultural stereotypes. What are some stereotypes that people have about your culture? How are these stereotypes incorrect?
5. In the fifth part of the reading, the authors say that sometimes you may want to criticize American culture. Do you have any criticisms? Are there some American behaviors or beliefs that you disagree with? Explain your answer.

VOCABULARY

Following is a list of vocabulary from the reading text in Unit IV, *Culture Learning*. To help you with pronunciation, each word is divided into syllables. The stressed syllable is marked with an accent mark ('). The words are grouped by part of speech (nouns, verbs, etc.) in the order in which they appear in the reading. *Practice saying these words after your teacher says them*. Each word is glossed (defined) at the bottom of the page the first time it appears in the reading. The definition gives the meaning of the word *as it is used in the reading*. These words also appear in post-reading activities.

PART I

Nouns
ATTITUDES at'-ti-tudes
VALUES val'-ues
CHALLENGE chal'-lenge
TASK task

Adjectives
ACCURATE ac'-cu-rate
MAINSTREAM main'-stream
CONSCIOUS con'-scious

Adverbs
FULLY ful'-ly

PART II

Nouns
CLUES clues
DISCOMFORT dis-com'-fort

Verbs
RESERVED re-served'
TREAT treat
SUSPECT sus-pect'

Adjectives
PERSONAL per'-son-al
TYPICAL typ'-i-cal
ONE ANOTHER'S one' an-oth'-ers
VALUABLE val'-u-a-ble

Two-word Verbs/Idioms
TEND TO tend' to
GONE WRONG gone wrong'

PART III

Nouns
EQUALITY   e-qual'-i-ty
RIGHTS   rights
PERSPECTIVE   per-spec'-tive
DIRECTNESS   di-rect'-ness

Adjectives
IDEAL   i-deal'
FRANK   frank

Adverbs
RARELY   rare'-ly

PART IV

Nouns
OVERGENERALIZATIONS   o'-ver
 gen-er-al-i-za'-tions
STEREOTYPES   ster'-e-o-types

Verbs
CONCLUDE   con-clude'

Adjectives
REGIONAL   re'-gion-al

Adverbs
FREQUENTLY   fre'-quent-ly

PART V

Nouns
JIGSAW PUZZLE   jig'-saw puzzle

Verbs
ADAPT   a-dapt'
EXAGGERATE   ex-ag'-ger-ate
ADMIRE   ad-mire'

Adjectives
UNWILLING   un-will'-ing

Adverbs
PARTIALLY   par'-tial-ly

Idioms
IT DEPENDS   it de-pends'
LET OFF STEAM   let' off' steam'
KEEP IN MIND   keep' in mind'

CONCLUSION

Nouns
CULTURAL IDENTITY   cul'-tu-ral i-den'-ti-ty

Reading Preview Suggestions

Before you begin to read the text, *Culture Learning,* do the following:

1. Read the titles of each part (Parts I, II, III, IV and V).
2. Read the subheadings within each part of the reading.
3. Read the sentences in the margin.
4. Read the first sentence of each paragraph.
5. Read the key concepts at the end of each part.
6. Read the glosses (definitions) at the bottom of the page.

READING TEXT: CULTURE LEARNING

Part I. U.S. Culture

Culture is shared knowledge.

1. What is culture? Culture is knowledge, beliefs, and behavior shared by a group of people. People use cultural knowledge and beliefs to understand their own experience and to guide their own actions and behavior. When people share a culture, this generally means that they have a shared language and communication style as well as shared customs, beliefs, *attitudes,* and *values.* This shared knowledge is learned and is passed on from generation to generation.

attitudes—what people think or feel about something
values—what people consider important, right, or good

There are many cultures in the U.S.

2. **A culture of cultures.** It is not possible to say that all Americans share the same culture. It is more *accurate* to speak about the many cultures of Americans. If you look at the following table, you can see why the U.S. is often described as a "culture of cultures."

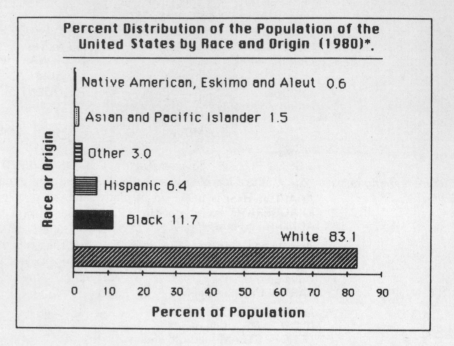

Percent Distribution of the Population of the United States by Race and Origin (1980)*.

Native American, Eskimo and Aleut 0.6
Asian and Pacific Islander 1.5
Other 3.0
Hispanic 6.4
Black 11.7
White 83.1

(y-axis: Race or Origin)
(x-axis: Percent of Population, 0 10 20 30 40 50 60 70 80 90)

*SOURCE: *1980 Census of Population,* volume 1. U.S. Department of Commerce, 1983.

Note: This information is from the 1980 U.S. census. People were asked to identify their own race. The category "White" includes people who identified themselves as White, as well as persons who identified themselves as Canadian, German, Italian, Lebanese, Polish, and so on. The category "Black" includes people who called themselves Black, as well as people who identified themselves as Jamaican, Black Puerto Rican, West Indian, Haitian, or Nigerian. The category "Asian and Pacific Islander" includes persons who identified themselves as Japanese, Chinese, Filipino, Korean, Vietnamese, Asian Indian, Hawaiian, or Samoan. Persons of Spanish origin form an important cultural group in the United States. The category "Spanish origin" includes persons who identified themselvs as Cuban, Puerto Rican, Mexican, Dominican, or other Spanish origin. The numbers add up to more than 100% because persons of Spanish origin are also included in other racial groupings.

There is a 'mainstream' U.S. culture shared by many Americans.

3. It is clear that not all Americans are blonde and blue-eyed. Yet, even though it is not possible to speak of a single American culture, Americans themselves do talk about a *"mainstream"* U.S. culture that is shared by a majority of Americans.

Americans are not fully aware of their cultures.

4. **"Submerged" culture.** In Unit I of this book, you read that culture is like an iceberg in that much of it is hidden from sight. As with people in most cultures, most Americans are not *fully* aware of their cultures. That is, their cultural knowledge is "submerged." They may not be fully *conscious* of their beliefs and their ways of thinking and communicating. They may not realize how their culture influences them.

accurate—correct; exact; with no errors

mainstream U.S. culture—customs, beliefs, and values shared by a majority of Americans. Mainstream U.S. culture is somewhat based on Northern European culture

fully—completely

conscious—aware; thinking about

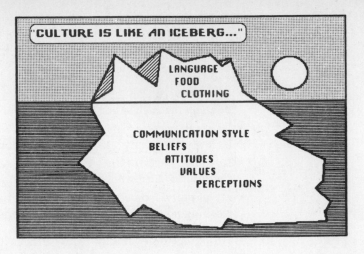

Culture learning takes time.

5. **Culture learning is a challenge.** Learning American culture is a *challenge*. The U.S. is made up of many kinds of people. People are not completely aware of their own culture and won't always be able to explain it to you. Culture learning takes time and patience, just as language learning does. When you first started learning English, you probably didn't expect to become fluent in a few weeks or months. Likewise, culture learning takes months and even years. Understanding how different groups of people think and behave is a challenging *task*.

Key Concepts in PART I _____

Culture: Culture includes communication style, customs, beliefs, attitudes, and values. People who share a culture use this knowledge to guide their own actions.

A culture of cultures: There are many different cultures in the United States. For this reason, America is often described as "a culture of cultures."

Mainstream U.S. culture: Although there are many American cultures, Americans do share certain customs, beliefs, values, and other aspects of culture. This general, shared U.S. culture is often called "mainstream" culture.

Culture learning: Just as we speak of language learning, we can also speak of culture learning. Both language learning and culture learning take time.

_____

Part II. Learning American Culture

Look for cultural clues to support your observations.

6. *Cultural clues.* Every person is influenced by his or her own culture, and every person has a unique personality. That is, not everything a person does is cultural. When you observe Americans and want to understand their behavior, you may sometimes have to ask yourself, "Is this *personal behavior,* or is it cultural? Is this just the way this one person usually acts, or is this *typical* American behavior?" It is often very difficult to answer these questions. You will usually need to meet several Americans before answering. Look for cultural *clues* which will help you to decide if the specific behavior you observed is an example of typical American behavior. For

challenge—something difficult that you must face
task—job; specific work to do
personal behavior—behavior of one person, not necessarily usual behavior of all people in this culture
typical—common or usual
clues—facts or ideas that help us understand something or answer a question

example, your teacher jokes with you and sometimes sits on his or her desk during class. You think, "Americans are often informal." Before you decide that this is true, look for other clues. Maybe you will observe Americans acting in the following cultural ways:

- In a conversation, speakers use *one another's* first name, even when they don't know each other well.
- In a business meeting, the boss doesn't always sit in the same place; a seat isn't always *reserved* for the most important person.
- In some parts of the U.S., people *tend to* touch one another on the shoulder or arm while speaking.
- At a party, someone might tell his or her employee, "Hey, it's after working hours. Don't *treat* me like your boss!"

By looking for everyday clues such as these, you can decide if your first observation was of typical American behavior, or just of personal behavior not necessarily typical of most Americans. Then you can safely say, "Americans are often informal."

Miscommunication can be an opportunity for culture learning.

7. **Learning from miscommunication.**   Careful observation can give you *valuable* cultural clues. A second way to learn American culture is through miscommunication or misunderstanding. That is, if you feel that something has *gone wrong* in an interaction with an American, you may have found an opportunity for culture learning. The following is an example of learning from cultural miscommunication.

> Minh is a young Vietnamese man living in California. Jim, an American friend, is going to meet Minh in the evening at Minh's house. They have decided to meet after dinner, at eight o'clock. When Jim arrives at Minh's house, Minh greets him at the door with, "Hi, Jim. Have you eaten yet?" Jim appears to be confused and a little uncomfortable. He doesn't directly answer Minh's question.

8. In this situation, Minh noticed Jim's *discomfort,* but he didn't understand it. This was an opportunity for learning something about American culture. For Minh, as a Vietnamese, "Have you eaten yet?" is a common way to greet someone. For Jim, and for many Americans, this is not a greeting and sounds unusual. Jim was especially confused since he and Minh had decided to meet after dinner.

9. Minh and Jim discussed what had happened and both laughed about it. The misunderstanding wasn't serious at all, but sometimes it can be. When you *suspect* that there is miscommunication or a misunderstanding with an American, you can ask yourself these questions:

When miscommunication happens, try to understand why.

- "Is this miscommunication or confusion due to a cultural difference or is it something personal?"
- "Who can I ask to help me understand what happened?"
- "Can I do anything to avoid it in the future?"

one another's—each other's (each person uses the other's first name)
reserved—kept free for a specific person (other people cannot sit there)
tend to—do something most of the time
treat (me like your boss)—act like I am your boss; act in a polite and formal manner
valuable—important and useful
(something has) *gone wrong*—something has happened that makes people uncomfortable or confused
discomfort—uncomfortable feeling
suspect—have a feeling that something is true

Key Concepts in PART II _____

Cultural clues: You may observe several different Americans acting in similar ways. Their actions can give you clues to help you decide, "This is typical American behavior and not just the way this one person acts."

Miscommunication: Sometimes miscommunication due to cultural differences can be a good opportunity for learning American culture.

_____

Part III. Is This Really American Culture?

There is a difference between ideal and real culture.

10. In learning American culture, your goal should be to learn the real culture, that is, what really exists. When Americans describe their culture, they may describe an *ideal* and not a real culture. For example, the following are often given as values of mainstream American culture:

- independence
- *equality* of all persons
- hard work
- *directness* in communication
- honesty

While many Americans do show these values in their actions, there are also times when they do not. That is, such values often describe an ideal way of living. They may describe what people think their culture should be like, and not what it is always like. An example of this can be seen in the important American value of the equality of all persons. The history of the United States shows Americans trying to change this value from an ideal to a real value. Today, Americans are continuing these efforts in the areas of racial equality and women's and men's *rights*.

A cultural description is rarely true for all people.

11. How can you learn the real culture of Americans? First of all, don't accept a cultural explanation from just one person. Ask several people the same question. Second, remember that a cultural description is *rarely* true for all people of a culture. For example, one person may tell you that Americans are *frank,* open, and direct in communication. Yet is this always true? Is it true for all the cultural groups in the United States? For women as well as men? For older people as well as younger people?

12. **Cross-cultural perspective.**   When you ask about culture, a person will probably answer you from a particular point of view. For instance, an American will probably try to give you information about the way Americans interact with other Americans. Sometimes, however, you may be more interested in how you can best interact with Americans. This is the cross-cultural *perspective.* Many Americans may not be able to give you very clear or helpful answers to questions about cross-cultural interactions. It is helpful, when you ask questions, to give specific information about the situation you are thinking about. For example, you might say "Why can't my boss explain things to me so that I can understand?" Better questions are, "How can I ask my boss to speak more slowly?" or "How can I ask my boss to use simpler words?" Although you are probably interested in American interaction with other

The cross-cultural perspective will help you understand how Americans interact with people from other countries.

ideal—best; perfect; not real
equality—everyone has the same rights and chances
directness—straightforward and clear; not vague
rights—political, social, or economic advantages
rarely—not often; usually not
frank—a frank person says what he really thinks, not just what is polite or what will make other people happy
perspective—understanding; point of view

Americans, you also want to know how Americans interact with people from other cultures.

Key Concepts in PART III

Ideal and real culture: Because people are largely unconscious of culture, they often describe an ideal when they talk about their culture. They often describe what they think their culture *should* be like (ideal culture) and not what it is actually like (real culture). It is a great challenge to learn the real culture of a group of people.

Cultural description: A cultural description is rarely true for all people in a group. That is, even if these people share some aspects of a culture, they will not share other aspects.

Cross-cultural perspective: It can be difficult to learn how people of one culture interact with people of other cultures. This is the cross-cultural perspective of culture learning.

Part IV. Avoiding Cultural Stereotypes

Stereotypes can create a false view of another culture.

13.   In culture learning, it is necessary to make general observations about groups of people. Let's say that you observe a few Americans doing something. For example, you have heard a few Americans saying "Sir" or "Ma'am" when speaking to someone older than they are. Then you ask yourself, "Is there something cultural about this behavior?" You decide that there is, and so you *conclude,* "All Americans act like this." Yet what you observed in this example is an aspect of *regional* culture. In the southern U.S. "Sir" and "Ma'am" are used more *frequently* than in other regions of the country. If you decide that something is "American" on the basis of what only a few people do, you may be making *overgeneralizations.* Some overgeneralizations can be completely incorrect. Others may not consider individual differences at all. They can prevent you from looking at people as individuals. These overgeneralizations, called *stereotypes,* often create a false view of another culture. Some stereotypes are positive, such as, "Americans are honest and hardworking." Other stereotypes are negative, such as "Americans appear friendly, but don't really want to have deep friendships." A stereotype, whether positive or negative, describes a group of people, but does not point out differences among individuals in that group.

14.   In talking about different cultures, we tend to look for general descriptions. Especially when one is new to a culture, it is easy to observe the actions of a few people and conclude that all people of the culture act in the same way. There are always differences among people in any group. For this reason, the authors stated in the first chapter of this book:

There are always differences among people.

> Remember that the information presented in this book about culture and communication in the U.S. is general. There are many kinds of Americans, and many ways of doing things. The information that follows is usually true for many Americans, but not for all Americans.

conclude—decide something must be true
regional—from a certain region or area of a country
frequently—often
overgeneralizations—general descriptions of something, often incorrect, made without enough information
stereotype—description, often negative and untrue, of a group of people; the description doesn't allow for differences among individuals

*Each American is
different, but some
general descriptions
can be made.*

It is rarely possible to describe Americans with expressions such as, "All
Americans . . . , " or "No Americans . . ."; or "Americans always . . . , "
or "Americans never . . ." Descriptions of Americans are more accurate if
they begin, "Many Americans . . . , " "Some Americans . . . , " or "Americans sometimes. . . ." Each American is different, just as each person in
every other culture is. However, some general descriptions can be made.

Key Concepts in PART IV

Stereotype: A stereotype is a general description of a group of people which does
not point out differences among individuals in that group. Stereotypes can be
positive and negative. Negative stereotypes, in particular, can give a false picture
of a culture.

Overgeneralization: It is not possible to talk about culture without making generalizations. Even so, the most accurate generalizations about American culture are
expressed in terms of "many" or "some" Americans. . . . Words such as "all,"
"no," "always," and "never" usually indicate an overgeneralization or a stereotype.

Part V. Culture Fatigue

*Culture fatigue is a
normal part of
adapting to a new
culture.*

15. As you are learning a language and culture, it is a good idea to stop from
time to time and ask yourself, "How am I doing?" Your answer won't
always be a positive one. One day your answer to this question might be,
"Not well. I'm tired of trying to do things the way Americans do them. I'm
tired of trying to *adapt* to American culture. I want to do things my own
way! And I'm tired of speaking English!" Culture learning, like language
learning, is hard work. It can be tiring. This tired feeling, or culture fatigue,
is a normal part of adapting to a different language and culture. If you are
experiencing culture fatigue you may find yourself needing exact answers
and losing patience when you don't get them.

16. In our own cultures, we are often sure of what to do or how to act. However, when we are trying to adapt to another culture, we are sometimes not
sure how to act. Even Americans will sometimes be unable to tell you
exactly how to act in a certain situation. You may find that, in answer to
questions about U.S. culture, Americans often answer, "Well, *it depends.*"
or "It's hard to say." For example, let's say that you ask, "Should I shake
hands with a woman?" You could get several answers, such as:

- "Well, it depends. If she's a young woman, you should probably shake
her hand. If she's an older woman . . . well, it depends on the situation."
- "If it's a business situation, yes, always shake hands. But if it's not business, it's hard to say."
- "That's a hard question. Personally, I wait to see if the woman puts out
her hand. If she does, I shake hands. But if she doesn't . . . I don't know.
It depends."

Your reaction to such answers might be, "I need to know exactly what to do
and what not to do." For someone learning a culture, an answer such as "It

adapt—change in order to fit into a new situation
it depends—I can't give you general information, because each situation is different

depends" can be frustrating. The situation is like trying to put together a *jigsaw puzzle* and discovering that you don't have all the pieces!

Learning a culture can be like trying to put together a jigsaw puzzle.

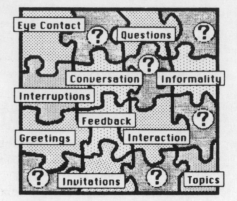

"It depends" is sometimes the best answer.

17. With culture learning questions, there is rarely one answer except "It depends." It is rarely possible to answer with, "Do this" or "Don't do that." Why? Because "Do this," for example, means, "Act this way in all situations with all Americans." As we have seen, all Americans are not the same and therefore all situations cannot be the same. "It depends" is sometimes the best answer.

It is easy to criticize aspects of another culture when you are experiencing culture fatigue.

18. One result of culture fatigue is that the person who is trying to adapt to a new culture may start asking for clear, definite answers to all questions. Another result of culture fatigue may be that the person begins to criticize many things about the new culture. In learning another culture, you may observe things which you do not like or which you do not want to accept. There are always things you can admire in another culture, but you will also see things you do not want to accept or should not accept. However, due to fatigue and frustration, some people become too critical of the new culture in which they are living. Examples of common criticisms of U.S. culture are:

- American food is terrible.
- Americans are only interested in money.
- Americans always *exaggerate*. To them, everything is "great" or "fantastic."

Criticisms are often negative stereotypes.

One good thing about such criticism is that it can help you to get rid of frustration. It can help you "*let off steam.*" On the other hand, *keep in mind* that general criticisms can often be negative stereotypes. As with all stereotypes, they can be *partially* true; but if they are partially true, then they are also partially false. So when you criticize an aspect of culture, ask yourself, "Is this true or is it a stereotype?" Remember, however, that adapting to a

jigsaw puzzle—a picture cut into small pieces with different shapes. One puts all the pieces together to make the picture again
exaggerate—describe something so that it seems bigger or more important than it really is
"let off steam"—let it out; don't hide your anger or frustration so that you will feel better
keep in mind—don't forget
partially—somewhat; not completely

Adapting to a culture does not mean accepting everything.

culture does not mean accepting everything in that culture. As you learn and adapt to American culture, recognize those aspects which you *admire* and which you want to accept, but also recognize those aspects that, because of your own cultural background, you are *unwilling* or unable to accept.

Key Concepts in PART V

Culture fatigue: Learning a new culture is hard work. Adapting to different ways of doing things can be tiring and, at times, frustrating. Culture fatigue, however, is a normal part of cultural adaptation.

Cultural adaptation: Adaptation is part of learning to communicate in a new language and in a new culture. Adaptation means recognizing similarities and differences, and learning how to act in different kinds of situations.

Definite answers: In order to escape culture fatigue, many people seek definite answers to "How should I act?" They want to be told, "Do this" or "Don't do this." Yet it is rarely possible to describe cultural behavior in such definite terms. "It depends" is sometimes the best answer.

Criticism: One positive aspect of criticism is that it can reduce some of the frustrations of cultural adaptation. On the other hand, some criticisms are negative stereotypes. This means that they may be only partially true.

Conclusion

19. You do not have to become a totally different person to be able to adapt to another culture. Yet you will have to learn new skills and make some changes. How you choose to change and adapt must be comfortable for you. You cannot be someone you are not; you have to be yourself.

20. Culture learning is gaining knowledge and skills. It is adapting to a different style of life and people in a way that is possible for *you* to do. The gain that comes from successful culture learning is the ability to communicate comfortably with people in your own culture and people in another culture. Culture learning, like language learning, is adding to what you already have. When you learn a second language, you do not lose or forget your first. You are able to talk to *more* people. With culture learning, you are able to communicate with and understand a group of people who may have beliefs, behavior, and a communication style very different from your own. If you can accept this point of view, then you don't have to feel that you are losing your *cultural identity*. Instead, you are gaining ways of understanding and communicating with people from different cultures.

Key Concepts in the Conclusion

Change and adaptation: It is necessary to make some changes in another culture. How you choose to change must be comfortable for you. You have to be yourself.

Culture learning as gain: When you learn a second language, you do not lose or forget your first. With culture learning, you can gain knowledge and skills without losing your own cultural identity.

admire—like; respect
unwilling—do not want to
cultural identity—the part of you that is influenced and shaped by your culture

My father travels a lot!   Hum !...

POST-READING ACTIVITIES

READING COMPREHENSION EXERCISES

True/False

Read each statement. Then, according to the reading, decide whether the statement is true or false. Write T (true) or F (false) in the space provided.

1. _____ It is possible to speak of a single American culture. (Part I)

2. _____ Most people are not fully aware of their own beliefs and values. (Part I)

3. _____ All behavior that you observe can help you understand cultures. (Part II)

4. _____ Miscommunication can help you understand cultural differences. (Part II)

5. _____ Honesty and directness of communication are described as American values or characteristics. (Part III)

6. _____ Any American you talk to can tell you about real American culture, because all Americans agree about American cultural values. (Part III)

7. _____ A stereotype is useful, because it is an accurate description that can help you to understand the culture of a group of people. (Part IV)

8. _____ "Regional culture" means cultural behavior that is found in every region of the U.S. (Part IV)

9. _____ It is normal to sometimes feel tired when you are learning another language and culture. (Part V)

10. _____ If you ask Americans what to do in a certain type of situation, they may answer, "It depends. . . ." (Part V)

Multiple Choice

Instructions: Circle the letter next to the one best answer. Try to answer each question without looking at the reading. Then, if you cannot answer the question, reread the paragraph indicated.

1. The U.S. can be called "a culture of cultures" because: (Paragraph 2)
   a) Americans are very interested in cultures.
   b) There are many different cultures in America.
   c) All Americans share the same culture.

2. Values are like the lower part of an iceberg because: (Paragraph 4)
   a) Values are easily seen.
   b) Values are not as important as the other aspects of culture.
   c) Values are hidden; people are not always aware of their values.

3. It is important to understand the difference between personal behavior and typical cultural behavior because: (Paragraph 6)
   a) Everyone in a culture likes to do things the same way.
   b) Sometimes what one person in a culture does is not the same as what most people in that culture would do.
   c) You need to know many different kinds of Americans.

4. Independence, hard work, honesty, equality, and directness in communication are: (Paragraph 10)
   a) Examples of ideal culture for all people.
   b) Examples of ideal American culture.
   c) Examples of real American culture.

5. A cross-cultural perspective on American culture is important because: (Paragraph 12)
   a) Each person you talk to will answer you from his or her own point of view.
   b) It is important to understand how Americans interact with people from other cultures.
   c) You need to know how people from the different American cultures interact with each other.

6. An example of a stereotype is: (Paragraph 13)
   a) Most Americans live in the U.S.
   b) Some Americans say "Ma'am" and "Sir" frequently.
   c) Americans are friendly, but don't want to have deep friendships.

7. The authors talk about shaking hands because: (Paragraph 16)
   a) They want to give an example of a cultural behavior that is not always the same in every situation.
   b) They want you to understand when to shake hands and when not to.
   c) They want to talk about men's and women's culture, and business and social cultures.

8. When people are adapting to a new culture, they often criticize that culture because: (Paragraph 18)

a) People need to "let off steam."

b) When people are tired, they often say things that they don't really mean.

c) People need to know that they do not need to accept everything in the new culture.

VOCABULARY EXERCISES

Matching

Draw a line from each verb in column A to the matching definition in column B. The first one is done for you.

	A		*B*
1.	adapt	a.	keep something free for a specific person; save something.
2.	reserve	b.	change in order to fit into a new situation.
3.	suspect	c.	describe something so that it seems bigger or more important than it really is.
4.	exaggerate	d.	decide something must be true.
5.	conclude	e.	have a feeling that something is true.

Word Forms

Choose the correct words in parentheses ( ) and fill in the blanks. The first one is done for you.

1. (accurate/accuracy)
    a) In science and mathematics, *accuracy* is very important.
    b) It is really not completely _____ to speak of "American" culture, because there are many different cultures in America. However, there is a mainstream culture.

2. (tend/tendency)
    a) If we compare Americans to people from many other cultures, we can say that Americans have a _____ to be more informal.
    b) Americans _____ to be confused or upset if they do not receive the kind of feedback that they expect.

3. (adapt/adaptation/adapting)
    a) While you are trying to _____ to a new culture, you may sometimes feel very tired.
    b) _____ to a new culture is a challenge.
    c) Cultural _____ can lead to culture fatigue.

4. (regional/region)
   a) If people act one way in a certain part of the country only, then we can say that their behavior is _____.
   b) In general, there is more formality in the southern _____ of the U.S. than in other parts of the country.

5. (admire/admiration)
   a) The school children have a lot of _____ for their teacher.
   b) You can _____ many things in another culture even if you don't want to accept them for yourself.

6. (reserved/reservation)
   a. She made a _____ at the restaurant for four people.
   b. You can sit wherever you want. There are no _____ seats.

7. (directness/direct/directly)
   a. Not all Americans are _____ when they communicate. Many are indirect.
   b. Generally, teachers and supervisors in the U.S. prefer that you speak to them _____ if you are having any problems.
   c. Some people appreciate _____ in communication; others do not.

8. (identity/identify/identification)
   a. We all have both a cultural and personal _____.
   b. You should carry your _____ papers with you at all times.
   c. Can you _____ any of these people? Have you seen them before?

Fill In the Blanks

From the list of nouns below, choose the correct word and fill in the blanks. Use each word only once.

attitude   clues
equality   perspective
stereotype   values
rights

1. _____ of all races is an ideal of American culture.
2. _____ is another way of saying point of view.
3. A positive _____ toward things that are different will help you to be more comfortable in a new culture.
4. An overgeneralization that is not true for everyone in a culture and is often negative is called a _____.
5. _____ help you understand or figure out a problem.
6. Cultural _____, or what people consider to be important, right, and good, are not always easy to identify.
7. Equal _____ for everyone in the U.S. is an ideal that people hope to achieve.

Choose the Best Explanation

Each sentence below contains an italicized word or phrase from the reading. Read each sentence and the three possible explanations. Choose the one explanation that best matches the meaning of the sentence. Circle the letter next to that explanation. The first one is done for you.

1. When two people have a good understanding of *one another's* culture, they have a better chance of good communication.
   a. one other
   b. other
   c. each other's

2. The statement, "English is the international language" is *partially* true. English is one language used internationally, but there are other languages that are used as well.
   a) not true
   b) completely true
   c) not completely true

3. Child: "Mommy, can I go swimming tomorrow?"
   Mother: "*It depends* on how you are feeling."
   a) Yes, if you don't feel sick.
   b) Yes, but don't swim in the deep end of the pool where you can't feel the bottom.
   c) Yes, if the water doesn't feel too cold.

4. Good teachers *treat* all their students with respect.
   a) teach
   b) act in a certain way
   c) give special foods

5. Many Americans feel it is healthy to *let off steam* sometimes.
   a) express anger or frustration
   b) take a hot bath or sauna
   c) turn off the heat and open the windows

6. *Keep in mind* that some Americans need help in learning how to talk to someone who doesn't speak English fluently.
   a) Don't worry if Americans use difficult words or talk too fast.
   b) You must continue to remind Americans to speak more slowly and explain clearly.
   c) Remember that you sometimes need to ask Americans to speak more slowly or use simple words.

7. Cultural generalizations are *rarely* true for all people in a culture.
   a) usually
   b) almost never
   c) never

GOING BEYOND THE READING

Each group of questions is based on a quote from the reading. Read the questions and then discuss them in small groups or with the entire class. After the questions have been discussed, choose a topic related to one of the questions and write a composition.*

1. "... *The U.S. is often described as a "culture of cultures."*
   (Paragraph 2)

   a) Talk about the history of people from your own culture who have come to live in the U.S. When and why did they first come? Where do they live now? What has their experience in the U.S. been?

   b) Talk about the immigrants who came from your culture to the U.S. In what different ways have the immigrants and their children and grandchildren adapted to American culture? What aspects of their own culture are still important to them?

2. *"Learning American culture is a challenge."* (Paragraph 5)

   a) Imagine that you are teaching a course on cross-cultural communication in your own country. Your students are a group of Americans, or people from other cultures, who need to understand your culture. What would you try to teach them? What are some examples that you would use to explain what you mean?

   b) What aspects of American culture do you need or want to learn the most? Why? Give specific examples. (For example, if you are working in an American company, maybe you need to understand how to interact with your co-workers. What are some specific situations you need to know about?)

3. *"In learning American culture, your goal should be to learn the real culture, that is, what really exists."* (Paragraph 10)

   a) From your own knowledge and experience, what are three or four values or behaviors that you feel are good examples of real American culture? Try to avoid stereotypes!

   b) Describe at least one *real* value of your own culture that you do not see in American culture, or that is somewhat different in American culture.

4. *"In culture learning, it is necessary to make general observations about groups of people."* (Paragraph 13)

   a) By now, you have probably studied much of this book, and you may also have had some experience with Americans in the U.S. or in your own culture. What are some generalizations that you can safely make about American values or behavior? Give examples.

   b) Had you heard any generalizations about Americans before you read this book, or before you came to the U.S. or met American people? Do you still feel these generalizations are true? Explain the generalizations and give examples to show why you think they are or are not true.

5. "... *recognize those aspects* [of culture] *which you admire and which you want to accept, but also recognize those aspects ... that you are unwilling or unable to accept."* (Paragraph 18)

   a) What are some aspects of American culture that you do not want to, or cannot, accept? Explain why you feel this way.

Note to the teacher: Some students may prefer to write out answers to questions that they feel are personal ones. In this case, you may want to use this exercise as a writing exercise.

    b) Perhaps you have children who are growing up in the U.S. What are some aspects of your own culture that you would want to teach your children to value? Are these also aspects of American culture?

    c) If there are aspects of American culture that you do not accept, how will this affect your ability to interact with Americans?

6. *"Culture learning, like language learning, is adding to what you already have . . . . If you can accept this point of view, then you don't have to feel that you are losing your own cultural identity."*   (Paragraph 20)

    a) Do you agree with the above statements? Why or why not?

    b) Do you feel that it is possible for a person to become "bicultural"? That is, can a person function well in two cultures and understand two cultural points of view?

    c) Talk (or write about) what you feel you've gained by knowing other cultural points of view and by being able to communicate with people from another culture.

About the Authors

Deena Levine has an M.A. degree in Teaching English as a Second Language (TESL) from San Francisco State University. She is an instructor of oral communication skills with the University of California, Berkeley Extension, and a cross-cultural training consultant for teacher-training programs, private industry, social service agencies, and hospitals. In addition, she has conducted cross-cultural and community human relations training for police officers in the San Francisco Bay Area. She worked as a cross-cultural training specialist for IRI International (formerly the Intercultural Relations Institute) in Redwood City, California, creating cultural awareness programs for supervisors and managers of non-U.S.-born employees in California's Silicon Valley. She was an instructor of ESL at De Anza Community College, Cupertino, California, and at the American Language Institute at San Diego State University, where she developed material for *Beyond Language: Intercultural Communication for English as a Second Language,* co-authored by Mara Adelman.

Jim Baxter has an M.A. degree in Modern English Language from the University of London and a License in linguistics from the University of Lyons in France. He is currently Manager of Corporate Training and Development at Advanced Micro Devices, a major U.S. semiconductor manufacturer, in Sunnyvale, California. He has had a variety of positions, both in the U.S. and abroad, including ESL instructor in France and in the U.S.; foreign lecturer at the University of Toyama, Japan; professional associate at the East-West Center in Hawaii; intercultural communication training specialist with IRI International in Redwood City, California; and adult education specialist in Vocational ESL. He has published articles and developed materials on communication skills such as interactive listening for ESL. At IRI International, he developed the "Take Two" methodology for teaching communication skills and directed the production of the videotape entitled, "Take Two: English for Intercultural Communication."

Piper McNulty has an MA degree in Teaching English as a Second Language from the School for International Training in Brattleboro, Vermont. She is currently a corporate business English and intercultural communication skills specialist with

IRI International in Redwood City, California, where she trains Japanese management employees and supervisors in Silicon Valley firms. She is also a cultural orientation/cross-cultural communication consultant for several San Francisco Bay Area refugee training programs. She has taught ESL to adults in New York City, the San Francisco Bay Area, Japan, Mexico, and Hong Kong. As a teacher-trainer/field representative for the Center for Applied Linguistics, she developed curricula and trained teachers for the United Nations High Commissioner on Refugees Intensive ESL and Cultural Orientation Program in Hong Kong. Her latest curriculum, developed for the Intercultural Studies Department at De Anza College in Cupertino, California, is an analysis of 38 case studies of intercultural miscommunication in the work place.